Instead of
Atonement

Instead of Atonement

The Bible's Salvation Story and Our Hope for Wholeness

TED GRIMSRUD

CASCADE Books • Eugene, Oregon

INSTEAD OF ATONEMENT
The Bible's Salvation Story and Our Hope for Wholeness

Copyright © 2013 Ted Grimsrud. All rights reserved. Except for brief quotations in critical publications or reviews, no part of this book may be reproduced in any manner without prior written permission from the publisher. Write: Permissions, Wipf and Stock Publishers, 199 W. 8th Ave., Suite 3, Eugene, OR 97401.

Cascade Books
An Imprint of Wipf and Stock Publishers
199 W. 8th Ave., Suite 3
Eugene, OR 97401
www.wipfandstock.com

ISBN 13: 978-1-62032-502-5

Cataloging-in-Publication data:

Grimsrud, Ted.

    Instead of atonement : the bible's salvation story and our hope for wholeness / Ted Grimsrud.

    x + 270 pp. ; 23 cm—Includes bibliographical references and indexes.

    ISBN 13: 978-1-62032-502-5

    1. Atonement 2. Nonviolence—Religious Aspects—Christianity I. Title.

BT265.3 G74 2013

Manufactured in the USA

*To my grandchildren,
Elias Pablo and Marja Lucy,
in hope for their wholeness*

Contents

Preface · ix

1 Introduction: "Gospel as Bad News"? Violence as a Theological Problem · 1

PART ONE: The Bible's Salvation Story · 23

2 Salvation in the Old Testament: Healing, Law, and Sacrifice · 27

3 Guardians for the Way of Wholeness: Salvation in the Prophets · 49

4 Jesus's Teaching on Salvation: Believe the Good News · 69

PART TWO: Jesus's Death and Salvation · 89

5 The Death of Jesus · 91

6 Jesus's Death and the Powers: Cultural Exclusivism (Law) · 111

7 Jesus's Death and the Powers: Religious Exclusivism (Temple) · 130

8 Jesus's Death and the Powers: Political Authoritarianism (Empire) · 149

9 Jesus Brings Salvation · 169

10 God's Saving Justice: Paul on Salvation · 186

11 Salvation through Revelation · 207

12 Conclusion: Is There an Atonement Model in This Story? · 226

Bibliography · 243

Author Index · 251

Scripture Index · 255

Subject Index · 265

Preface

There is a saying, perhaps going back to Leonardo da Vinci, that there are no finished projects, only abandoned ones. I feel the truth of this statement strongly with this book. Partly because I have lived with it so long, I have found it difficult to let it loose.

My first step was taken over thirty years ago when, as a student at the Associated Mennonite Biblical Seminaries, I wrote a paper, "Discipleship and Atonement in the Synoptic Gospels," for Professor Willard Swartley's New Testament Theology and Ethics course. Willard gave me much appreciated encouragement to keep working on this theme and even to consider working on a doctorate.

About ten years later I read something by Paul Ramsey, the influential advocate for the just war tradition, where he agreed that the core difference between his thought and that of my pacifist Mennonite mentor John Howard Yoder had to do with their respective christologies. At that point I decided to focus on that issue. It has taken awhile (and many changes in focus along the way), but here is fruit of that decision.

It is also the case, as it usually is when I complete a writing project, that I keep learning of more materials I should take into account. It is hard to resist the lure to keep attending to important newly discovered resources—until I remember that the new resources enter the scene faster than I can read them all anyway. So, it is time to move on with what I've got.

My need to abandon this project serves as a good reminder, though, of the limited and focused agenda I have had with it. I have not actually intended to do everything. I simply want to tell a story about what the Bible seems to me to teach. And I want to link this story with our problem with violence, partly as a challenge to traditional Christian theologies that have not addressed that problem (and may, actually, have exacerbated it). I tell this story as a thought experiment more than as a comprehensive and definitive analysis.

Preface

I have approached this material as a theological ethicist, a preacher, a teacher of undergraduate college students, and a concerned world citizen. I have, as a non-specialist, mined biblical scholarship as a resource to help in what ultimately is advocacy work—an effort to contribute to peace on earth.

I have debts beyond recalling to teachers, friends, writers, and students. I do want explicitly to mention several crucial ones, though. I appreciate Eastern Mennonite University's willingness to grant me a sabbatical for the school year 2003–2004 that allowed me to write the first draft of this book. During the spring semester of that school year, I met regularly with Dan Umbel, then a precocious college senior, to share and discuss drafts of my chapters. Dan's many insights strengthened the book. Several years later, when the project was trending toward moribund, Vic Thiessen, at that time director of the London Mennonite Centre, invited me to present a day-long seminar at the Centre on this material. That most helpful experience helped rekindle my motivation.

Most of all, going back to when I first began to think about salvation and peace in the early 1980s, my life partner Kathleen Temple has listened, talked, challenged, and affirmed through all the stages of reading, writing, preaching, lecturing, and rewriting. She shares the hopes I express as I dedicate this book to Eli and LouLou.

ONE

Introduction: "Gospel as Bad News"?
Violence as a Theological Problem

WE GENERALLY ASSOCIATE THE term "gospel" or "good news" with the message of Jesus and the Christian faith. We have strong biblical grounds for doing so. The early Christian document we know as the Gospel of Mark gets right to the point in its very first verse—announcing the agenda for what follows: "The beginning of the *gospel* of Jesus Christ, the Son of God."

The Greek word here that is translated "gospel" (or "Good News" in the NRSV's preferred rendering) is *evangel*, the root for "evangelism" and "evangelical." Mark makes the basic claim, along with the rest of the New Testament, that the story he tells of the ministry of Jesus contains the good news of God's healing work for humanity. This work provides our hope for healing and reconciliation.

Mark's "good news" may be closely linked with the central motif in the Old Testament related to salvation: *shalom*, or "peace." Mark explicitly connects the good news of Jesus with the story that began with the children of Israel. Mark's second verse contains a quote from one of Israel's greatest prophets, Isaiah, presented as a prophecy concerning John the Baptist. Mark thus makes clear that the story that Isaiah was part of (Abraham, Moses, and their descendants) continues with Jesus, in whom the hopes of Israel are fulfilled.

Jesus enters the scene, in Mark's account (1:15), with a powerful proclamation: The time is fulfilled (i.e., the story is reaching its climax). The kingdom of God (i.e., the promised time of shalom, the purpose of the story) is at hand (i.e., is now present). Repent (i.e., turn from your idols and turn toward God) and believe in (i.e., trust, accept, welcome into your hearts) the good news (i.e., the announcement that the king's kingdom is victorious).

The present tense of this proclamation is unmistakable. Jesus makes God present in a powerful way and the world will never be the same. However, when we 2,000 years later place the fulfillment of the promises with Jesus, we face many questions. In what sense did this fulfillment actually happen? Are we to understand that Jesus meant what he said in a literal sense? Has the community Jesus established to embody what he announced conveyed truly good news to the world—or has the message been profoundly mixed with bad news?

This is not the place to make the case for a specific conclusion regarding the dynamics of the connection between Christianity and violence.[1] However, we may assume a consensus that the Christian movement has had a problematic relationship with violence throughout its history—think of support for warfare, treatment of alleged heretics and other offenders, and harsh discipline of children as an expression of God's will, among other examples.

If *shalom* (peace) stands as a close synonym with salvation in the Old Testament, the relationship has become more complicated in Christian history and theology. In fact, an important body of historical analysis has lately been suggesting that many traditional understandings of salvation may actually underwrite violence.[2]

Numerous public opinion surveys as well anecdotal evidence support the impression that in our present time in the United States, being a self-identified Christian makes a person more likely to support warfare, harsh criminal justice practices, and corporal punishment of children.[3]

Is there a direct connection between understanding salvation in terms of God's retributive justice and support for inter-human violence?

---

1. This book will focus on biblical materials, but will be followed by a sequel that will focus on understandings of salvation during the past 2,000 and will be attentive to the evolving relationships between Christian churches and violence.

2. See for example, Gorringe, *God's Just*; Hardin and Jersek, eds., *Stricken*; and Weaver, *Nonviolent*.

3. For just one example, see a 2006 Baylor Religion Survey that reported that while 45 percent of the general United States population supported the United States war on Iraq, of those who believed in an "Authoritarian God" (mainly evangelical Protestants), 63 percent supported that war. Cited in Belousek, *Atonement*, 29. These Christians are likely to affirm salvation theologies that understand God in strongly retributive terms—a God who *punishes* and who requires sacrifices to satisfy the needs of justice.

Introduction: "Gospel as Bad News"?

British theologian Timothy Gorringe suggests there is. He argues that Christian atonement theology, articulated influentially by Anselm of Canterbury, dovetailed with the emergence of more retributive criminal justice practices in Europe to underwrite state-sponsored violence.[4] Harry Potter, a British historian, illustrates this dynamic in his history of the move to abolish the death penalty in Great Britain, a process slowed significantly by church leaders who argued theologically in favor of the death penalty long after general public sentiment in Britain supported abolition.[5]

According to American theologian Donald Capps, the history of Christianity has witnessed numerous "theological legitimations for the physical and emotional abuse of children" under the rubric of "punishment, tough love, or teaching the child a lesson."[6] Capps argues that the abuse that has resulted from such treatment of children has been made even worse by the religious justifications given for it.[7]

These concerns about the possible complicity of Christian salvation theology with violence provide the impetus for the rereading of the biblical materials in what follows in this book. What do we find as the Bible's core salvation story if we read it front to back without the lenses of post-biblical (possibly pro-violence) theology? Does the Bible indeed contain a salvation story with shalom-oriented emphases instead of the possibly more violence-oriented emphases of traditional atonement theologies based on understanding God in terms of retributive justice? Does the Bible actually present salvation in ways that focus on life in the present instead of on death in the present and life in "heaven" after death as in traditional atonement theologies?

In calling this book *Instead of Atonement: The Bible's Salvation Story and Our Hope for Wholeness*, I have a specific use of the term "atonement" in mind. I do not mean to suggest that salvation has nothing to do with "atonement" in any possible meaning that might be given to the term. Rather, I use "atonement" in the title in the sense of the popular meaning of the term as referring to sacrificial payment that makes salvation possible.

D. Stephen Long's dictionary definition of "atonement" is typical: "The atonement is how Christ accomplished our justification (i.e., 'being

---

4. Gorringe, *God's Just*.

5. Potter, *Hanging*. See also American theologian Wayne House's argument in favor of the death penalty: House and Yoder, *Death Penalty*.

6. Capps, *Child's Song*.

7. See also many books by Alice Miller, especially *For Your*.

found just or righteous before God') through his sacrifice on the cross."[8] Implied in this understanding of "atonement" is that God's ability to provide salvation is constrained pending the offering of an appropriate sacrifice. I will suggest later in this chapter that such an understanding of God being constrained is based upon a notion of God's justice or holiness or honor carrying tremendous weight in God's ability to relate to sinful human beings. It seems inevitable that violence play a role in satisfying the demands of God's character—and that violence is part of God's response when the satisfaction is not forthcoming.

It is "atonement" in this sense to which I will counter-pose the salvation story I believe that the Bible tells. With the phrase "instead of atonement," I mean to suggest that salvation in the Bible is not dependent upon atonement—that is, dependent upon adequate sacrifices being offered (including the ultimate sacrifice of God's Son, Jesus) as a condition for salvation. I also mean to suggest that in the overall message of the Bible, God's response to sin is not violence (see the concise statement in support of this suggestion in Hos 11:1-9).

However, before we turn to this book's main agenda, the recounting of the merciful, shalom-oriented story of salvation the Bible tells, we need to linger a bit longer with the question of how violence is a theological problem.

The Logic of Retribution

Despite the widespread occurrence of inter-human violence throughout most of recorded history, the case may be made that most human beings tend to want to avoid lethal violence toward other human beings. In human experience we usually need some overriding reason to go against the tendency to avoid lethal violence. To act violently toward, especially to kill, other human beings is serious business, undertaken because some other value or commitment overrides the tendency not to be violent.

Almost all violence emerges with some kind of rationale that justifies its use. Psychiatrist James Gilligan argues, based on his extensive work with extremely violent offenders, that even the most seemingly pointless acts of violence usually nonetheless have some justification in the mind of the perpetrator.[9]

---

8. Long, "Justification," 79.
9. Gilligan, *Violence*.

Introduction: "Gospel as Bad News"?

Most socially accepted uses of violence (e.g., warfare, capital punishment, corporal punishment of children) follow a fairly self-conscious logic. At the core of this "logic" usually rests a commitment to the necessity of retribution; using violence is justified as the appropriate response to wrongdoing. When the moral order is violated by wrongdoing, "justice" requires retribution (defined as repayment of wrongdoing with violent punishment, or pain with pain).

We find deeply ingrained in the religious consciousness of the United States the belief that retribution is God's will. I will argue that roots of that belief owe more to extra-biblical influences and are not based on the best reading of the biblical materials. Yet we cannot deny the close link between Western Christianity as it has come to be and the strong support for retribution (that is, for justifying violence as the appropriate response to wrongdoing).

A theologically grounded "logic of retribution" underlies rationales for using violence. In "the logic of retribution," when all is said and done, people understand God most fundamentally in terms of impersonal, inflexible holiness. They see God's law as the unchanging standard by which sin is measured, and believe God responds to violations of the law with justifiable violence.

According to the most popular account of this framework, human beings are inherently sinful. Jesus' death on the cross offers a sacrifice that provides the only basis for sinful humans to escape deserved punishment. Most violence is justified as in some sense being an expression of this deserved punishment ("punishment" defined as inflicting pain in response to wrongdoing). Violence in response to wrongdoing is required by the logic of retribution.[10]

The theological rationale for retributive punishment asserts that appropriate punishment reflects God's character. The first, most basic,

---

10. Knowledgeable readers may recognize that my account of retributive theology relies on sources mainly from those who affirm a "penal substitution" view of the atonement (on this view, see Thomas Schreiner's contribution to Beilby and Eddy, eds., *Nature*, and Cole, *God the Peacemaker*).

In scholarly circles, this is considered to be an extreme view. However, in popular Christianity since the Reformation—the kind of Christianity that has the biggest impact on the wider culture—this has been the dominant view. And, though this view departs in many ways from Anselm's original "satisfaction" view, it still fits within the satisfaction model broadly speaking—especially in echoing Anselm's view on the constraints God's honor (or justice or holiness or wrath) places on God's mercy. I use "penal substitution" writers in order to make clearly apparent the retributive dynamics of satisfaction atonement theology and to make as obvious as possible the links between this theology and violent criminal justice practices.

attribute of God is holiness—which means that God simply cannot countenance any kind of sin. If God has direct contact with sin, God must destroy it. A modern evangelical theologian, Millard Erickson, echoes ideas from Augustine, Anselm, Luther, and Calvin: "The nature of God is perfect and complete holiness. This is . . . the way God is by nature. He has always been absolutely holy . . . . Being contrary to God's nature, sin is repulsive to him. He is allergic to sin, so to speak. He cannot look upon it."[11]

Erickson most directly follows John Calvin in how he articulates this view. Calvin wrote in his *Institutes of the Christian Religion*, "there is a perpetual and irreconcilable disagreement between righteousness and unrighteousness" (II.xvi.3). Hence, Christ has "to undergo the severity of God's vengeance, to appease his wrath and satisfy his just judgment" (II.xvi.10).[12]

Human beings have been told what we must avoid doing in order to keep from violating God's holiness. When humans sin, we are diverging from God's laws. Since the laws come from God, we sin directly against God. Erickson writes, "The law is something of a transcript of the nature of God. When we relate to it, whether positively or negatively, . . . it is God himself whom we are obeying or disobeying. Disobeying the law is serious . . . because disobeying it is actually an attack upon the very nature of God himself."[13]

In this view, when human beings violate God's holiness, God must (due to God's holiness) punish them. Violated holiness must be satisfied. According to the logic of retribution, then, God (in effect) is governed by inflexible holiness and human beings invariably violate that holiness. Because of the fundamental nature of this holiness, God is not free to act with unconditional mercy and compassion toward rebellious human beings. Simply to forgive would violate God's holiness. Compassion without satisfaction is not possible for God. To quote Erickson: "For God to remove or ignore the guilt of sin without requiring a payment would in effect destroy the very moral fiber of the universe, the distinction between right and wrong."[14]

Justice, in this framework, works to sustain the balance of the universe. If the balance is upset, justice requires recompense to restore the

---

11. Erickson, *Christian*, 802. For a more recent articulation of this theology, see Jeffrey, et al., *Pierced*.

12. Cited in Stott, *Cross*, 120.

13. Erickson, *Christian*, 803.

14. Ibid., 816.

balance, payment to satisfy the requirements of the balance. This payment is made through punishment, pain for pain.

In much Christian theology, here is where the doctrine of the atonement enters. Due to the extremity of the offenses by human beings against God's law, the only way God can relate to human beings is if there is death on the human side to restore the balance. The only way this can happen is through the enormity of the death of God's own son, Jesus, whose own holiness is so powerful that it can balance out the unholiness of all of humanity.

Jonathan Edwards wrote that the crucifixion of Jesus "was willed and ordered by God" as "the most admirable and glorious of all events" because only in this way could human beings be granted salvation.[15] When we confess our helpless sinfulness, we may claim Jesus as savior from God's righteous anger. Jesus satisfies God's retributive justice on our behalf.

Within the logic of retribution, salvation (i.e., the restoration of harmony with God) is achieved as the result of violence. Such a means to salvation is consistent with the view of the basic nature of the moral universe as founded on impersonal holiness. Salvation happens only because God's holiness or honor is satisfied through the ultimate act of violence—the sacrificial death of Jesus Christ. In light of this understanding of the nature of God and of the fundamental nature of the universe, the logic of retribution indeed leads to acceptance of "justifiable violence." Violence may be the best response to wrongdoing.

Retributive Responses to Crime[16]

Let us look more closely at one particular expression of retributive violence, the dynamics of criminal justice in the United States. Criminal justice is only one issue among many where the logic of retribution exerts a major influence—but it may be the most easily perceived.

Punishment involves the intentional infliction of pain and is, thus, a form of violence. Punishment by the state, then, requires some justification as it involves the state acting violently, something normally considered morally and socially unacceptable. Because violence requires a rationale, punishment has given rise to a huge variety of justifications for delivering such pain.

---

15. Cited in Greven, *Spare*, 50.
16. This section is drawn from Grimsrud and Zehr, "Rethinking."

In our criminal justice tradition, the overriding justifications given for harsh punishments, even to the point of death, have and continue to be tied to an understanding of ultimate reality that believes that this reality requires retributive justice when fundamental natural or divine laws are violated. Such "retributive justice" is seen to restore the moral balance.[17] Most obviously, the death penalty provides a way to balance the "scales of justice" that "demand a life for a life, the ultimate punishment for the ultimate crime."[18]

This understanding is to a large extent rooted in a particular understanding of God as ultimate reality: retribution is needed to "satisfy" the requirement God has that violations be paid for with pain. When someone commits a wrong, it is assumed, the central question of justice is "What does she or he deserve?" The assumed answer is punishment.

So, in the arena of criminal justice, the issue of authorized human beings inflicting punitive pain (including death) on other human beings has theological as well as philosophical and political significance. In saying that violence is a theological issue, I use "theology" in a broad sense to refer to beliefs about ultimate reality, foundational beliefs about the nature of the universe. I use "God" as the common human symbol for ultimate reality.[19] The issue of punishment has to do with how human beings understand the world we live in, the values by which we shape our lives. Beliefs about God and God's character shape our concept of retribution or punishment as justice.

Part of the theology underlying retributive justice speaks of how God was (and is) understood. There are some key aspects of the view of God generally characteristic of medieval Europe that shaped (and were also shaped by) the emerging punitive practices of criminal justice and that continue to be foundational in present-day practices of retributive justice. God's will for violent punishment provides a crucial impetus for the overriding of our tendency to need justification for killing or in other ways acting violently toward human beings.

Retributive theology has infused the social, political, and cultural life of the West in very fundamental ways going back not just to the medieval period but into antiquity. Timothy Gorringe makes a strong case for the

---

17. See United States Supreme Court Justice Antonin Scalia's essay, "God's Justice." A Roman Catholic, Scalia interestingly rejects the Vatican's recent anti-death penalty statement, *Evangelium Vitae*, and uses the Bible (specifically Romans 13) to justify his pro-retributive justice convictions.

18. Garland, *Peculiar*, 64.

19. Kaufman, *In Face*.

Introduction: "Gospel as Bad News"?

atonement theology of Anselm of Canterbury (c.1033-1109) providing a crucial link in applying this view of God to the practice of punitive criminal justice.[20] However, surely the roots of such an application of these theological themes go much further back, to the infusion of Greek philosophy and Roman political thought into Christian theology, fostered especially by the extraordinarily influential writings of Augustine of Hippo.

The key impact Greek philosophy had on theology may be seen in emerging notions of God's impassivity, the growing abstraction of concepts of justice, and the objectifying or "othering" of offenders. The Greek-influenced theology provided a notion of God's impersonal holiness and retributive response to violations of that holiness. In the early Middle Ages, this theology merged with Roman legal philosophy, which was also centered on impersonal principles. Instead of being based on custom and history, law in this perspective stood alone.[21]

Justice became a matter of applying rules, establishing guilt, and fixing penalties—without reference to finding healing for the victim or the relationship between victim and offender. Canon law and the parallel theology that developed began to identify sin as a collective wrong against a moral or metaphysical order. Crime was a sin, not just against a person but against God, against God's laws, and it was the church's business to purge the world of this transgression. From this understanding of sin, it was a short step to assume that since the social order is willed by God, crime is also a sin against this social order. The church (and later the state) must therefore enforce that order. Increasingly, focus centered on punishment by established authorities as a way of doing justice.

By the end of the sixteenth century, the cornerstones of state justice were in place in Europe, and they drew deeply from the underpinnings of retributive theology. New legal codes in France, Germany, and England enlarged the public dimensions of certain offenses and gave to the state a larger role. Criminal codes began to specify wrongs and to emphasize punishment.

The primary instrument for applying pain came to be the prison. Part of the attraction of prison was terms that could be graded according to the offense. Prisons made it possible to calibrate punishments in units of time, providing an appearance of rationality in the application of pain.

20. Gorringe, *God's Just*, 85-125. For Anselm's treatment of atonement theology, see "Cur Deus Homo?" in Evans and Evans, eds., *Anselm*. For a recent critique of Anselm, see Weaver, *Nonviolent*.

21. I am especially drawing here on Berman, *Law*; Bianchi, *Justice*; and Zehr, *Changing*.

Instead of Atonement

Between the mid-1800s and the 1970s, the practice of criminal justice in the United States evolved away from strictly retributive justice. David Garland, in his important book, *The Culture of Control*,[22] argues that the "penal-welfare" model gained ascendancy among criminal justice professionals, with a concern for rehabilitation of offenders and a diminishment of focus on strict punishment. This model, however, never received widespread support among the general population. Because politicians for a long time found it disadvantageous to try to intervene in criminal justice issues due to conventional wisdom that criminal justice was a no-win issue to be identified with, the prison system was allowed to pursue its own agenda.

However, with a significant increase in the crime rate in the United States after World War II, politicians discovered that "law and order" rhetoric actually gained them popularity. The criminal justice system tended to be centralized and bureaucratic and not noticeably effective in reducing the incidents of crime. Hence, when strong critiques were raised in the 1960s and 1970s, the somewhat ineffective focus of rehabilitation was soon significantly lessened.

The logic of retribution that became embedded in our criminal justice practices by the nineteenth century, even though it was mitigated against somewhat during the penal-welfare era, has returned with a vengeance in the last quarter of the twentieth century and the early years of the twenty-first. As summarized by legal scholar William Shuntz, "No previous generation of Americans embraced the version of retributive justice that has held sway in the United States over the past thirty years.... Only in the last decades of the 20th century did most American voters and the law enforcement officials they elect conclude that punishing criminals is an unambiguous moral good. The notion that criminal punishment is a moral or social imperative—the idea that a healthy criminal justice system should punish all the criminals it can—enjoyed little currency before the 1980s."[23] In the retributive model of justice, crime has come to be defined as against the state, justice has become a monopoly of the state, punishment has become normative, and victims have been disregarded.

Going back to the Middle Ages, penal theory helped reinforce the punitive theme in theology—e.g., a satisfaction theory of atonement that emphasized the idea of payment or suffering to make satisfaction for sins. Retributive theology, which emphasized legalism and punishment, deeply

---

22. Garland, *Culture*.
23. Shuntz, *Collapse*, 55–56.

influenced Western culture through rituals, hymns, and symbols. An image "of judicial murder, the cross, bestrode Western culture from the 11th to the 18th century," with huge impact on the Western psyche. It entered the "structures of affect" of Western Europe and "in doing so, . . . pumped retributivism into the legal bloodstream, reinforcing the retributive tendencies of the law."[24] The result was an obsession with retributive themes in the Bible and a neglect of the restorative ones—a theology of a retributive God who wills violence.[25]

This view is embedded in the Western criminal justice system through our modern paradigm of retributive justice, which might be characterized like this:

1. Crime is understood primarily as a violation of the (unchanging, impersonal) law, and the state is the victim.

2. Offenders must get what they deserve. The aim of justice is to establish blame and administer pain in order to satisfy the demands of the moral balance in which the violation is countered by the punishment.

3. The process of justice finds expression as a conflict between adversaries in which the offender is pitted against state rules, and intentions outweigh outcomes and one side wins while the other side loses.

A Recipe for Alienation

The paradigm of retributive justice that dominates Western criminal justice is a recipe for alienation. By making the "satisfaction" of impersonal justice ("God's holiness") the focus of society's response to criminal activity, the personal human beings involved—victims, offenders, community members—rarely find wholeness.

Moreover, the larger community's suffering often only increases. Instead of healing the brokenness caused by the offense, we usually increase the spiral of brokenness. Many victims of violence speak of being victimized again by the impersonal criminal justice system.[26] Offenders, often alienated people already, become more deeply alienated by the punitive practices and person-destroying experiences of prisons.

---

24. Gorringe, *God's Just*, 224.

25. See H. Wayne House's biblically based theological argument in favor of capital punishment in House and Yoder, *Death Penalty*, 1–104.

26. See Zehr, *Transcending*.

Garland portrays our "culture of control" in criminal justice as a new form of segregation. We focus not on rehabilitating and reintegrating offenders, but on identifying and isolating offenders. "The prison is used today as a kind of reservation, a quarantine zone in which purportedly dangerous individuals are segregated in the name of public safety."[27] That this "segregation" has a decided racial aspect in the United States is confirmed in Michelle Alexander's powerful book, *The New Jim Crow*.[28]

Present dynamics emphasize the difference between offenders and law-abiding citizens. Garland writes, "being intrinsically evil or wicked, some offenders are not like us. They are dangerous others who threaten our safety and have no call on our fellow feeling. The appropriate reaction for society is one of social defense: we should defend ourselves against these dangerous enemies rather than concern ourselves with their welfare and prospects for rehabilitation."[29]

James Gilligan, former director of psychiatry for the Massachusetts prison system, draws on his experience working closely with violent offenders to critique retributive justice in the our criminal justice system. "A society's prisons serve as a key for understanding the larger society as a whole."[30] When we look through the "magnifying glass" of the United States prison system, we see a society focused on trying to control violence through violence, a society that willingly inflicts incredible suffering on an ever-increasing number of desperate people.

Despite our democratic principles and our belief that a person is innocent until proven guilty, our per capita prison rate is one of the highest in the world. And our rate continues rapidly to grow. Between 1924 and 1975, the rate of incarceration remained fairly steady at around 100 prisoners per 100,000 population—a rate at that level higher than most industrialized nations. But between 1975 and 2007, the rate increased by more than seven times, to 700 per 100,000.[31]

This exploding prison population faces increasingly worsening conditions. According to Gilligan, prisons have become "cruel, inhumane, and degrading, with severe overcrowding, frequent rapes and beatings, prolonged and arbitrary use of solitary confinement, grossly unsanitary,

---

27. Garland, *Culture*, 178.
28. Alexander, *New Jim Crow*.
29. Garland, *Culture*, 184.
30. Gilligan, *Violence*, 185.
31. The United States, with 6 percent of the world's population, in 2007 held 25 percent of the world's prisoners (Logan, *Good*, 1).

Introduction: "Gospel as Bad News"?

disease-inducing living conditions, and deprivation of elementary medical care."[32]

Underlying our society's tolerance of these dehumanizing conditions is a "rational self-interest" theory of violence.[33] According to this theory, people decide to use violence based on a rational calculation of costs and benefits. If the costs of wrongdoing are understood to be high enough, that should deter such wrongdoing. At least implicitly, assumptions follow from this theory that to allow our prisons to be hellholes will serve to prevent violence by deterring would-be wrongdoers (similar logic applies to the rationale for the death penalty).[34]

THE LOGIC OF RETRIBUTION IN PRACTICE: A STORY

Robert Hughes, in his account of the settling of Australia, illustrates this theory.[35] Great Britain founded Australia as a penal colony in the late eighteenth century. The British encouraged a terrible reputation for Australia, better to help deter crime. Over time, though, life in Australia proved to have its attractions, so officials decided to establish a prison within the prison that would indeed be worthy of even the most hardened criminal's terror.

Norfolk Island sits 1,000 miles east of Australia. The British leaders ordered Thomas Brisbane, Australia's governor, to "prepare a place of ultimate terror for the incorrigibles of the System."[36] He established on Norfolk Island a prison of last resort from which no escape would be possible. Brisbane intended this island to serve as "the nadir of England's penal system," the lowest level of hell. In Hughes's words, "Although no convict could escape from it, rumor and reputation would. In this way, the 'Old Hell,' as convict argot termed it, would reduce mainland crime by sheer terror."[37]

The settlement of the island began in 1825. The government's philosophy was concisely expressed: "Our object was to hold out that settlement

---

32. Gilligan, *Violence*, 23–24. See also Garland, *Culture*, 130.
33. Gilligan, *Violence*, 94–95.
34. Garland, *Peculiar*, 62–63.
35. Hughes, *Fatal*, see especially pages 460–551. See also Hirst, "Australian," especially 260–62.
36. Hughes, *Fatal*, 455.
37. Ibid., 456.

Instead of Atonement

as a place of the extremist Punishment, short of Death."[38] This object was achieved; Norfolk Island became "the worst place on earth." The hellishness of Norfolk Island may be seen in this example. A group of prisoners would draw lots, one became the murderer, the second the victim, and the rest witnesses. The prison's chief did not have the authority to try capital crimes; the murderer and the witnesses had to be sent to Sydney for trial. The prisoners "yearned for the meager relief of getting away from the 'ocean hell,' if only to a gallows on the mainland."[39] After several years of such "murders," the government began sending judges to the Island to try, convict, and hang the murderers there.

Hughes quotes a leading Scot churchman of the time, Reverend Sydney Smith, who asserted that a prison should be "a place of punishment from which men recoil with horror—a place of real suffering painful to the memory, terrible to the imagination, a place of sorrow and wailing, which should be entered with horror."[40]

In 1837, the British government sent Alexander Maconochie, a British naval commander and college professor, to investigate the treatment of prisoners in Australia. He wrote a report that condemned the System, that he believed "debased free and bond alike."[41] This report ended up in the hands of John Russell, the official in charge of the British penal system. Russell, who himself opposed the system of transportation of convicts to Australia, saw Maconochie's report as ammunition for his quest to reform, so he made sure that it was widely distributed.

Then in 1840, Russell appointed Maconochie head of Norfolk Island. Maconochie's initial encounter with the prisoners gave him hope. "He had the Old Hands mustered in the jail yard at Kingston and strode in to confront the collective stare of 1,200 men, nameless to him, masks of criminality and evasion, burnt by sun and seamed by misery, the twice convicted and doubly damned, Scottish bank clerks and aboriginal rapists, Spanish legionnaires and Malay pearlers, English killers and Irish rebels. 'A more demonical-looking assemblage could not be imagined,' he later wrote, 'and nearly the most formidable sight I ever beheld was the sea of faces upheld to me.' They looked at their new commander with utter skepticism."[42]

38. Ibid., 457.
39. Ibid., 468.
40. Ibid., 484.
41. Ibid., 490.
42. Ibid., 502.

Introduction: "Gospel as Bad News"?

As Maconachie explained that his role was not to be their torturer but to help the men change their lives, the prisoners began to cheer. According to one witness, "from that instant all crimes disappeared. The Old Hands from that moment were a different race of beings."[43]

Maconachie brought many books to Norfolk Island for the prisoners to read and sought, as his main form of therapy, to encourage the inmates to make music. He dismantled the gallows and discarded the whips used by floggers. He built two churches, Protestant and Catholic, whereas before there had been none. "He gave every man a plot of rich soil, set up classes in vegetable and fruit gardening . . . and encouraged them to sell their surplus to the officers."[44]

Maconochie met with remarkable success as he sought to rehabilitate the "worst of the worst." Under his administration, 920 prisoners were discharged to freedom. Only a small handful returned to prison.[45] However, this success did not insure Maconochie's continued role. The government recalled him in 1843, after only three years. Crime rate increases in Britain during the 1830s and early 1840s led to more harsh prison practices and support for having a symbol of the threat of extreme terror as a crime deterrent such as Norfolk Island.

Maconochie's successors returned to the harshness of the prison before his tenure. One's term concluded in 1846 with a mutiny that resulted in the execution of twelve Norfolk Island prisoners. Another's extraordinarily brutal punishments led to protests from a few ministers who visited Norfolk Island and observed his handiwork first hand. This led governmental leaders, who did not necessarily themselves oppose such treatment of prisoners, to fear that the prison "might become a serious embarrassment to the Crown" and to remove this head from the position in 1853. The government closed the prison on Norfolk Island shortly thereafter.

Norfolk Island, as became clear with the rejection of Maconochie's fruitful efforts to rehabilitate the prisoners, never had the purpose of reforming offenders or protecting society from the dangers of recidivistic convicts. Rather, Norfolk Island served as the symbol of ultimate terror—regardless of the costs to the actual prisoners who suffered mightily at the hands of the brutal administrators of the Island.

---

43. Ibid., 502–3.
44. Ibid., 510.
45. Ibid., 519.

Social Consequences

Ironically, it would appear that the effect of treating prisoners with brutality and other dehumanizing tactics actually serves to put the broader society more at risk.

James Gilligan argues, "if the purpose of imprisonment were to socialize men to become as violent as possible—both while they are there and after they return to the community—we could hardly find a more effective way to accomplish it than what we do."[46] Treating people violently makes them more violent. About nine out of every ten prisoners eventually return to society; treating prisoners violently and thereby making them more violent endangers all of us.

Gilligan states that the strongest predictor for people being violent is their being treated violently, especially as children.[47] "Violence does not occur spontaneously or without a cause, it only occurs when somebody does something that causes it. Therefore, all we need to do to prevent violence is to stop doing what we have been doing to cause it."[48] The logic of retribution is not an answer to the problem of violence; it is one of the central causes.

Nonetheless, we remain in the grip of that logic in our criminal justice practices—with many negative consequences.

1. Our culture in increasingly characterized by growing social fragmentation, exacerbated by the "othering" of convicted criminals. "To treat them as understandable is to bring criminals into our domain, to humanize them, to see ourselves in them and them in ourselves. The criminology of the other encourages us to be prepared to condemn more and understand less."[49]

2. We pour ever more governmental resources into our prison system. Ironically, by reducing public investments in education, job creation, and other factors that heighten the stake citizens have in our society we make crime more attractive for ever more needy people.

3. With the growing privatizing of prisons, we encourage a more austere system with fewer resources available to make prison life humane

---

46. Gilligan, *Violence*, 155.
47. Ibid., 25.
48. Gilligan, *Preventing Violence*, 20.
49. Garland, *Culture*, 184.

and a means for rehabilitation—plus, we make corruption and profiteering more likely.[50]

4. The combination of the growth of the imprisonment rate with punitive laws that permanently, in many states, disenfranchise convicted criminals, leads to a rapidly growing segment of the population that has no sense of being vested in the wider society. This sense of alienation, ironically fostered in the name of public safety, actually makes all of us less secure. "If the goal is to prepare people to live as law-abiding, contributing citizens, then objective data suggests that our prison system is a stellar example of failure."[51]

5. More broadly, beyond literal disenfranchisement, all convicts are given a lifetime stigma few will escape. They will spend the rest of their lives with the identity of "ex-con" living with a "debt to society" they are never allowed to repay.[52]

6. In general, the prison system increasingly serves as a breeding ground for more violence. We may see a direct relationship between the reduction of the role of prisons as a context for education in usable life skills (apparently the best predictor that convicts will not return to prison after release is if they have earned a college degree while in prison[53]) and the increase in the role of prisons as a context for education in violence.

7. Disturbing evidence continues to grow that shows that our present population of long-term prisoners is becoming a ticking time bomb due to high incidents of terrible communicative diseases that are likely to spread to the wider population in time. One example is the high incidence of Hepatitis C cases among prisoners.[54]

---

50. See, for example, Schlosser, "Prison-Industrial," and Logan, *Good Punishment*, chapter one, "Re/producing Criminality and the Prison-Industrial Complex."

51. Santos, *Inside*, xxiii.

52. McHugh, *Christian*, 148. As Herman Bianchi writes, "once a crime has been committed there is no forgiveness, and no activity of the offenders can bring them back into the community, not even passive submission to the harm we inflict on them" (*Justice*, 29–30).

53. Gilligan, *Preventing Violence*, 98–99. According to Gilligan, separate studies in the Massachusetts, Indiana, and California prison systems all showed that "not one prisoner who had acquired a college degree while in prison had been reincarcerated for a new crime."

54. Hylton, "Sick."

Instead of Atonement

Gilligan concludes, ultimately, that nothing stimulates crime as powerfully and effectively as punishment. "Punishment is a form of violence in its own right, but it is also a *cause* of violence." Punishment makes people more violent.[55] One main reason punishment has this impact is because punishment humiliates its recipient and has the ironic impact of heightening shame in a way that actually reduces a person's sense of guilt and responsibility. People who feel profound shame, Gilligan argues, are especially prone to acting violently, especially when the inhibiting influence of guilt is absent.

He describes how the dynamic tends to work:

> Man's greatest pain, whether in life or in prison, is the sense of personal insignificance, of being helpless and of no real value as a person, an individual—a man. Imprisoned and left without any voice in or control over the things that affect him, his personal desires and feelings regarded with gracious indifference, and treated at best like a child and at worst like an animal by those having control of his life, a prisoner leads a life of acute deprivation and insignificance. The psychological pain involved in such an existence creates an urgent and terrible need for reinforcement of his sense of manhood and personal worth. Unfortunately, prison deprives those locked within of the normal avenues of pursuing gratification of their needs and leaves them with no instruments but sex, violence, and conquest to validate their sense of manhood and individual worth.[56]

The spiral of violence intensifies—people hurt others, then the state steps in and hurts the violator. Part of this state-sanctioned hurting takes the form of setting the violator in a culture of extreme violence (the prison) that further socializes the violent person to be violent. Eventually, often more severely damaged than when entering prison, the violator returns to society primed for more violence.

Against Retribution: The True "Good News"

The notions of God and ultimate reality that underlie the retributive paradigm outlined above are not set in concrete. If we would return to Christianity's founding documents, the writings of the Bible, and try to read them afresh, free from the filters of later retributive paradigms, we

---

55. Gilligan, *Violence*, 184 (Gilligan's italics).
56. Ibid., 181.

might well discover the bases for a different understanding of justice, ultimate reality, and God. This alternative reading of the Bible provides the basis for constructing a new understanding of justice. We may call this new understanding "restorative" justice rather than retributive justice. Restorative justice offers us a different perspective on how we may respond to violence. Perhaps with a new perspective, we may be able to imagine responses to violence that break the cycle, and strive for healing rather than punishment of wrongdoers.

To put it another way, one of the sources of our problem (i.e., Christian theology) might actually provide a way to overcome the problem. Dutch law professor Herman Bianchi has argued that we should apply "homeopathic therapy" to our situation. Maybe it will take a dose of what made us sick to cure us. Since an interpretation of theology helped get us into this "illness" we have outlined above, Bianchi suggests that it may well take a dose of theology to heal us.[57]

In what follows, I will try to provide some resources for the work Bianchi suggests may be necessary—a biblical and theological rationale for rejecting the logic of retribution in favor of a logic of mercy, a rationale to replace "bad news" theology with "good news" theology. I will focus on one specific theological theme—salvation. We may see at the heart of the retributive paradigm an understanding of God's holiness and justice that bases salvation on sacrificial violence. In this paradigm, God's ability to save requires violence. In such a world, as Timothy Gorringe shows, we find inevitable links between the belief that God requires violence in response to violence and the justification of human beings (acting as God's representatives) being the agents of such required violence against other human beings.

If, as an alternative to a retribution-oriented understanding of salvation, we may construct an understanding of salvation that has no need for violence (ultimately, even, no room for violence) we may be in a better position to create peaceable ways of dealing with wrongdoing.

In what follows, I will provide a reading of biblical salvation that is non-retributive. So, first I will look at what the Old Testament tells us about salvation.

When I started my research several years ago, I expected that I would find that the role of sacrifice in the Old Testament economy of salvation would be similar to how it is portrayed in Christian substitutionary atonement theology. I expected to develop an argument that would give priority

---

57. Bianchi, *Justice*, 2.

to the prophets (especially Amos, Hosea, and Micah—the "eighth-century prophets") over the earlier sacrificial ideas—and see the prophets being the source for Jesus's own teaching on salvation. That is, I expected to have to read the Bible against the Bible.

However, while certainly the Bible does not offer a simple, totally unified understanding of salvation, I have found less of a gulf between the Old Testament portrayal of sacrifice (as sacrifice was intended to be) and the prophetic perspective than I expected. A case may be made (and I will attempt to make it) that the Old Testament actually presents sacrifice in ways analogous to how it presents the law. In both cases, what we have are not means to salvation so much as responses to God's saving initiative. And in both, we also have problems when the order is reversed and either the law or the sacrifice is seen as means to gain leverage over against God.

From start to finish the Old Testament does not present salvation as linked with a will of God for violence.[58] Rather, at its most basic level salvation in the Old Testament emerges from God's mercy, period. And sacrifice plays the role of providing a way for people to show their commitment to God as a *response* to God's saving works—just as following the law is meant to be how people show their commitment to God as a response to God's saving works (on this see most clearly Exodus 20:1–2, where Moses prefaces the Ten Commandments with a confession of God's saving work already expressed).

Human beings do not sacrifice nor follow the law in order to change God's attitude toward them (as in satisfying God's honor or justice). Sacrifice is a response and following the law is a response, meant to express the human choice to trust in God and follow God.

To understand sacrifice in this way significantly impacts how we read the critique of sacrifice in the eighth-century prophets. The prophets do not reject the rationale for sacrifice as provided for in Torah. Rather, they reject the way sacrifice and religiosity in general later found expression in their context. Sacrifice, according to Amos, became a means of making claims on God's favor that were separated from the demands of the core of the law for just living as *the* central required response to God's mercy. When sacrifice co-exists with profound injustice, it has been cut off from its life-source and rationale. When sacrifice is not a response to mercy that leads to just living, then that proves that the mercy has not been accepted.

---

58. This, of course, is not to claim that the Old Testament explicitly rejects all violence. However, if salvation itself is understood as being nonviolent, the way is cleared to see Jesus' rejection of violence as in continuity with the core biblical salvation story—in fact, as its logical outcome.

Introduction: "Gospel as Bad News"?

The prophetic understanding of salvation, then, does not a repudiate sacrifice per se, but rather underscores that salvation from the beginning in the Old Testament comes as a gift from God, initiated by God, and appropriated first by trust in God alone and a rejection of idols, and then actualized through sacrifice and obedience to the law.

We will find Jesus' own teaching to be compatible with the Old Testament's understanding of salvation. Interestingly, little attention in the history of theology has been paid to what Jesus himself said, directly and indirectly, about how human beings find harmony with God.[59] What was Jesus' own soteriology (doctrine of salvation)?

As near as I can tell, Jesus' teaching does not link salvation with the logic of retribution—in contrast with how the satisfaction atonement view presents salvation. Jesus himself did not teach about a God who needed an act of violence in order to establish a restored relationship with human beings. Jesus echoes the ideas of the prophets (and actually, the ideas of most of the Old Testament) when he twice quotes Hosea's words, "I desire mercy and not sacrifice" (Hos 6:6; Matt 9:13; 12:7).

In following this direction of thought, we will see that Jesus's death is not best understood as being a necessary sacrifice in order to satisfy God's honor, placate God's holiness, or balance the scales of justice. If God's mercy provides the basis for salvation, then Jesus' death loses much of the theological meaning that traditional theology assigns it.

This leads to the next step in my argument. The New Testament and Christian tradition obviously do place great importance on Jesus's death. If we seek to delink Jesus's death from traditional notions of necessary violence in order to satisfy God's holiness, might we still see Jesus's death as having importance for our beliefs and practices?

I will look at the story of Jesus's death attempting to answer this question. Why did Jesus die, according to the Gospels, and what meaning did that death have? I will argue that Jesus died due to the combined violence of cultural exclusivism (seen in the Pharisees and focused on the issue of the law), religious institutionalism (seen in the leaders linked with the temple), and political authoritarianism (seen in the occupying Roman

---

59. See Wright, *How God*: "There has been an assumption, going back at least as far as the Reformation, that 'the gospel' is what you find in Paul's letters. . . . This 'gospel' consists normally of a precise statement of what Jesus achieved in his saving death ('atonement') and a precise statement of how that achievement could be appropriated by the individual ('justification by faith'). Atonement and justification were assumed to be at the heart of 'the gospel.' But the 'gospels'—Matthew, Mark, Luke, and John—appear to have almost nothing to say about those subjects" (6).

colonial hierarchy, especially the governor, Pontius Pilate). That these forces conspired to kill Jesus is not without significance for our soteriology, even if considering these factors does lead to a dismissing of much about traditional soteriology connected with the belief in satisfaction atonement.

The basic saving significance of Jesus's death, I will suggest, may be found in how his death exposes the Powers that put him to death and reveals these Powers as rivals to the true God. We find in Jesus's death the bases for anti-idolatry, disillusionment with the central Principalities and Powers that seek to dominate human life and to separate people from God. The death of Jesus reveals the difference between the reign of God and the rule of evil. Evil uses violence; God's reign does not. The story of Jesus death does not tell of necessary violence as an expression of God's holiness, justice, and honor as a requirement for human salvation. Rather, the story of Jesus's death repudiates violence. It reveals that the Powers' claim to need to use violence is pure rebellion against God.

The next step in the argument will be to look at the story of Jesus's resurrection. The saving significance of the resurrection may be found in how it vindicates Jesus's life, reveals the Powers as idols, and promises that trust in God's love is the source of empowerment to find freedom from idols and restoration of harmony with God.

Then, finally, we will look at how this story of Jesus and salvation was presented in two crucial apostolic writings—Romans and Revelation. We will see how profoundly these books underscore the message of the Old Testament and Jesus about salvation.

So, I will show in this book that the Bible portrays the means of salvation as free from sacred violence. We may appropriately affirm that God's will does not ever include violence. Our affirmation of God's rejection of violence, finally, takes the ground out from the logic of retribution. We may, in God's name, actively seek alternatives to the various ways of justifying violence as the appropriate response to wrongdoing.

PART ONE

The Bible's Salvation Story

I INTEND THIS BOOK to be a Christian reflection on understanding salvation as a gift—and how this understanding might help us break free from the violence that is encouraged by acceptance of the logic of retribution. I focus on biblical theology for two main reasons.

First, the Bible powerfully shapes Christian beliefs and practices. Christians confess a commitment to listen to the Bible. All Christian theology and ethics remain accountable to the Bible. A second reason, using Dutch jurist Herman Bianchi's imagery, is a sense that our society needs something analogous to homeopathic treatment of our violence problem.[1] Since a significant historical source for our society's current retributive mindset has been Christian theology, then perhaps we need a theological antidote.

As seems clear, in the present as well, much of the social impetus for retributive responses to offenders (be they convicted criminals, straying children, or alleged "terrorists") is fueled by religiously oriented arguments.[2] A reconsideration of biblical materials, thus, provides the potential to think of alternatives to the logic of retribution from within the same framework that has reinforced that logic. Such refection also directly challenges present-day theologically grounded justifications of retribution.

The sheer breadth of biblical materials makes it impossible to fit every part in equal measure into one synthetic "biblical perspective." We need to be self-conscious with the ways we find the approximate coherence necessary to make the Bible usable. In what follows I will privilege the life and teaching of Jesus as providing our basic criteria for interpreting the rest of the Bible.

1. Bianchi, *Justice*, 2.
2. See Scalia, "God's Justice."

Some of these criteria include:

(1) The God of the Bible is most clearly revealed in the life and teaching of Jesus. Hence, biblical materials consistent with this revelation—those that portray God as merciful, as seeking to bring healing to human beings, as welcoming vulnerable people, as critical of human power politics—should be seen as providing the core of biblical revelation. And those materials in tension with such a portrayal will be seen as less central.

(2) The Bible presents a single basic story, beginning with the calling of Abraham and Sarah, proceeding through the history of Abraham and Sarah's descendants in the ancient Near East, and culminating with the ministry of Jesus and the emergence of the community of Jesus-followers. This single story provides the orienting point for all biblical materials—and establishes that biblical revelation is first of all narrative.[3]

(3) God's primary representatives throughout the story act from outside the power structures of Israel and the nations. Abraham and Sarah were "wanderers," Moses a fugitive from Egypt. Most prophets spoke as independent voices, Jesus as an itinerant rabbi. Hence, authoritative biblical speech is grounded in content, not the official status of the speaker.

I will present the Bible as a coherent collection of faith-stories first told to inspire adherence to God's reign among human beings. My concern will be with the basic plotline of the material when read as a whole. Reading the Bible theologically and ethically differs from reading it historically (the way critical scholars and evangelical-fundamentalist apologetes tend to read it). In focusing on the story, I will not spend time on discussions of authorship and specifics of historical context, but focus on the narrative itself.

Hence, in what follows, my concern will center on how the Bible itself presents salvation. I will tend toward looking at the big picture and the development of the over-arching story, more than isolating specific parts. However, I am not looking to harmonize all the differences or impose a rigid uniformity on the materials.

Due to the limitations of space, I will not spend the energy I could (with great profit) on reflecting on the tensions within the story. My concern here is with identifying the main storyline and reflecting on how we may see salvation portrayed there.

For this approach to be valid, we must assume that casting the net ever wider over the diversity outside the main story line would still ultimately reinforce that story line. I hope to work more on that task in the

---

3. See Josipovici, *Book*, and Schneidau, *Sacred*.

future, and I will be delighted if what I write here stimulates others to test my arguments more broadly in the Bible.

For now, I self-consciously present an argument meant to suggest more than prove. I offer what follows as a contribution to a much-needed, ongoing process of discernment and reflection among people of good will—an attempt to appropriate the biblical story in a way that will foster life and wholeness.

TWO

Salvation in the Old Testament
Healing, Law, and Sacrifice

We may see the Bible as a collection of writings on the theme of how human beings may live on earth in relationship with God, the creator of heaven and earth. When this relationship is strong, human life is whole—healthy, balanced, creative, expansive, vital, peaceful. Salvation has to do with how this wholeness might happen.

From Cain's murder of Abel at the beginning of Genesis to visions of bloodletting in Revelation, violence undermines human wholeness. Salvation and violence have much to do with one another. Salvation frees people from threats of violence. At the same time, quite often violence seems to be a tool that effects salvation—holy wars, judgment versus wrongdoers, violence that cleanses the earth of evildoers, the violent sacrifice of innocent life.

The Bible links salvation with God—in a paradoxical way. God intervenes to provide what we need for wholeness. But do we also need to be saved from God? Are we condemned to suffer God's wrath unless God's disposition toward us might be changed? Does God require sacrificial violence for this disposition to change, operating according to the logic of retribution?

Does the portrayal of salvation in the Bible provide us a model of the need to respond to violence with violence—a retributive model? Or, does the portrayal of salvation in the Bible provide a model of how violence must be dealt with in a way that ends the violence—a restorative model, a God who orders the cosmos in terms of mercy and a desire to heal the wrongdoer and community when there is a violation?

PART ONE: The Bible's Salvation Story

Clearly, the Bible gives mixed signals. We see this ambiguity in the extreme diversity throughout Christian history among biblical interpreters concerning these questions. However, I believe that the crises of our present world, the extent of violence and brokenness, do not allow us to throw up our hands in relativistic despair in face of the diversity within the Bible and the diversity among Christian interpreters. I will read the Bible in a way that does draw conclusions. I will argue that the overall (though not unanimous) testimony of the biblical writings—Old and New Testaments together—points against retribution.

I read the Old Testament as a Christian, through the lens of Jesus. Reading the Old Testament in this way simply means allowing Jesus's values to guide how I sort through the various witnesses. I still try to read the Old Testament on its own terms. However, I make choices among this diversity to place the highest priority on themes that reflect Jesus's priorities.

In this chapter and in chapters three and four, I show the coherence among (1) the "primal story line of the Old Testament,"[1] (2) the presentation of the law and sacrifice, (3) the message of key prophets, and (4) the teaching of Jesus concerning salvation.

In a nutshell, all of these sources, in general terms, portray salvation as a simple act of God's mercy. All of these sources assume a God who does not first need to be persuaded by human acts in order to make whatever provisions are necessary for salvation to occur. All of these sources present salvation as being free from the logic of retribution.

What Is Salvation?

Salvation has to do with wholeness. To gain salvation leads to harmony with God, other human beings, and with the rest of creation. We need salvation when we live with disharmony, when we experience brokenness instead of wholeness.

The Old Testament begins with a portrayal of creation at peace. However, after the beginning, the Bible presupposes disharmony and brokenness—and focuses on the struggle for salvation. Salvation results in healed brokenness, restored health and wholeness. The Bible presents salvation on three levels: (1) salvation as liberation from Powers of brokenness, (2) salvation as restoration of harmony with God, and (3) salvation as

---

1. This is Walter Brueggemann's phrase. See Brueggemann, *Bible*, 45–50. Brueggemann defines "the primal narrative" as "that most simple, elemental, and non-negotiable story line which lies at the heart of biblical faith," 45–46.

restoration of harmonious human relationships. The Old Testament story places priority on salvation in the first sense (liberation). The other two follow from and depend upon the first. Because God acts to deliver, people are then freed to respond to God and restore harmony in their relationships with God and to live at harmony with one another.

The Healing God

"The primal story line of the Old Testament is a sequence of events through which Yahweh intervenes in the life of Israel in order to effect rescue, deliverance, and emancipation. These actions are nameable, concrete, and decisively transformative, and are termed 'salvation' or 'deliverance' (see Isa 52:7,10; Pss 27:1; 78:22)."[2]

In presenting salvation the way it does, via concrete events communicated in stories, the Old Testament locates this salvation in history and not in a cosmic, transcendent context. Salvation in the Old Testament is not about some transaction in the heart of God or some sort of weighing of the cosmic scale of justice. Rather, salvation has to do with flesh and blood actions.

Let me sketch a short version of the primal story line of the Old Testament—with its basic concern for portraying God as savior within Israel's story.[3] I will mention eight main aspects of this story line, following the order in which the story is told.[4] The primal story serves as our main source for the biblical understanding of salvation.

(1) *Creation*. What is, is good, created good by a loving God committed to a genuine relationship of freedom with humankind. This God, we see in Genesis one, loves the entire created order—an important prelude to the soon-to-come focus on one particular people.[5]

(2) *Disruption*. Adam and Eve break the harmony when they reject the limitations that God placed on them. We then see a spiral of violence—their son Cain murders his brother Abel, the Flood of Noah, the building of the Tower of Babel. Yet, God remains committed to human beings. We see this commitment, for example, in the rainbow God gives after the Flood.

---

2. Brueggemann, *Reverberations*, 184.
3. I essentially follow Brueggemann's outline in *Bible*.
4. This section draws on Grimsrud, *God's Healing*.
5. Birch, *Let Justice*, 71.

PART ONE: The Bible's Salvation Story

(3) *God's healing strategy.* This strategy begins with the calling of Abraham and Sarah to found a community of faith. God promises this community that it will bless all the families of the earth. "The movement into particularity (the beginning of Israel's story) is to be read within the frame of God's universal purposes (the beginning and well-being of all things)."[6]

(4) *Exodus.* God's healing strategy continues with Abraham's descendants' liberation from slavery in Egypt. The exodus frees the people to enter the promised land that God gives them so they may establish their community. In leaving Egypt, they reject the values of Egypt.

(5) *Nationhood.* The exodus leads to the establishment of a Hebrew kingdom in the promised land. On the journey to the land, the people are given the law for shaping their common life in line with the will of this liberating God. Under Joshua's leadership, the people enter the land.

The Hebrews' kingdom departs from God's will. The elders decide they need a king. David becomes Israel's greatest king, in many ways living faithfully—"after God's own heart." However, David sins grievously when he commits adultery with Bathsheba and has Bathsheba's husband killed. David's son, Solomon, decisively moves human kingship in the direction of authoritarianism. Israel's movement away from the vision of Moses continues under the kings who succeed Solomon, as the society becomes more and more like Pharaoh's Egypt.

(6) *Prophetic witness.* God remains involved with the Hebrews, especially through the prophets. The prophets keep alive Torah's central thrust: the ideals of peace, justice, compassion for the weak and needy, and accountability to God. These "radical conservatives" attempted to hold Israel to the main tenants of Torah. The prophets challenge corrupt kings (e.g., Elijah), critique injustice (e.g., Amos), and speak of God's ongoing love (e.g., Hosea).

(7) *Exile.* The Babylonian empire conquers the Hebrew kingdom, destroying the temple and king's palace. Israel's leadership class is sent into exile. Prophets say God judges due to the nation disobeying God's will. However, even in the context of judgment and exile, God still speaks words of hope to people of faith (see especially Isa 40–55). These words point forward to new expressions of God's healing strategy. In the end, God does not abandon God's people but continues to use them as channels for whole-making love.

---

6. Ibid., 107.

(8) *Return.* After the Assyrians defeat Babylon, many of Israel's exiles return to their homeland. They seek to sustain the faith community in the context of living as a subject people. They rebuild the temple (though without its former splendor) and (more importantly) focus on the recovery of Torah-centered life. God sustains the community even as the people struggle to keep the promise alive.

THE PRIMAL SALVATION STORY

When we get to the New Testament, we will find that Jesus and his followers express their understandings of salvation in terms of the Old Testament's primal story. Salvation in the New Testament is also narrative. Salvation has to do with the concrete lives of God's people—not cosmic transactions. In relation to salvation, God acts, mercifully. God's character is revealed to be gracious and focused on healing—not retributive and focused on balancing the scales of justice and satisfying the dictates of honor. We learn all we need to know about salvation by tracing the story.

In this primal salvation story, the key saving act of God comes in the exodus. However, the exodus presupposes God's initial call of Abraham and Sarah that establishes them as a people meant to bless all of the families of the earth (Gen 12:3).

The biblical story of salvation channeled through a particular people begins with Genesis 12. In response to the brokenness of creation, God seeks patiently to heal. Genesis 12:1–3 tells of the beginning of God's strategy for healing. God's strategy is summarized in the words to Abraham in verse three: "In you all the families of the earth shall be blessed." Through what happens with you and your descendents, salvation will spread to all corners of the earth.

God encourages healing when God calls a people and establishes a community to know God. God's strategy to bring about peace leads to another act of creation, the creation of a community. People of faith living together, face-to-face, as they learn to love and give and take, will make peace for all the families of the earth.[7]

---

7. We must acknowledge, as well, the inherent dangers in the calling of a particular community. Too easily—as we see in the biblical accounts and in the years since then—the sense of calling to be God's people becomes distorted. When this sense of calling is separated from the mandate to "bless all the families of the earth," the called community may become self-centered and more easily violent toward those outside the community (and even toward those within the community who do not adequately conform to the community's norms). This issue will arise numerous times in the pages to come.

PART ONE: The Bible's Salvation Story

How might this be? Isaiah 2:2–4 gives an answer:

> In days to come the mountain of the Lord's house shall be established as the highest of the mountains, and shall be raised up above the hills. Peoples shall stream to it, and many nations shall come and say, "Come, let us go up to the mountain of the Lord, to the house of the God of Jacob; that he may teach us his ways and that we may walk in his paths." For out of Zion shall go forth instruction, and the word of the Lord from Jerusalem. He shall judge between the nations, and shall arbitrate between many peoples; they shall beat their swords into plowshares, and their spears into pruning hooks; nation shall not lift up sword against nation, neither shall they learn war any more.

In Isaiah's vision, people from all nations come to the house of Jacob (Israel) to learn the ways of peace—because they have seen such peace expressed in the lives of the people of Israel. The importance of this vision may be seen in its being repeated almost exactly in Micah 4:1–3.

Genesis traces the fate of Abraham's direct descendants. The last part of the book tells how his great-grandson Joseph ended up in Egypt, sold into slavery. In time, though, Joseph gains his freedom and rises to leadership in Egypt as the right-hand man of the king (Pharaoh). Joseph's father, Jacob, his brothers, and their families eventually follow Joseph to Egypt. At first they are in Pharaoh's favor. However, after many years, Egypt comes under the rule of a new king, "who did not know Joseph" (Exod 1:8). This Pharaoh returns the Hebrews to slavery.

Exodus 2:23–25 tells of their situation. "The Israelites groaned under their slavery, and cried out. Out of the slavery their cry for help rose up to God. God heard their groaning, and God remembered God's covenant with Abraham, Isaac, and Jacob. God looked upon the Israelites, and God took notice of them." God remembered the promise given Abraham.

The next several chapters tell how God liberates the children of Israel from slavery. Moses's part of the story begins with his personal exile from Egypt, his childhood home. Moses then returns and becomes a leader of the Hebrew people, who are slaves in Egypt under the iron hand of Pharaoh. Moses asks Pharaoh to let the Hebrews go; Pharaoh refuses. God performs several wonders designed to get Pharaoh to change his mind. God turns water into blood, then brings frogs, gnats, flies, disease, boils, thunder and hail, locusts—and finally dense darkness. Pharaoh at first refuses to reconsider, then says the people can go but not the livestock. Moses says this is not good enough, thereby enraging Pharaoh, who says he will not reconsider any more.

Salvation in the Old Testament

So, the final plague occurs. Every first-born child and every first-born animal in Egypt is put to death—except those of the Hebrews, because the death angel "passed over" them. Pharaoh finally relents and lets the Hebrews go. Then he changes his mind and chases them. As the Egyptian army readies to pounce on the Hebrews, whose backs are to the Red Sea, the sea opens up and the Hebrews pass through. When the Egyptians follow, the sea crashes down on them. Finally, Pharaoh faces defeat and the Hebrew people are set free. Exodus 15 celebrates that final victory: "The Lord has triumphed gloriously" (15:1).

The Exodus was a crucial part of God's healing strategy and an important memory for biblical faith. Old Testament writers often evoke, or report the evoking of, the memory of God's deliverance (see, especially, Pss 22; 77; 78; 105; 106; 114; 136). God loved you, God delivered you, God brought you salvation—praise God. Let God's love for you move you to love others. Remember how God treated you when you were being oppressed, and see that you do not oppress others (see Lev 19:33–34).

The God of the Exodus is not the God of people in power. This God, unlike other gods, is not a projection from the king who reinforces the king's power. The God of the Exodus is a God of slaves who gives life to the lifeless. This God hears the cries of those being treated like non-persons, like tools to increase the king's wealth.

The Hebrews did not defeat Pharaoh by their own strength. God's miracles (the plagues, the parting of the Red Sea) brought about liberation. The center of power in this new society lay not with generals and warriors, but with the peoples' God.[8] Thus, that which God values most (mercy, compassion, caring for the powerless and outcast, just distribution of resources) matters most in the society—not the increase of wealth and power for the already wealthy and powerful. The people with the most power are the weaponless prophets, those who best discern the will of the liberating God.[9]

We see in the Old Testament "salvation story" two distinct themes. First God calls Abraham and Sarah and promises salvation: a gift of newness in the context of barrenness. God plans to use the community of faith to bring newness to all the families of the earth. This call begins a long process where God's persevering love brings salvation. Second, God intervenes in the exodus to bring salvation to God's people. God is a God who

---

8. See Millard C. Lind's treatment of the Exodus as the paradigmatic Old Testament "Holy War" wherein the key point lay not with inter-human violence but with God's intervention against militarism in Lind, *Yahweh*.

9. Lind, "Concept."

PART ONE: The Bible's Salvation Story

liberates the oppressed. God's salvation does not come through human power politics. God's salvation leads to a rejection of the values of empires such as ancient Egypt.

Behind God's gifts and God's demands lay God's mercy. Salvation does not rest on human purity or satisfaction of god's needs. Salvation comes from God's infinite store of mercy that leads to God's persevering and patient love finding expression in Israel's history. Salvation arises as God's initiative and God's unilateral intervention to heal.

The "salvation story" tells us: (1) God, in love, commits to a long healing process with humankind and (2) God's healing work involves at its core a counter-cultural sensibility that exalts the oppressed and vulnerable and defies power politics.

As the Hebrews traveled through the wilderness on their way to the promised land, God spoke to them through Moses and gave them the law—God's directives for faithful living. The law provides social structure for the delivered slaves to sustain the effects of that deliverance. The law provides a framework for ongoing faithful living according to God's shalom. As Norman Gottwald writes, "Yahweh not only sets these former 'nobodies' on a new foundation that gives them identity and self-worth, but grants them alternative social and economic forms of life so they need not lapse back into tributary domination or unbridled self-seeking."[10]

In addition, God gave the promised land so these people could settle down and establish a society that would live out the fruit of the exodus liberation. The ongoing faithful living required a place.[11]

Numerous times throughout the Old Testament, writers recall the basic outline of this primal story of salvation. As a rule, the God of this story is a God of unmerited love, a God who simply chooses to deliver God's people. A typical recounting of God's work comes in Hosea 11, set fairly late in the eighth century BCE. At the beginning of this chapter, Hosea recites the basic story of ancient Israel. He starts with the assumption that Israel is God's child. The parent-child dynamic—the tender love of a mother and infant, the father teaching the child to play games, the parents providing food and shelter, affection and discipline, education and exhortation—captures at least something of how God and Israel were connected.

"When Israel was a child, I loved him, and out of Egypt I called my child" (Hos 11:1). Throughout, the Old Testament sees exodus as central

10. Gottwald, *Hebrew Bible*, 353.
11. See Brueggemann, *Land*, especially pages 43–65.

to Israel's identity and Israel's understanding of God. God freed the poor enslaved Hebrews from Egypt. The Hebrews did not have to prove themselves before God would love them. God took the first step out of pure mercy: "Out of Egypt I called my child." However, God did ask that these former slaves follow Torah—ordering their communal life justly, treating each other with the care and respect God had shown them. By following Torah they would show their commitment to the one true God.

The story tells us, though, that Israel did not remain committed to God's ways. "The more I called them," God says in Hosea, "the more they went from me; they kept sacrificing to the Baals [to other gods], and offering incense to idols" (Hos 11:2).

The chapter makes the point, though, that ultimately God's healing love remains decisive. Exodus may be followed by brokenness, but God still works to heal. God asks, "How can I give you up, Ephraim? How can I hand you over, O Israel?" (11:8). Ephraim is one of Israel's tribes. God asks the people of the covenant this basic question, Can I simply write you off?

"How can I make you like Admah? How can I treat you like Zeboiim?" (11:8). These were two cities, according to Genesis 19, destroyed along with Sodom and Gomorrah. Can I simply wipe you out in judgment? If we were dealing with a God whose primary characteristic was adherence to the logic of retribution, the answer would be yes.

However, God does not intend retribution here. "My heart recoils within me; my compassion grows warm and tender. I will not execute my fierce anger; I will not again destroy Ephraim; for I am God and no mortal, the Holy One in your midst, and I will not come in wrath." God says, in effect, no, I will not simply act in anger and vengeance. I will not treat you like Sodom and Gomorrah. What will determine my actions is my compassion, my love for you.

Why does God do this? Because "I am your God and no mortal" (11:9). God does this because of God's character. God does this because ultimately God is a compassionate God. God desires healing, not retribution. God desires salvation, not punishment.

Hosea 11, then, portrays the basic salvation story in terms of God's love that liberated the Hebrews, plus God's patience in remaining committed to the people's salvation even as they pursue self-destructive idolatrous paths, plus God's "warm and tender" compassion that ultimately provides the people with a future. This future, though, did include severe trauma.

With the book of Jeremiah, several generations after Hosea, we read that the Hebrew kingdom's severe trauma arrived—as well as why. The

PART ONE: The Bible's Salvation Story

Babylonians invaded, destroying the center of Israel's religious life, the temple, and the center of their political life, the king's palace. They killed many people and shipped many others away to Babylon to live in exile.

Jeremiah's theology emphasizes God's involvement in these terrible events. He refused to see the Hebrews' defeat as God's defeat. In fact, as Jeremiah presents it, God instigated the Hebrews' defeat due to their unfaithfulness. Their God is vindicated in their own failure.[12] However, God's intentions toward the Hebrews still remained redemptive:

> The days are surely coming, says the Lord, when I will make a new covenant with the house of Israel and the house of Judah. It will not be like the covenant that I made with their ancestors when I took them out of the land of Egypt—a covenant that they broke. . . . This is the covenant that I will make with the house of Israel after those days, says the Lord: I will put my law within them, and I will write it on their hearts; and I will be their God, and they shall be my people. No longer shall they teach one another, or say to each other, "know the Lord," for they shall all know me, from the least of them to the greatest, says the Lord; for I will forgive their iniquity, and remember their sin no more. (Jer 31:31–34)

A generation later, in the despair of exile, with two of the main pillars of Hebrew identity (temple and palace) in rubble, God gave the people a gift of hope through the words recorded in Isaiah, beginning in chapter 40: "Comfort, O comfort my people, says your God. Speak tenderly to Jerusalem, and cry to her that she has served her term, that her penalty is paid."

It is clear that the "penalty" here is mainly a figure of speech. It is not that God has literally received a "payment" of retribution that now allows God to forgive. Rather, Israel's recognition of God's healing love took this time of exile and suffering ("penalty") to become clear.[13] Even after the failures of the Hebrew kingdom and without actual moral compensation or proof of purity, God still loves God's people and offers them healing.

Isaiah 43 contains powerful words from God. You have been suffering, you exiles, "but now thus says the Lord, he who created you . . . do not fear for I have redeemed you; I have called you by name, you are mine" (43:1). "But now" things have changed. Through the brokenness comes hope for wholeness and healing; through the confusion comes clarity as to God's love.

---

12. Schwartz, *Curse*, 44.
13. Brueggemann, *Isaiah 40–66*, 18.

Isaiah 51:1–3 challenges: "Look to the rock from which you were hewn, and to the quarry from which you were dug. Look to Abraham, your father and to Sarah who bore you; for he was but one when I called him, but I blessed him and made him many. For the Lord will comfort Zion; God will comfort all her waste places, and will make her wilderness like Eden, her desert like the garden of the Lord; joy and gladness will be found in her."

Look to God as your creator who made you and blessed you as good and gave you responsibilities to share God's care and love with the world. Look to the way God has cared for those who have gone before and look to the tradition of God's people of which you are part. Look to the promises of God to bring healing, joy, and gladness. Clarity about our identity as God's people feeds hope, feeds a sense that the future is meaningful and will be fruitful.

Israel experienced a shattering loss of its physical home. The Temple, the king's palace, the great city of Jerusalem all lay in ruins. The people suffered in exile. Yet, in this context of deep trauma—the loss of their world, actually—the prophet once again proclaimed God's love. When God says to the people, "You are precious in my sight, and honored, and I love you" (43:4), God does not speak to faithful people. God speaks to the people who have been judged and traumatized because of their lack of faithfulness. It is to the unworthy people that God says, "You are precious in my sight, and honored, and I love you."

Isaiah 54:9–10 sums up this message of hope: "This is like the days of Noah to me: Just as I swore that the waters of Noah would never again go over the earth, so I have sworn that I will not be angry with you and will not rebuke you. For the mountains may depart and the hill be removed, but my steadfast love shall not depart from you, and my covenant of peace shall not be removed, says the Lord, who has compassion on you."

The Hebrews have done nothing to earn what seems like a change in God's disposition—any more than people in the time of Noah had (see Gen 8:21, God's statement of human sinfulness after the flood leading into the rainbow covenant). The mercy is gratuitous and becomes clear only when God's love continues in the midst of great trauma.

The heart of the Old Testament's primal story may be seen as three key saving moments: the calling of Abraham and Sarah (Gen 12), the liberation of the Hebrews from slavery (Exod 1–15), and the proclamation of mercy to the Hebrew exiles (Isa 40–55). The following conclusions concerning salvation and the logic of retribution follow from the primal story.

PART ONE: The Bible's Salvation Story

(1) God gives salvation in each of these key moments to unworthy recipients. Abraham and Sarah have no particular virtues; they are simply "wanderers." The Hebrews in Egypt were demoralized slaves who showed no evidence of worshiping the God of their ancestors. And, the exiles of Isaiah 40–55 had lost their pillars of identity due to their unfaithfulness to Torah.

The explicitness of the unworthiness of those being saved by God makes clear that they had done nothing to earn God's favor. The logic of retribution tells us that God must act to destroy the unworthy, that God cannot save them unless somehow God restores the "balance of the scales of justice" through punitive acts. The actual story tells us something quite different.

(2) God the savior acts in these moments purely out of God's own good will. In each case God supplies most of the action. The saving acts came unilaterally from God, due to God's free choice to intervene. The recipients did nothing to "purchase" God's favor, nothing to obligate a legalistic God to act. God required no human acts to balance the scales of justice. "God's deliverance is not compelled or made necessary; it is unrelated to any special merit on Israel's part (cf. especially Deut 7:8). The Exodus experience is an initiative of God's grace, a divine action freely taken for the sake of establishing relationship and community."[14]

These three salvation moments show that when God wants simply to intervene and bring healing to the world, God freely does so. God is not constrained by a holiness that needs to have its demands for an evenly balanced "justice" satisfied before offering transforming mercy.

(3) At its core, according to the primal story, salvation has to do with a loving, passionate God desiring a personal connection with humanity. God's work to sustain these relationships emerges from this personal, passionate, and loving disposition. God's desire for relationships with God's people fuels the saving acts of God. God's intervention is personal, born out of compassion and love, leading to liberating acts that effect and sustain human/divine relationality.

This portrayal contradicts the logic of retribution that posits an impersonal, legalistic, detached dynamic at the heart of salvation. The saving God of the Old Testament does not follow the dictates of abstract justice and static holiness, but follows the dynamics of concrete, personal, and creative restorative justice and healing holiness.

---

14. Birch, *Let Justice*, 116.

(4) According to a typical account of the primal story, Hosea 11, God's holiness fuels mercy, not retribution. Hosea recites God's saving acts, then critiques the Hebrews for turning from God. But God, in agony over the broken relationship, asserts that because of holiness, God will not come in punitive wrath but rather will act with warm and tender compassion.

From Hosea's perspective, God's holiness does not force God to destroy sinners. Rather, God's holiness is precisely the attribute that pushes God to intervene, to become involved *with* sinful humanity in order to bring healing. The sin problem, then, does not lead to divine action to punish and destroy but to divine action to heal and restore.

Salvation comes first in this story—and it comes directly from the intervention of a merciful God bringing healing to undeserving humanity. God simply acts to save. This simple initiative of God determines the nature of biblical salvation. God gives the gift of salvation to empower the embodiment of shalom. The gift means to enable the response.

This basic dynamic of gift and response provides the necessary context for understanding two important Old Testament institutions—Torah (the law) and sacrifices. Human obligation to keep Torah and to keep sacrifices follows from the gift of salvation. Human beings are not required to follow Torah or offer sacrifices in order to gain God's favor. Rather, human beings keep Torah and offer sacrifices because they have already received God's favor.

At least, according to the story, this is how Torah and sacrifices were meant to operate. In chapter three, we will look at the prophetic response to the failure of these institutions to operate as they were meant to. And, in that response we will see the primal story's portrayal of salvation reiterated. But first, we must look at law and sacrifice as they were meant to be.

THE ROLE OF THE LAW

Following the Exodus, as the Hebrews traveled through the wilderness on their way to the promised land, God spoke to them through Moses, giving them the law (Torah). God gave the law to provide social structure for the delivered slaves so that the effects of that deliverance could be sustained. The law provides a framework for ongoing faithful living. In addition, God gave the promised land so these people could establish an ongoing society that would live out the fruit of the exodus liberation. The ongoing faithful living required a place. "The liberating act of God constitutes freedom from socio-economic, physical, and psychological oppression and has as

PART ONE: The Bible's Salvation Story

its goal life in the land of promise." God's liberation finds concrete expression in the gift of Torah at Sinai.[15]

God gave these gifts so the people would spread God's shalom to all the families of the earth. The context for the law included two crucial affirmations: (1) God saves by grace, in mercy, with acts of deliverance. The law comes after—not as a means of earning salvation but as an additional work of God's grace, a resource for ordering peaceable living in the community of God's people.[16] (2) God intends to create universal shalom, to bless the families of the earth (God's healing strategy). Exodus 19:6: "The whole earth is mine. . . . You shall be for me a priestly kingdom." The Hebrews are called to mediate God's presence to the "whole earth."[17]

As a whole, Torah (when understood in context) is far from the rigid, fearful, legalistic, burdensome set of rules as presented in many Christian stereotypical portrayals.[18] In many ways, Torah is radical and creative.[19] The books of the law (Exodus, Leviticus, Numbers, and Deuteronomy) present the words of the law coming to the Hebrews through a prophet, not a king. The law is not the tool of an all-powerful, dominating king buttressed by state-generated violence. Rather, the law reflects the free and creative will of the slave liberating, Pharaoh-defying God of the Hebrews. "Moses was not a warrior and led no army. He was sent forth only as a messenger . . . who must fear God rather than the military might of Pharaoh."[20]

As well, the law supports, reinforces, and sustains the social radicalism of the leader who brings it to the people.[21] The content of the law and the challenge to the Egyptian status quo both find expression in Moses. The exodus and the giving of the law cohere in their purpose. At the heart of Torah, symbolizing this overturning of Empire values but also with major practical ramifications, lies God's direct concern for vulnerable people.[22]

The law makes specific provision to protect the well-being of widows, of orphans, of other vulnerable ones among the Hebrews, and of resident aliens among the Hebrews. The law anchors this call for the Hebrews to be

---

15. Van Wijk-Bos, *Making Wise*, 15-16.
16. Birch, et al., *Theological Introduction*, 151.
17. Ibid., 139.
18. For a sharp critique of Christian misunderstandings of Judaism, see Yoder, *Jewish-Christian*, especially chapter 1, "It Did Not Have to Be."
19. Hanson, *People*, 45-52.
20. Lind, *Monotheism*, 124.
21. Gottwald, *Hebrew Bible*, 353.
22. Birch, *Let Justice*, 162.

Salvation in the Old Testament

concerned for vulnerable ones in their midst in God's care for the Hebrews while they were slaves in Egypt. "The alien who resides with you shall be to you as a citizen among you; you shall love the alien as yourself, for you were aliens in the land of Egypt; I am the Lord your God" (Lev 19:34).

The law not only argued on behalf of vulnerable people presently among the Hebrews, it also sought to prevent the creation of new groups of vulnerable people. "The reason the commands are sought and insistent is that they are Yahweh's (and therefore Israel's) strategy to fend off a return to pre-Exodus conditions of exploitation and brutality within the community."[23]

The law established a decentralized social structure supporting economic viability for each household. The inheritance law meant to keep families on the land over the generations by preventing dispossession from the land and the resultant maldistribution of power and wealth. At its heart, Torah was not about picky, legalistic rules that must not be violated out of fear of harsh punishment. Rather, Torah sought healthy communal relationships for all in the community. Torah had a constructive, relational, and life-embracing concern.[24]

Power, according to the law, did not rest primarily in the hand of a few political leaders. Social life was not oriented around a king. At one point, the law does allow for a human king (though this is a very brief reference, Deut 17:14–20). But even then, kingship for Israel is redefined over against the empire way. Deuteronomy tells us the king must not gather weapons of war or wealth. The king must remain submissive to the law, "neither exalting himself above other members of the community nor turning aside from the commandment" (Deut 17:20).

According to Torah, to do justice is the responsibility of every person in the community. Justice is not a monopoly of the state, hired enforcers who "do justice" when they wield the punitive sword. Justice was for everyone, its enactment decentralized and meant to heal the community, not "protect the honor" of the state or some abstract ideal of holiness and balanced pain paid for pain. "By investing greatly in the creation of a covenantal brotherhood of individuals bound by law and theology, the Pentateuch envisions an ideal society that holds together on the merits of its members, rather than on the basis of the authority of its power brokers."[25]

---

23. Brueggemann, *Theology*, 184.

24. I am indebted to Millard Lind's work on the law in what follows. See especially his programmatic essay, "Law."

25. Berman, *Created*, 169.

PART ONE: The Bible's Salvation Story

The laws directly address each Hebrew: "*You* shall . . . ," "*You* shall not . . ." The personal nature of the laws reflects the basic dynamic of God's involvement with the Hebrews.[26] Because God, the lawgiver, is personal, and seeks to create healthy communities, then the Law is also at its heart personal. The purpose of justice is to serve the relationships of the community. The goal when there is brokenness is the restoration of relationships.

This is all the case because ultimately, the law stems from God's will to liberate. The Hebrews' motives for following the Law are love for this God who liberates. The first word, when the Law was presented by Moses, is this: "I am the Lord your God, who brought you out of the land of Egypt, out of the house of slavery" (Exod 20:2). "Again and again in the statutes and ordinances that spell out the specifics of living by the commandments, one encounters a recollection or a call to remember how the Lord led them out of Egypt, out of the house of slavery (Lev 25:42; Deut 13:5; 15:15; 20:1; 24:18, 22; et al)."[27]

To follow the law does not lead people to salvation. Salvation leads people to follow the law. The first act is God's—a merciful act of gratuitous liberation. In God's free and sovereign love, God may simply act to liberate. Then, as a further act of mercy, God gives the law as directives for how a liberated people ought to act.[28] The law is not a legalistic blueprint that, when violated, triggers God's wrath and renders God unable (due to God's holiness) to act directly with pure mercy. Rather, the law is, simply, the loving gift of a merciful God for the sake of the life of God's people.

We saw in chapter one how theologians who follow the logic of retribution understand the law as a standard that marks the purity expected of all people; its violation leads to God's punitive response. However, this is not biblical law. Biblical law offers a vision of God's will for life in the here and now. The problem with violations of the law is not so much harm to God's purity but harm to others in the community. Violations lead to responses that intend to bring healing to victim, offender, and community. "Observance of the Mosaic Torah is the opposite of an obstacle to a loving and intimate relationship with God. It is the vehicle and the sign of just that relationship."[29]

Most fundamentally, biblical law has its roots in God's love. It expresses God's mercy meant to empower people of faith to live joyful,

---

26. Lind, "Law," 66.
27. Miller, *Ten Commandments*, 16.
28. Birch, *Let Justice*, 154.
29. Levenson, *Sinai*, 45.

healthy lives in community. Law, for the logic of retribution in contrast, has its roots in God's "holiness."[30] It expresses God's strict justice meant to communicate to human beings the appropriateness of God's punitive wrath as a response to human failure to follow the law.

When we read the story from its beginning, we will see that the first move in creating a community centered on Torah was for God unilaterally to bring liberation to slaves apart from their merit or faithfulness. Torah came as a gift, not as the basis for the initial salvation but as guidance for how the saved people might live as God's people and bless others.

The Role of Sacrifices

Sacrifices are present from the very beginning and then throughout the Old Testament story—starting with Cain and Abel's famous encounter in Genesis 4. However, we find very little overt reflection on what sacrifice meant and what it hoped to accomplish.[31] It seems likely that the Hebrews borrowed their sacrificial practices from surrounding cultures. However, the meaning of sacrifice among the Hebrews must be seen as ultimately following from their view of their own peculiar God (Yahweh) and from their understanding of the nature of their covenant with Yahweh.[32]

Sacrifices are not theologically central to Old Testament salvation, though they are commonly practiced. In numerous instances forgiveness and, even more, deliverance, do not depend upon sacrifices. The basic dynamic, on Yahweh's side, is the decision to save simply because that is the kind of god Yahweh is. The basic dynamic, on the human side, is repentance and trust. The sacrifices then follow, as the means to concretize the reception of the gift.

According to the story, the first step in God's saving work is deliverance. The calling of Abraham and Sarah and God's acts to free their descendants from slavery follow from God's free will to bring healing, first to the Hebrews and ultimately to all the families of the earth (Gen 12:1-3). The second step, following deliverance from Egypt, came when God provided the gift of Torah to provide direction for how common life as God's people would be ordered. To follow the Law does not effect

---

30. That is, "holiness" defined as God's abhorrence of sin and impurity. As seen in Hosea 11 and Leviticus 19, "holiness" may be defined in terms of God's transformative compassion and care for vulnerable people.

31. Daly, *Origins*, 16.

32. Brueggemann, *Reverberations*, 182.

PART ONE: The Bible's Salvation Story

salvation; rather, because of the gift of salvation, faithful Hebrews joyfully shape their lives according to Torah as people in a covenant relationship with the liberating God.

The rationale for sacrifices emerges in the context of Torah's expectations. Sacrifices are the third step—the rationale for their use emerges as part of the Hebrews' joyful response to the healing, transforming initiative of Yahweh.[33] The call to offer sacrifices is something that comes from God in order to enhance the well-being of the Hebrews in their common life.[34] Sacrifices do not establish the relationship with God. God provides for sacrifices as means to sustain the already-created life lived in joyful response to Yahweh's purely gracious work of deliverance and sustenance.[35] The context for sacrifice in the Old Testament story is relational—not impersonal and legalistic.

Contrary to the logic of retribution, we find mercy at the very core of Old Testament sacrifice theology. Sacrifices do not appease an angry and punitive God; rather their practice enters as gifts from a consistently loving God to sustain relationships established already by God initiating healing, delivering love.[36]

The first seven chapters of Leviticus report the Hebrews' approach to sacrifice. These chapters follow shortly the act of rebellion of Exodus 32, where the people defied Yahweh's commands and worshiped idols. Persuaded by Moses's intercession, Yahweh determined to stay in relationship with the Hebrews. The Levitical legislation that concerned sacrificial practices may best be understood as Yahweh's attempt to prevent a recurrence of the golden calf apostasy.

The sacrifices, as presented in Leviticus 1–7, were of two general types. The first type included offerings that express commitment, loyalty, and gratitude. With these offerings, grateful community members returned to God part of the fruits of their labor. In so doing, worshipers expressed thanksgiving and cemented their commitment to Yahweh and to the covenant they had made with Yahweh.[37]

These routine offerings concretize the basic dynamic of gift and response that typify faith. The saving initiative lay with Yahweh, who brings deliverance, provides guidance, and sustains life. Salvation is pure

---

33. Rogerson, "Sacrifice," 57–58.
34. Birch, et al., *Theological Introduction*, 159.
35. Ibid., 135.
36. Ibid., 159–60.
37. Ibid., 160.

gift—but Yahweh expects a response that will concretize and sustain the gift. Yahweh brought healing so the people might live lives of justice and shalom in order to bless all the families of the earth.

The offerings of thanksgiving and commitment, then, reflect the merciful dynamic of God's deliverance and sustenance of a people of peace. In God's wisdom, these rituals keep before the people's eyes the nature of their God and the intended nature of their community: a God of healing love and a community of genuine shalom.

The second type of offering presents a more complicated picture. These are the "sin offerings," expressions of repentance, regret for wrongdoing, and resolve to return to a viable relationship with Yahweh (see especially Leviticus 4–6). The sin offerings most routinely served as means for people who inadvertently violated Torah or people who for reasons outside of their control (e.g., women menstruating) had entered an unclean state to express their commitment to Yahweh. These sacrifices, too, were provided for by the merciful God of Israel's covenant. They provide concrete expressions that kept before the people's eyes the importance of their relationship with God—a relationship created and sustained by God's merciful initiative.[38]

For advertent violation of Torah, sin offerings were also provided, but only after the offender had made restitution with the community.[39] The acts of restitution constituted concrete expressions of repentance that restored relationships; the sacrifices then served as expressions of recommitment to the covenant. That is, the sacrifices were not the means to re-establish the relationship but after-the-fact concretizations of the reality of the re-established relationships.

The sin offerings served to foster wholeness in the covenant community. Impurity and evil, even when inadvertent, were highly contagious, potentially damaging the shared life[40]—as had happened with the golden calf incident. So the sin offerings served to stop the contagion early on by bringing to overt expression the people's commitment to God and the covenant.

The Old Testament does not explain the place of blood in the sin offerings. The most explicit description, Leviticus 17:11, seems to say that the key is that the blood symbolizes *life* (not death). The "power" in the

---

38. Young, *Sacrifice*, 28.
39. Brueggemann, *Theology*, 667; Rogerson, "Sacrifice," 53.
40. Milgrom, *Leviticus*, 256.

PART ONE: The Bible's Salvation Story

blood, then, is not related to death or punishment. Blood is a reminder of the power of life (and of the Giver of life) to overcome sin and evil.[41]

Even at the beginning of the story, salvation is not death-focused. The acts of "atonement" in the sin offering were not practiced with the expectation that the death of a sacrificed animal would provide satisfaction to an angry or dishonored deity and in that way make salvation possible. Salvation was made possible by God's mercy instead of atonement. The sin offering provided for recognition of the mercy already given—not for satisfaction that then enables the mercy to be expressed.

As the Old Testament story proceeds, the role of sacrifices evolves. The emergence of kingship and the centralized temple correspond with a social evolution away from the relative egalitarianism of the Torah provisions for the Hebrews' common life.[42] Sacrifices continued apace in the midst of the Hebrews' social and religious life, but the health of the covenant community nonetheless deteriorated.

As a consequence of the social problems that emerged in the kingship era, prophets emerged and raised voices of confrontation. Their perspective, apparent overtly in the "writing prophets" of the eighth century, tends toward hostility regarding sacrifices. These prophets did not necessarily totally reject the sacrificial cult out of hand so much as critique its abuse.[43] The prophetic critique illumines the intended meaning of sacrifice in the covenant community.

Sacrifices, clearly, were not intended to be autonomous and intrinsically efficacious expressions of commitment to Yahweh. Valid sacrifices took place in a broader context, as supplements to a holistic practice of faith in the covenant community.

Torah meant for sacrifices to cultivate justice in the covenant community—wherein all members of the community are given access to the means of life and health. Sacrifice in an unjust community is worse than worthless. Amos asserts that to offer sacrifices while oppression reigns is sinful. The means of dealing with sin had become itself an occasion for sin.

Torah intended sacrifices to express commitment to Yahweh as the one (and only) true God. The Levitical legislation sought to prevent a repeat of the golden calf incident, but according to Hosea, the Hebrews did return to idol worship. The community turned the intent of sacrifices to

---

41. Daly, *Christian*, 119–20; Rogerson, "Sacrifice," 53.
42. Miller, *Religion*, 87–88.
43. Milgrom, *Leviticus*, 482.

express grateful commitment to Yahweh on its head when the sacrifices took place amidst social injustice and Baal worship.

Torah included sacrifices to concretize gratitude to the Hebrews' liberating God. By the eighth century, Amos and other prophets claimed that such faithfulness had been forgotten and the sacrifices had become autonomous (and empty) religious acts—wrenched from their faithfulness-to-Torah context.

The underlying dynamic for sacrifices in their intended expression was God's love and the call for the Hebrews to love God and one another. This love was missing, according to the prophets. Lack of love for Yahweh was seen in Baal-worship. Lack of love for one another was seen in rampant injustice. Prophets such as Amos, Hosea, and Micah saw sacrifices as part of the problem. The people offered sacrifices outside of commitment to Yahweh and to justice, gratitude, and love.[44]

Valid sacrifices follow from and help concretize God's work that restores the individual and community to life and health in relationship to God and to one another. "If any idea captures the essence of the sacrificial ritual, it is God's saving action, which restores the individual and community to life and health in relationship to God and to one another."[45]

Salvation and Retribution

We see a basic message in the primal story of salvation in the Old Testament, and in the role of Torah and sacrifices in relation to salvation. Salvation comes from God's mercy. Time after time, throughout the story, God initiates healing prior to Torah faithfulness and sacrificial offerings.

For salvation to enter the Hebrews' world, nothing is needed that would change God's disposition. The Hebrews are not called to find ways to appease God's anger, to satisfy the demands of God's balance-the-scales justice or God's honor, or to find ways to avoid impurities that violate God's absolute holiness. The called-for actions, rather, include the Hebrews responding to God's merciful acts by acting mercifully themselves. The people should seek to follow Torah regulations that provide guidance for such merciful actions and intend to form Israel into a merciful society. As well, Torah calls the Hebrews concretely to express their gratitude and commitment to Yahweh by ritualistic offerings of their produce (grain and animal).

---

44. Levenson, *Sinai*, 54–55.
45. Birch, et al., *Theological Introduction*, 160.

PART ONE: The Bible's Salvation Story

So the portrayal of salvation in the Old Testament story does not support the logic of retribution. The story does not link salvation with punishment, appeasement, and purification as means to achieve reconciliation with God. Rather, it links salvation with unilateral merciful acts by God and the joyful response to those acts with expressions of commitment to God. The most important expressions of commitment are lives lived in harmony with God's will as expressed in Torah (a will coherent with continued health for all the people in the community). A secondary expression of commitment is found in the sacrifice rituals—that in time become corrupted as they are separated from Torah faithfulness.

The primal story begins with God's direct liberating mercy that finds fruit in the exodus, giving of the Law, and establishment in the promised land. It continues on, of course, to show that the relationships between God and the Hebrews deteriorate. So in the next chapter we will turn to the challenges offered to the Hebrews from several prophets. When there is disharmony within the covenant community, how is that understood and how is it dealt with?

THREE

Guardians for the Way of Wholeness
Salvation in the Prophets

IN CHAPTER TWO, WE saw that at key moments in the story (such as the calling of Abraham, the exodus, and the renewal of life in exile), God acts out of mercy. God provides salvation as a gift—given out of God's healing love—unearned, even unmerited by the people.

The story presents two institutions linked with salvation, Torah and sacrifice. Both initially served as responses to the gift. First, the people received God's acts of deliverance, then came gratitude. Such gratitude led to responses of obedience to God's will for social life, in following Torah and in ritualized expressions of commitment to God via sacrifice.

As the Hebrews' political structures expanded and became centralized under the office of the king, their religious structures concomitantly became centralized around the temple. With this, practices in relation to the law and to sacrifices changed from their original purposes.

Torah originated as the framework for the Hebrews to concretize their liberation. Torah arranges for the economic viability of each household, resisting social stratification. Inheritance legislation, Sabbath year laws, and the ideal of the Year of Jubilee all pushed in the direction of widespread participation in economic well-being. The law also placed special emphasis on tending to the welfare of vulnerable people—widows, orphans, and aliens ("for you too were aliens in Egypt before God delivered you," Lev 19).

As Walter Brueggemann writes: "Something like 'God's preferential option for the poor' is deeply rooted in Israel's testimony, so deeply rooted as to be characteristic and definitional for Israel's speech about God. The claim is not a belated, incidental addendum to Israel's ethical reflection, but belongs integrally and inalienably to Israel's core affirmation of the character of Yahweh."[1] The sacrificial practices, above all else, were intended to be linked with the faithful responses of the people, in gratitude, to God's liberating work.

Problems with Law and Sacrifices

The books of Moses meant neither the law nor the sacrifices to be means to salvation but rather responses to the saving works of God. These books meant the law and sacrifices to enhance justice in the community. Once they were established, though, the danger inevitably arose that either or both would be separated from their grounding in God's merciful liberating works.

As the intent of the law faded, the story tells of the community's tendency to focus on external expressions, easily enforced and susceptible to becoming tools of people in power. These tendencies led to legalism and, eventually, in the prophets' views, to removing the law from its living heart: liberation from slavery and concern for the well-being of vulnerable people.

As the community lost the original intent of sacrifices, many Israelites treated sacrifices as means of salvation, ritual acts separated from practical justice in the community. Especially, as they centralized religious structures, people in power used sacrifice as a tool to enhance their standing. Presenting sacrifice as a necessary means to salvation enabled people who controlled access to sacrificial rituals in the temple to exercise enormous power in the community.

Voices of accountability arose to challenge such distortions, the voices of the prophets. The prophets emerged as the voice of loyalty to Torah following the establishment of kingship. They challenged Israel's practices that contradicted the covenant relation. "The prophets repeatedly utilize the old legal traditions to determine the present status of Israel."[2]

One great kingship-era prophet, Elijah, established the basic prophetic concern. Elijah challenged Israel's king when the king departed from God's ways—and pointed back to the law of Moses as the basis for his challenge. A poignant story in 1 Kings 21 illustrates this dynamic.

---

1. Brueggemann, *Theology*, 144.
2. Brueggemann, *Tradition*, 21.

Israel's king, Ahab, desired the fruitful vineyard of the Israelite Naboth. At first, Ahab offers to buy the vineyard. His offer, however, reflects his lack of respect for the inheritance practices of Israel. The land does not simply belong to Naboth. He refuses to sell it because it belongs to God and is for the use also of Naboth's parents and his children and their children. It is his inheritance. This term "inheritance" contrasts with Ahab's term, "vineyard."[3]

"Inheritance" recognizes the land as the Lord's, cultivated by the family through the generations for their livelihood. The Lord wills that the land stay with family members so that they will not be dispossessed and future generations made landless.[4] When all have vine and fig tree to cultivate, the community will be healthy. That health is why inheritance matters.

"Vineyard," on the other hand, as used by King Ahab, views the land as a commodity, something simply to be bought and sold with little concern for the wholeness of the entire community. Those who are wealthy and powerful may accumulate more and more. The other people become landless, disinherited—a recipe for poverty and vulnerability.

Naboth refuses to part with his inheritance. Ahab falsely convicts Naboth of blasphemy and executes him. Ahab takes the land. He assumes that since he is the king he may do whatever he wants. The main weapon God has against corrupt kings such as Ahab simply is the word of the prophets, reminding people of God's will and exposing the violence and injustice of this corruption for what it is.

King Ahab goes down to the vineyard to take possession of it (1 Kgs 21:16). But, he meets an old acquaintance when he gets to the vineyard, the prophet Elijah. Elijah had confronted Ahab before and had to flee for his life. Ahab remembers Elijah. "Have you found me, O my enemy" (1 Kgs 21:20). Earlier, Ahab called Elijah a "troubler of Israel" (1 Kgs 18:17). Indeed I have found you, says Elijah. The Lord has told me the injustice you have done to Naboth. You are the troubler of Israel. You are the one who has disregarded the Lord's commands. You are the blasphemer, not Naboth. You, King Ahab, will suffer consequences.

To his credit, Ahab responds. When Elijah speaks for God in promising that immediate devastating judgment will fall on Ahab and his house, Ahab "humbled himself" before God (1 Kgs 21:29). As a consequence, the judgment is postponed. "I will not bring disaster in his days." The

---

3. Brueggemann, *1 & 2 Kings*, 257–59.
4. Seow, "First and Second," 156.

prophet's word did have power. Elijah, as the prophets to follow, reminds people. He reminds Ahab of God's will for human life, as expressed in God's commands. He sets out the template later prophets will follow: Be suspicious of people in power. Do not blindly trust their claims but test them thoroughly. But also remember who God is, what God has done for you, and what God's will for your life is.

In Brueggemann's words: "Prophets arise in Israel when covenantal modes of existence are endangered. It is the work of the prophets to insist that all of Israel's life is to be lived in relation to and in response to Yahweh's will and purposes, and to enunciate the consequences of a life lived without regard to this defining relationship. The prophets are to invite a 'turning' in Israel, a turn from pride to trust, from despair to hope, from abusiveness to covenantal neighborliness."[5]

In challenging the distortions of law and sacrifice, the prophets reiterate the meaning of salvation. They re-emphasize that salvation is God's liberating gift, and that following Torah and offering sacrifices are responses to God's gift, not means to try to gain it.

In this chapter, I will focus on the first "writing prophets." Their proclamations were gathered into books bearing their names—Amos, Hosea, and Micah. These prophets' message set the tone for much of the prophetic critique to come. Even more important, in terms of what is to come, these prophets exerted a profound influence on Jesus. I will argue that salvation according to these prophets and salvation according to Jesus are very closely related.

One basic issue facing the Hebrew people, according to prophetic witness, is that the community has departed from the will of their liberating God. "The more I call them, the more they went from me" (Hos 11:2). Hosea frames the "departure" in terms of idolatry. Amos focuses more on injustice. Micah emphasizes both.

Originally, the people needed liberation from non-being, the barrenness symbolized by Abraham and Sarah's lack of a future. God provided this family with a child. Around them, the Promise arose. However, within a few generations, the people stood in need of liberation. They again faced non-being, this time as slaves in Egypt. God again gave them a future—this time as a nation with its own unique law-code, its unique religious rituals, and eventually its own land.

At the time of Joshua, the story portrays the Hebrews living in a state of wholeness, with a world of potential for creative growth and witness.

---

5. Brueggemann, *Theology*, 697.

They lived at that point with a large measure of harmony with God, due to God's generosity. "The gracious gifts assured by the prophets derive not from what Israel does but from who Yahweh is."[6] However, as the generations passed, this harmony turned to disharmony.

WHAT CAUSES THE DISHARMONY?

All three of the eighth-century prophets, Amos, Hosea, and Micah, spoke in response to the disharmony they perceived among the Hebrew people.

The earliest of the three, Amos, had lived in the southern kingdom of Judah but traveled north to Israel to speak the words recorded in the book that bears his name. Amos prophesied during the time of King Jeroboam II of Israel, who ruled from 786 to 746 BCE. Scholars place Amos's prophecies at around 760 BCE. Amos presented himself as an independent "lay-prophet." He had no official standing, relying solely on the power of his words.

As his basis for critique, Amos drew on the shared traditions. He several times reminded his listeners of their belief that Yahweh had brought the Hebrews out of Egypt and placed them in the land (Amos 2:9-10; 3:1-2; 9:7-8). The Hebrews' "immoral and unethical treatment of those who are unable to defend themselves is juxtaposed [to God's] protective treatment throughout their early history when they were unable to defend themselves."[7]

Amos prophesied, assuming that the people of Israel would share his starting point. Their liberating God had directly given them Torah with its clear instructions regarding the nature of covenantal life. Liberation and land are linked inextricably with Law. Yahweh delivered the people from the injustice of Egypt's slavery and for justice in the covenant community.

In prophet's view, the people have always known that Yahweh expected justice. Amos breaks no new ground in terms of moral and legal expectations. He draws directly on tradition, taking for granted that the people would know Torah. He expected no debate about the centrality of justice for the covenant community—only over the extent of injustice current in Israel.

Likewise, Hosea also draws directly on the liberation story that formed the core of Hebrew consciousness. His indictment in chapter 11 begins with these words: "When Israel was a child, I loved him, and out

---

6. Brueggemann, *Tradition*, 79.
7. Paul, *Amos*, 87.

of Egypt I called my son" (11:1). Hosea then goes on to outline how the people did not remain faithful to the ways of their loving God.

Hosea came on to the scene about a generation later than Amos. He prophesied in the northern kingdom in the years just prior to the Assyrian empire laying waste to Israel in 721 BCE. Whereas Amos spoke directly about injustice in Israel and used legal types of imagery, Hosea relied more on personal relationship-type imagery. Israel broke Yahweh's heart by cultivating relationships with other gods.

The third of these prophets, Micah, prophesied in Judah, the southern kingdom. He entered the scene in the years shortly after the northern kingdom's fall. His period of prophecy ended around 701 BCE. Like Amos and Hosea, Micah centrally emphasized the exodus and Torah and basically ignored the Davidic-Zion kingship tradition. For Micah, unlike many of his fellow Judeans, Jerusalem was not inviolable. In Micah's view, violating the covenant, in the way his contemporaries had, rendered the nation's future uncertain.

It is not that Yahweh had changed from loving to wrathful; rather, a society founded on Torah-justice will become deathly ill when it disregards Torah-justice. To draw on Amos's imagery, we may say that where there is justice there is life; the community will be strong and healthy. Injustice, on the other hand, is inherently unhealthy.

All three of these prophets saw the key for the Hebrew's health to be Yahweh's love and liberating work. This divine, life-giving initiative of God—Torah—included detailed guidance for liberated living in justice and Shalom. "The reason the commands are so urgent and insistent is that they are Yahweh's (and therefore Israel's) strategy for fending off a return to pre-Exodus conditions of exploitation and brutality within the community."[8]

Certainly the prophets do speak words of threat, anger, even judgment. However, they understand themselves to speak out of Yahweh's love. They speak because they believe God desires the community's healing. All three books conclude with hopeful visions of such healing. The prophets confront the people in hope that the community will return to trust in their liberating God.

These prophets themselves had no recourse to means that would literally punish anyone. They had no interest in marshalling the power of the sword against wrongdoers. They relied on rhetoric, on their vision of Torah and of Yahweh's justice, to seek to effect healing—not to inflict pain for pain.

---

8. Brueggemann, *Theology*, 184.

The people's break with the covenant with Yahweh may be seen in terms of the expressions in their communities of injustice, violence, idolatry, and vain religiosity.

Injustice

According to these prophets, the people had changed their original social structure. Torah had provided for a decentralized social order characterized by widespread land ownership. Within this, all were to be given access to means that would sustain their livelihoods. None were to gain the extreme wealth that may be accumulated via the disinheritance of large numbers of community members. By the eighth century, a transformation had occurred that led to increased social stratification—a few wealthy, many poverty-stricken. Amos and Micah zeroed in on this stratification as evidence of a fundamentally unjust social order.[9]

God's judgment on Israel is immanent, "because they sell the righteous for silver, and the needy for a pair of sandals—they who trample the head of the poor into the dust of the earth, and push the afflicted out of the way" (Amos 2:6–7). This injustice goes contrary to the will of God expressed in Torah and, indeed, in creation itself. "Do horses run on rocks? Does one plow the sea with oxen? But you have turned justice into poison and the fruit of righteousness into wormwood" (Amos 6:12).

Micah also speaks of the corruption of the community departing from God's will: "Alas for those who devise wickedness and evil deeds on their beds! When the morning dawns, they perform it, because it is in their power. They covet fields, and seize them; houses, and take them away; they oppress householder and house, people and their inheritance" (Mic 2:1–2). Micah lays responsibility for this corruption directly at the feet of Judah's leaders: "Listen, you heads of Jacob and rulers of the house of Israel! Should you not know justice?—you who hate the good and love the evil, who tear the skin off my people, and the flesh off their bones; who eat the flesh of my people, flay their skin off them, break their bones in pieces, and chop them up like meat in a kettle, like flesh in a caldron" (Mic 3:1–3).

Judah's rulers practice injustice, not justice. They turn their responsibility as agents of Torah on its head. "Hear this, you rulers of the house of Jacob and chiefs of the house of Israel, who abhor justice and pervert all equity, who build Zion with blood and Jerusalem with wrong! Its rulers

---

9. Horsley, *Jesus and the Powers*, 56–58.

give judgment for a bribe, its priests teach for a price, its prophets give oracles for money" (Mic 3:9–11). Though Hosea focuses more on idolatry than injustice, he sees the two as interrelated in his challenge to Israel's leaders. "You have plowed wickedness, you have reaped injustice, you have eaten the fruit of lies" (Hos 10:13).

The presence of widespread injustice among the Hebrews contradicted the dynamics of liberation that characterized Yahweh's original intervention. Much earlier in the story, when the Hebrew elders expressed their desire for a king "like the nations," Samuel warned of a return to Egypt. The king will take and take, and the people will again "cry out" as they had when they were slaves (1 Sam 8:10–18). Yahweh formed this community to be an alternative to Egypt's injustice. According to the prophets, this alternative was no more.

Violence

All these prophets identified violence as a key manifestation of disharmony. Amos begins his prophecies with several statements against the practices of Israel's neighbors, focusing on their violence. Among other images, we read of Edom pursuing his brother with the sword (Amos 1:11) and of the Ammonites ripping open pregnant women in Gilead (Amos 1:13).

Amos then emphasizes Israel's guilt. Of Israel we read: "See what great tumults are within it, and what oppressions are in its midst. They do not know how to do right, says the Lord, those who store up violence and robbery in their strongholds" (Amos 3:9–10).

Hosea, of the three prophets, speaks of the curse of violence the most forcefully and extensively. The Lord's first words to Hosea refer to the house of Jehu's responsibility for "the blood of Jezreel" (Hos 1:4). This reference alludes to the violence of the Northern Kingdom's kings in their practice of power politics. King Ahab, under the influence of his Baal-worshiping Phoenician wife, had murdered Naboth in order to expropriate his vineyard (1 Kgs 21). Ahab's action then set in motion more violence in Israel. Jehu arose to instigate a bloodbath to avenge Naboth's murder. Jehu assassinated King Joram in Naboth's former home property and followed that by killing Judah's King Ahaziah, who had been visiting Joram. Jehu then killed Ahab's widow, Jezebel, and oversaw the massacre of Ahab's seventy sons (2 Kgs 9–10).

Hosea is not convinced that Jehu's violence was justified, and he presents God as condemning it.[10] Hosea seems to believe that all Jehu actually did was contribute to the ever-deepening spiral of violence in Israel that may soon result in the nation's final demise.

Hosea reiterates the indictment in chapter four: "Hear the word of the Lord, O people of Israel; for the Lord has an indictment against the inhabitants of the land. There is no faithfulness or loyalty, and no knowledge of God in the land. Swearing, lying, and murder, and stealing and adultery break out; bloodshed follows bloodshed" (Hos 4:1-2). The problem with violence is that it does not lead to resolution; "bloodshed follows bloodshed."[11]

According to Hosea 6:9, "priests are banded together [to] murder on the road to Shechem, they commit a monstrous crime." Hosea links together violence with rejection of Israel's old Mosaic traditions. Shechem was a city valued by pilgrims loyal to the old tradition. It was the location of an ancient sanctuary of Yahweh.

The reference to Gibeah in Hosea 10:9 ("Since the days of Gibeah you have sinned, O Israel") is likely alluding to the terrible violence of Judges 19-21, when the tribes united to lay waste to Benjamin in retaliation for the murder of the Levite's concubine.

Violence only leads to violence; preparing for war leads to war. If you trust in the sword you shall die by it. Hosea continues: "You have plowed wickedness, you have reaped injustice, you have eaten the fruit of lies. Because you have trusted in your power and in the multitude of your warriors, there the tumult of war shall rise against your people, and all your fortresses shall be destroyed" (Hos 10:13-14).

Micah also critiques the role of violence in the Southern Kingdom. "You rise up against my people as an enemy; you strip the robe from the peaceful, from those who pass by trustingly with no thought of war" (Mic 2:8). Those who seek to remain faithful to Yahweh's shalom are themselves treated violently.

Micah's vision of peace, of swords being beaten into plowshares (4:1-5), contrasts with Judah's present violent reality. It reiterates Micah's own loyalty to the old tradition's sense of Yahweh's purposes in liberating the Hebrews and giving them the land. Yahweh seeks peace for all the

---

10. For a discussion of this fascinating case of a biblical prophet critiquing the Bible, see Brenneman, "Prophets."

11. Limburg, *Hosea—Micah*, 16-17.

PART ONE: The Bible's Salvation Story

families of the earth (Gen 12:1-3) and seeks to use the Hebrews to spread this peace.

In working for this goal, Yahweh's judgment on Judah focuses on the nation's war-making resources. "In that day, says the Lord, I will cut off your horses from among you and will destroy your chariots" (Mic 5:10). The accumulation of horses and chariots reflects the priorities of Judah's elite classes. "Your wealthy are full of violence; your inhabitants speak lies, with tongues of deceit in their mouths" (Mic 6:12).

As does the problem of injustice, so also the problem of violence brings into clear focus Yahweh's intended priorities in calling the Hebrews. According to Abraham Heschel, "the prophets were the first [people] in history to regard a nation's reliance upon force as evil."[12] Yahweh's priorities, according to these prophets, included, at their core, justice and peace.

To the prophets, the covenant community, with its injustice and violence, denies the character of its founding God. They see Yahweh not first of all as a wrathful, angry, retributive God. To the contrary, the prophets see Yahweh as a loving, gracious, merciful God. Yahweh liberated these vulnerable people from slavery with the plan that the people would be agents of liberation for the whole earth. Yahweh's anger stems from grief at the failures of the people to live out their liberation. The prophetic rhetoric of judgment does not stem from God's retributive eye-for-an-eye justice that must punish wrongdoing. No, this rhetoric stems from God's continuing love and is meant to call the people back (see Hos 11:8-9).

Unbelievably, though, from the prophets' point of view, the people steadfastly loved by Yahweh do not trust in Yahweh as God. The prophets link the injustice and violence with idolatrous trust in other gods.[13] And they merge them all together to insist that the Hebrews' religious practices serve the opposite of their intended effect; (vain) religiosity actually becomes an occasion of further sin, not a means of reconnecting with Yahweh.

Idolatry

Interestingly, Amos's sharp critique of Israel says little about idolatry. The most urgent problem was to be found in their injustice and violence. Clearly, a people cannot worship Yahweh while it practices such blatant and widespread oppression.

12. Heschel, *Prophets*, vol. 1, 166.
13. Brueggemann, *Theology*, 697.

Guardians for the Way of Wholeness

On the other hand, Hosea does place the central focus on idolatry. Idolatry seems to be the root cause for the injustice and violence. The book begins with a direct reference to idolatry, "the land commits great whoredom by forsaking the Lord" (Hos 1:2). Hosea portrays Yahweh as deeply attached to the Hebrew covenant community. This close attachment explains Yahweh's deep hurt when the people turn to Baal and violate their covenant with Yahweh. "The Lord loves the people of Israel, though they turn to other gods" (Hos 3:1).

Baal was a Canaanite god, "clearly the most active and prominent." He was often portrayed as the great storm god on whom the fertility of the land depended.[14] The Hebrews found Baal worship attractive, given their own dependence upon the rains and their being surrounded by cultures deeply shaped by Baalism. The Baal religion likely threatened the Hebrews' exclusive Yahwism more than any other Ancient Near Eastern faith.[15]

Just as the prophets hold the political leaders responsible for leading the Hebrews into the paths of violence when the leaders were called to cultivate peace, so Hosea presents the priests as responsible for leading the Hebrews into the paths of idolatry (5:1). Instead of seeing the harvest of fruits from their fields as a time to remember Yahweh's work on their behalf and to offer sacrifices of thanksgiving that would reinforce the people's commitment to lives lived according to Torah, the people, according to Hosea, make their offerings to Baal (9:1–9).

As Psalm 135:18 points out, people become like that which they worship.[16] So, to offer sacrifices to Baal instead of Yahweh leads to a society becoming violent instead of peaceable, given Baal's status as the source of violent storms.

Hosea critiques Judah's practices. "Do not rejoice, O Israel! Do not exult as other nations do; for you have played the whore, departing from your God. You have loved a prostitute's pay on all threshing floors" (9:1). Grain piled on threshing floors is "prostitute's pay" because Israel takes the harvest as the gift of Baal.[17] Micah also points to idolatry as a central concern of Yahweh's in relation to Judah. "I will cut off your images and your pillars from among you, and you shall bow down no more to the work of your hands" (Mic 5:13).

---

14. Daly, "Baal," 545.
15. Ibid., 547.
16. See Beale, *We Become*, 45–46.
17. Mays, "Hosea," 1340.

PART ONE: The Bible's Salvation Story

Vain Religiosity

All three prophets forcefully express their rejection of the possibility that the Hebrews' rituals effectively connect them with Yahweh.[18] However, they do not reject religious or cultic practices per se; they reject religious practices separated from their original intention. "For them, worship and ritual were means; justice and righteousness were ends."[19]

The prescribed religious rituals, in, say, Leviticus, meant to reinforce justice for all in the covenant community. The rituals meant to be linked inextricably with Yahweh's liberating love, especially oriented toward widows, orphans, and resident aliens. With this link broken, the rituals become worse than simply ineffective. They become themselves occasions for sin and alienation from God. They reinforce the illusion that the covenant community can tolerate injustice, violence, and idolatry and still connect with Yahweh through ritual.

As Abraham Heschel writes: "Amos and the prophets who followed him not only stressed the primacy of morality over sacrifice, but even proclaimed that the worth of worship, far from being absolute, is contingent upon moral living, and that when immorality prevails, worship is detestable."[20]

Amos begins his critique when he shockingly names Israel's profound trouble as due to its identity as Yahweh's elect, not despite this status. God holds the people accountable to their commitment to Torah. "Hear this word that the Lord has spoken against you, O people of Israel, against the whole family that I brought up out of the land of Egypt: You only have I known of all the families of the earth; therefore I will punish you for all your iniquities" (Amos 3:1-2).

Amos mocks the Israelites: "Come to Bethel—and transgress; to Gilgal—and multiply transgression" (4:4). Bethel and Gilgal were traditional sanctuaries. In Amos's view, Israel's worship and transgression have become synonymous. "The more the people attend the cultic rites, and the more zealous they are in performing the manifold attendant rites, the more they continue to offend and transgress."[21] In a famous assertion, Amos presents God's perspective on unjust Israel's religiosity: "I hate, I despise your festivals, and I take no delight in your solemn assemblies.

---

18. Brueggemann, *Theology*, 678.
19. Paul, *Amos*, 139.
20. Heschel, *Prophets*, vol. 1, 195.
21. Paul, *Amos*, 139.

Even though you offer me your burnt offerings and grain offerings, I will not accept them; and the offerings of well-being of your fatted animals I will not look upon. Take away from me the noise of your songs; I will not listen to the melody of your harps" (5:21–23).

Hosea echoes Amos's warnings. God places special responsibility upon the leaders, the ones called to insist that the link between religious practices and the demands of Torah remain central in the awareness of the people. "My people are destroyed for lack of knowledge; because you [O priest] have rejected knowledge, I reject you from being a priest to me. And since you have forgotten the law of your God, I will also forget your children" (Hos 4:6).

When Israelites present their sacrifices to God, Hosea warns, they will be to no avail. "With their flocks and herds they shall go to seek the Lord, but they will not find him; he has withdrawn from them" (Hos 5:6). In fact, the attempts to sacrifice, in the context of unfaithful living, only make things worse. "When Ephraim multiplied altars to expiate sin, they became to him altars for sinning. . . . Though they offer choice sacrifices, though they eat flesh, the Lord does not accept them. Now he will remember their iniquity, and punish their sins; they shall return to Egypt" (8:11, 13)—reiterating Samuel's prophecy about the return to slavery.

Like Hosea and Amos, Micah sees simply offering of sacrifices as of little avail. He follows Torah in understanding right living as the core of authentic faith. He references God's liberating work, "I brought you up from the land of Egypt, and redeemed you from the house of slavery" and gave you the promised land, "that you may know the saving acts of the Lord" (Mic 6:4–5). But the people seem not to remember. Micah asks, how might life be renewed in the context of alienation? "With what shall I come before the Lord, and bow myself before God on high? Shall I come before him with burnt offerings, with calves a year old? Will the Lord be pleased with thousands of rams, with ten thousands of rivers of oil? Shall I give my firstborn for my transgression, the fruit of my body for the sin of my soul?" (6:6–7). The answers are no, no, no. These are ritualistic tactics tried and failed due to the injustice of the community.

The disharmony the prophets perceive will never be healed through rituals in and of themselves. Contrary to the logic of retribution, the Lord does not require sacrifices. The Lord's favor is not to be regained by sacred violence within the community.

PART ONE: The Bible's Salvation Story

How Is Harmony Restored?

The prophets raised their critiques for the purpose of helping the Hebrews find healing. They "sought to bring the people to realize that at the depth of the catastrophes which shook their lives and brought intense suffering, God was present, providing the impulse for the return from a road leading to ruin and offering a new life."[22]

The prophets reject a sacrifice-centered approach to restoring harmony. The proper role of sacrifice is as a response to God's initiative, not as a means to turn God back toward the people. The prophets assume that God remains the source of wholeness, that God still loves the people in the same way as God had in the time of Moses. Hence, the restoration of harmony is not complicated nor is it something God withholds. Hosea 12:6 captures what is needed in a nutshell: "Return to your God, hold fast to love and justice, and wait continually for your God." Repent. Do kindness and justice. Trust.

Repent

Behind the prophetic call to "return" or "repent" lies the presumption of God's availability. The alienation follows from what happens on the human side. God simply wants a turning back from problematic beliefs and practices, and then offers mercy. Hosea articulates this in the conclusion of his prophecies:[23] "Return, O Israel, to the Lord your God, for you have stumbled because of your iniquity. Take words with you and return to the Lord; say to him, 'Take away all guilt; accept that which is good, and we will offer the fruit of our lips. Assyria shall not save us; we will not ride upon our horses; we will say no more, "Our God," to the work of our hands. In you the orphan finds mercy' " (14:1–3).

When Amos speaks against vain religiosity, he offers as an alternative that the people "seek the Lord and live" (5:6). "Seek" may be understood as a kind of technical term for turning to God in a service of prayer; in this context such turning is contrasted with making pilgrimage to the main religious sites.[24] The call to repent or return rests upon a certainty of God's receptivity. In Amos, especially, the weight of inequity is so heavy that

---

22. Anderson, *Eighth-Century*, 34.
23. Limburg, *Hosea*, 51.
24. Paul, *Amos*, 162.

Israel seems doomed. But the way out is simple—"seek the Lord and live," that is all.[25]

Justice

Should the people truly seek God, their lives would bear the fruit: justice and mercy (as complementary virtues). According to Amos, when the people seek God their common life will be transformed in practical ways. In order to live, the people must "seek good and not evil, that you may live; and so the Lord, the God of hosts, will be with you, just as you have said. Hate evil and love good, and establish justice in the gate" (Amos 5:14–15).

This call to seek the good simply calls to return to observing Torah. The love of Yahweh had created this community and provided clear guidance for its functioning. To live justly does not gain God's favor; it rather returns to living consistently with the favor already granted.

Micah contrasts empty rituals with authentic faith. "With what shall I come before the Lord, and bow myself before God on high? Shall I come before him with burnt offerings [and other sacrifices]? He has told you, O mortal, what is good; and what does the Lord require of you but to do justice, and to love kindness, and to walk humbly with your God?" (Mic 6:6, 8). Hosea also links living justly and righteously with salvation. "Sow for yourselves righteousness; reap steadfast love; break up your fallow ground; for it is time to seek the Lord, that he may come and reign righteousness upon you" (Hos 10:11–12).

In calling Israel to justice, the prophets do not call for impersonal "fairness" nor for eye-for-an-eye vengeance. They call to covenant community. Doing justice relates to salvation. Saved people know themselves to be loved by the justice-seeking God, and out of this love, walk in God's paths.[26]

Kindness

Hosea and Micah both call upon the people to do kindness (that is, to do mercy and to practice steadfast love) as part of their core proclamation regarding salvation. They link this call to kindness with justice as two closely related and complementary emphases.

---

25. Paul, *Amos*, 162.
26. Grimsrud, "Healing."

"Hold fast to kindness and justice" (Hos 12:6). The Lord requires the people "to do justice and to love kindness" (Mic 6:8). "I desire kindness and not sacrifice, the knowledge of God rather than burnt offerings" (Hos 6:6). "Sow for yourselves righteousness; reap steadfast kindness" (Hos 10:12). The call to do kindness, like the call to do justice, directly alludes to Torah. At their heart, the Law and the Prophets unite in calling the Hebrews to healthy and strong relationships in which all people (including, especially, vulnerable ones such as widows, orphans, and resident aliens[27]) receive care.

Salvation, then, in the context of the disharmony the prophets spoke so strongly against, led to the healing of relationships within the community. Gift and obligation are inextricably united. Because Yahweh liberated the Hebrews they have the obligation to share life together in ways that insure the well-being of all.

Salvation comes as a gift from God. Salvation obligates its recipients to live together justly and kindly. Salvation, in the context of disharmony, requires repentance, a turning from injustice and idolatry. The prophets assumed this salvation could be present. "God's love and kindness indicate a road. It is a road not limited to a particular area in space nor to exceptional miraculous happenings. It is everywhere, at all times."[28]

Trust

Because of Yahweh's own love and justice that restore relationships, the prophets assure their hearers that they may (and must) trust in Yahweh. The basic dynamic includes the interplay of these elements: Repent, turn from idolatry and toward God. Let justice and mercy characterize your lives. Trust in your loving and faithful God. And that is it. Sacrifice, if present, comes later. Living in trusting reliance upon Yahweh leads to human fulfillment. "To be fully human, so Israel testifies, is to have a profound, unshakeable trust in Yahweh as reliable, present, strong, concerned, engaged for; and to live and act on the basis of that confidence."[29]

For all his confrontational language and extraordinarily strong warnings, Amos in the end portrays Yahweh as merciful. Yahweh remains trustworthy, faithful to the promise to bless all the families of the earth. "I will restore the fortunes of my people Israel, and they shall rebuild the

---

27. Heschel, *Prophets*, vol. 1, 167.
28. Ibid., 211.
29. Brueggemann, *Theology*, 466.

ruined cities and inhabit them; they shall plant vineyards and drink their wine, and they shall make gardens and eat their fruit. I will plant them upon their land, and they shall never again be plucked up out of the land that I have given them, says the Lord your God" (Amos 9:14-15).[30]

Hosea emphasizes the trustworthiness of God's love for the people throughout his book. The threats and warnings, the tragic consequences of the Hebrews' injustice and idolatry, do not overturn Yahweh's dependable love. Hosea most fundamentally proclaims not Israel's doom but God's love that provides for a future.[31] "In the place where it was said to them, 'You are not my people,' it shall be said to them, 'Children of the living God.' The people of Judah and the people of Israel shall be gathered together, and they shall appoint for themselves one head; and they shall take possession of the land, for great shall be the day of Jezreel" (Hos 1:10-11).

Jezreel was Naboth's inheritance that was taken from him by Ahab (1 Kings 21). Hosea's vision of taking "possession of the land" might allude to reinstating the inheritance laws and restoration of land to the landless among the Hebrews.

The promise of Yahweh both points back to Yahweh's work of liberation and provision of Torah and points forward to a time of genuine peace:

> I will now allure her, and bring her into the wilderness, and speak tenderly to her. From there I will give her vineyards, and make the Valley of Achor a door of hope. There she shall respond as in the days of her youth, as at the time when she came out of the land of Egypt. On that day, says the Lord, you will call me, "My husband," and no longer will you call me, "My Baal." For I will remove the names of the Baals from her mouth, and they shall be mentioned by name no more. I will make for you a covenant on that day with the wild animals, the birds of the air, and the creeping things of the ground; and I will abolish the bow, the sword, and war from the land; and I will take you for my wife in righteousness and in justice, in steadfast love, and in mercy. I will take you for my wife in faithfulness; and you shall know the Lord. (Hos 2:14-20)

---

30. Scholarly consensus concludes that Amos 9:11-15 most likely was added to the book, perhaps sometime not too long before 515 BCE (Willoughby, "Amos," 211). However, as I use a reading strategy of that takes "the Bible whole," that is, as it comes to us—focusing on it as story more than history—I choose to read Amos's final vision as part of the book's overall message. Plus, most of the reasons given to bracket Amos 9:11-15 from the rest of the book are based on assumptions about internal consistency that are open to challenge.

31. Heschel, *Prophets*, vol. 1, 43.

PART ONE: The Bible's Salvation Story

Micah similarly asks Yahweh for deliverance and evokes past memories. "Shepherd your people with your staff, the flock that belongs to you, which lives alone in a forest in the midst of a garden land; let them feed in Bashan and Gilead as in the days of old. As in the days when you came out of the land of Egypt, show us marvelous things" (Mic 7:14–15).

Then, Micah gives this promise: "He does not retain his anger forever, because he delights in showing clemency. He will again have compassion upon us; he will tread our iniquities under foot. You will cast all our sins into the depths of the sea. You will show faithfulness to Jacob and unswerving loyalty to Abraham, as you have sworn to our ancestors from the days of old" (Mic 7:18–20).

Because of Yahweh's trustworthiness with the Hebrews, going back to the liberation from Egypt, the people have every reason to trust Yahweh in the present and for the future. Such trust is central to their experience of salvation. What does the Lord require? Justice, mercy, "and to walk humbly with your God" (Mic 6:8). That is, bow before your God in trust and humility.[32] God desires steadfast love, not sacrifice, "the knowledge of God rather than burnt offerings" (Hos 6:6). "Knowledge of God" here may be defined as living with dependence upon and trust in the steadfastness of God. To "know" God is to trust in God above all else.

Salvation in the Prophets

These three eighth-century prophets often assert that God initiates salvation out of love for the Hebrew people. The key work of salvation was the deliverance of the slaves from Egypt. Everything follows from God's initiative. Because of God's healing love, unearned by the people, God holds the people accountable to love and to do justice themselves.

For these prophets, salvation comes straight from God, at God's free initiative, and due to God's transforming mercy. God's frustration with the people stems not because of their inherent impurity when they violate God's holiness, but because the people fail to remain true to God's loving provision for holistic life.

These prophets portray the Law as a gift, meant for sustenance of the covenant community. Far from being legalistic and impersonal, they saw Torah as relational, stemming from God's loving concern for the people. The prophets understand themselves not as radical innovators but as "conservatives," calling the people back to the covenant commitments

32. Limburg, *Hosea*, 192.

their ancestors made. Torah serves the relationship, providing guidance for just, whole, and peaceable communal life. This community includes all, making special provision for those vulnerable ones often pushed to the margins (such as widows, orphans, and resident aliens).

These prophets criticize sacrificial practices—not, though, because the sacrifices were inherently wrong. Rather, the prophets presuppose the original hope that sacrifices would remind the people to be grateful to God, to share with others, and to be committed to Yahweh alone as God. In the context of injustice and oppression (that reflect a lack of gratitude toward God) and worship of other gods, the purpose of sacrifices had been turned on its head when the Hebrews combine a self-satisfied attitude about worship with insensitivity toward social injustice.

The prophets, preoccupied with the covenant, portray the terrible disharmony they expose in terms of violated relationships. The people violate their relationship with Yahweh with idolatry and when they ignore Torah's call for justice among those in the community. The sin is not about broken rules per se, but about breaking relationships and thereby causing harm. The use of rituals came to be separated from the relationships. Making sacrifice impersonal (and hence, empty) ritual became part of the problem, not part of the solution.

The prophets show us a God angry not because the legalistic scales of justice have been unbalanced. Rather, God's anger stems from violation of the interpersonal dynamics of just relationships through oppression and violence. "God's concern is the prerequisite and source of [God's] anger. It is because [God] cares for [humans] that [God's] anger may be kindled against [humans]." God's anger and God's mercy are not in conflict with each other but directly link, as both stem from God's will to heal the world.[33]

Because the problem lies with violating relationships and doing harm, these prophets present the solution in terms of seeking to restore the relationships. And this restoration is uncomplicated. The God of the prophets remains the loving liberator of the Exodus. The restoration of the Hebrews' relationship with God essentially depends only upon their remembering who God is. This remembrance entails a simple turn—from false trust and back to trust in God. With renewed trust, justice and mercy in social relationships inevitably returns.

A key assumption lies behind how the prophets understand the hope for restoration of harmony with God. God does not require sacrifices to

---

33. Heschel, *Prophets*, vol. 2, 66. See also, Anderson, *Eighth-Century*, 82.

PART ONE: The Bible's Salvation Story

change God's disposition toward God's people. God remains, as always, favorably disposed—so long as human beings simply recognize that and trust—and ready and willing to heal the sin-caused brokenness. "Sin is not a *cul-de-sac*, nor is guilt a final trap. Sin may be washed away by repentance and return, and beyond guilt is the dawn of forgiveness. The door is never locked, the threat of doom is not the last word."[34]

The prophetic stance, then, as reflected in these three prophets, contrasts sharply with the logic of retribution. In Abraham Heschel's words, "the ultimate power is not an inscrutable, blind, and hostile power, to which [humans] must submit in resignation, but a God of justice and mercy to whom [humans are] called upon to return."[35]

For the prophets, salvation results from God's loving initiative. God delivers, forebears, restores. This initiative is a constant. Nothing is needed to change God. The only needed changes are on the human side. Return to Yahweh. Trust in Yahweh, not in other gods, not the works of your hands. Sacrifices are not needed to balance the scales of justice. At most, they simply serve to remind the people of God's generosity and to stimulate rededication to Yahweh.

The prophets see reality as personal and concrete. They know nothing of a detached inner life of God, of cosmic scales of justice, or of impersonal, abstract laws that transcend mundane life. Yahweh feels, responds, loves, and grieves. The entire context for theological reflection concerning salvation must be seen in terms of the covenant relationships God has established with God's people. Justice is not about God's internal processes and impersonal holiness. Rather, justice encourages health in the community of people who seek to live together in a way that glorifies God.

All three prophetic books underscore God's overarching healing love. Each presents God seeking healing, but also—in its overall structure—makes clear that the portrayal of anger and wrath work as rhetoric meant to encourage a return to trust in the Hebrews' loving, patient, and healing God. The prophets do not portray an angry, wrathful God. Rather, they show us a God who out of committed love feels anger at the people's self-destructive behavior. God expresses this anger, but it ultimately serves the love and seeks to make a return more likely.

---

34. Heshcel, *Prophets*, vol. 1, 174.
35. Heschel, *Prophets*, vol. 2, 20–21.

FOUR

Jesus's Teaching on Salvation
Believe the Good News

THE STORY TOLD IN the Gospels places itself in the heart of the traditions of Israel. Jesus presents himself in this story as embodying the promises of Yahweh to his forebears—from Abraham and Sarah on down through Moses, Elijah, and the later prophets.

So, contrary to later Christian soteriologies, for Jesus the Old Testament's salvation story remains fully valid. He does not tell a different story, but proclaims the truth of the old story. "Jesus continues the work of the prototypical prophet, Moses, because he uses Torah to disclose the will of God and to define the justice of God."[1]

THE BIRTH STORIES

The stories of Jesus's birth already make clear the continuity of the story of Jesus with the story of the Old Testament. I will summarize themes, jumping from one Gospel to another with a special emphasis on Luke, rather than take a rigorous historical-critical approach. I do this, in large part, because this is how the common Christian reader tends to approach the Gospels.

Luke begins by telling of John the Baptist. John's father "belonged to the priestly order of Alijah" (1:5). Both parents are faithful to Torah. In his portrayal of John, Jesus's mentor, as fully in continuity with Israel's story, Luke makes clear Jesus's connection with that story. The angel tells John's

---

1. Herzog, *Jesus*, 66.

PART ONE: The Bible's Salvation Story

father Zechariah that John "will turn many of the people of Israel to the Lord their God. With the spirit and power of Elijah he will go before him, to turn the hearts of parents to their children, and the disobedient to the wisdom of the righteous, to make ready a people prepared for the Lord" (Luke 1:16–17; for the link between John and Elijah, see also Matt 11:13; 17:9–13; and Mark 6:14–15).

These words from the angel allude to the final words of the Old Testament book of Malachi: "Lo, I will send you the prophet Elijah before the great and terrible day of the Lord comes. He will turn the hearts of parents to their children and the hearts of children to their parents, so that I will not come and strike the land with a curse" (4:5–6). Luke presents John the Baptist as a prophet in the direct line of the Old Testament prophets, the guardians of Yahweh's message of salvation.

When Luke turns the focus toward Jesus himself, he reiterates the connection with the Old Testament story. The angel Gabriel speaks to Mary, telling her she will bear a son to be named Jesus. The name "Jesus" is a Greek form of the Hebrew name "Joshua," that means "Yahweh saves."[2] This Jesus will be called "Son of the Most High," an echo of language used about Israel's kings, and will, in fact, receive the throne of his ancestor David. Jesus "will reign over the house of Jacob forever" (Luke 1:31–33).

Mary's song of response, the Magnificat (Luke 1:46–55), teems with allusions to the Old Testament salvation story. Mary's words echo those of Hannah, the mother of the great prophet and judge, Samuel (see 1 Sam 2:1–10). In speaking of God exalting the lowly and scattering the proud, she repeats images from the Exodus and numerous of the Psalms (see, for example, Ps 89:10, 13 and Exod 6:6).

Mary concludes by making the connection explicit: "The Lord has helped his servant Israel, in remembrance of his mercy, according to the promise he made to our ancestors, to Abraham and his descendants forever" (Luke 1:54–55). Salvation here, as with the Old Testament story, is an act of God's pure mercy, given as a gift in continuity with God's gracious call of Abraham. Whatever will happen with Jesus, Luke makes it clear at the start that the salvation Jesus brings is of a piece with the salvation Yahweh brought of old.

The next song of praise in Luke one, Zechariah's upon the birth of his son, John, also directly draws on the Old Testament. "Blessed be the Lord God of Israel, for he has looked favorably on his people and redeemed them" (1:68). Zechariah's song points to the salvation Jesus will bring, for

---

2. Meyer, "Jesus," 773.

which John will pave the way. In doing so, Zechariah connects Jesus with the Old Testament's paradigmatic king, David (1:69), and Yahweh's "holy prophet from of old" (1:70) in presenting this salvation in terms of deliverance "from our enemies" (1:71).

The Lord's work in bringing this salvation fulfills "the mercy promised to our ancestors" as God remembers the holy covenant made with Abraham (1:72–73). Zechariah concludes his prophecy by alluding to various Old Testament hopes: "By the tender mercy of our God, the dawn from on high will break upon us, to give light to those who sit in darkness and in the shadow of death, to guide our feet into the way of peace" (Luke 1:78–79).

Luke's story of Jesus's birth begins with another link to the legacy of King David. A government census requires Joseph and Mary to go "to the city of David called Bethlehem, because [Joseph] was descended from the house and family of David" (Luke 2:4). Jesus is born in David's "city." After Jesus's birth, an angel appears to nearby shepherds and tells them that in fulfillment of the people's hopes, their God has brought a savior into the world—one who is linked with David, being born in Bethlehem and named "the Messiah" (Luke 2:11). David himself, of course, had also been a shepherd.

Joseph and Mary, as people of the covenant, have their newborn circumcised after eight days (Luke 2:21). They then take "him up to Jerusalem to present him to the Lord (as it is written in the law of the Lord, 'every first born male shall be designated as holy to the Lord'), and they offered a sacrifice according to what is stated in the law of the Lord, 'a pair of turtledoves or two young pigeons' " (Luke 2:22–24). This birth comes fully within Israel's covenant with Yahweh.

Luke confirms the deep rootage of Jesus in Old Testament salvation traditions by telling of two elderly prophets who confirm God's presence in this young child. Simeon, "righteous and devout, looking forward to the consolation of Israel," had been shown "by the Holy Spirit that he would not see death before he had seen the Lord's Messiah" (Luke 2:25–26). When Joseph and Mary, in obedience to the Law, took Jesus to the temple, Simeon saw him. Simeon alludes to Isaiah's prophecies (Isa 40:3–5; 49:6) when he praises God for bringing a salvation "prepared in the presence of all peoples" that will be "a light for revelation to the Gentiles and for glory to your people Israel" (Luke 2:28–32).

The second prophet, Anna, a member of the ancient Israelite tribe of Asher (2:36), worshiped "night and day" in the temple. When she saw

PART ONE: The Bible's Salvation Story

Jesus, she "began to praise God and to speak about the child to all who were looking for the redemption of Jerusalem" (2:38).

Luke's birth story sets the stage for a proper understanding of Jesus's life and the meaning of his role as savior. In the birth story we learn that indeed something new is at hand, a "new thing" in full harmony with the Old Testament portrayal of salvation. Israel's God has "remembered" the promise to Abraham (Luke 1:54–55), the covenant with Abraham's descendents, and hence acts anew with profound mercy.

There is no hint here that something has to happen to God to make restoration possible. God initiates the reconciliation. God unilaterally declares that salvation has come and is especially available to the vulnerable and marginalized people—those with ears to hear the good news. The birth of Jesus is not presented as linked with the logic of retribution. The birth story's announcement of salvation's presence contains no hint of a new approach to satisfy God's aggrieved holiness or violated honor or to balance the scales of justice with ultimate innocent sacrifice. The story points only to God's initiating mercy and forgiveness.

Jesus's Self-conscious Link with the Old Testament

As Jesus begins his public ministry, he expresses his own sense of continuity with the Old Testament salvation story. Just prior to "going public," Jesus encounters a series of temptations in the wilderness related to his own sense of vocation. Yes, he is called to a messianic role—but what kind of Messiah will he be? Jesus responds to the tempter, according to Luke's account, by quoting from Israel's scriptures. "It is written . . ." he begins each time in resisting the temptations (Luke 4:1–13). He anchors his identity in Israel's story.

Then Jesus returns to his home territory, begins to teach in the synagogues, and soon gains attention. His words in his hometown of Nazareth express his self-understanding concerning his vocation. He reads from Isaiah and then makes the audacious claim, "today this scripture has been fulfilled in your hearing" (Luke 4:21). Linking himself with the text from Isaiah, Jesus identifies himself with Israel's hopes and Yahweh's promises. The fulfillment of those promises stems from Yahweh's initiating mercy.

Throughout his teaching as presented in the Gospels, Jesus quotes and alludes to and paraphrases the Old Testament. He never hints that he might understand his teaching as anything but in full continuity with Israel's scriptures. Jesus "interprets his own actions in terms of the fulfillment, not of a few prophetic proof-texts taken atomistically, but of the entire story-line which Israel had told herself, in a variety of forms, over and over again."[3]

Matthew presents Jesus making this point explicitly: "Do not think that I have come to abolish the law or the prophets; I have come not to abolish but to fulfill. For truly I tell you, until heaven and earth pass away, not one letter, not one stroke of a letter, will pass from the law until all is accomplished" (Matt 5:17–18). Jesus did find himself in conflict with religious leaders over differing interpretations of scripture. But these conflicts must not prevent us from recognizing that in his own self-understanding, he affirms the law and the prophets.

Later in Matthew, Jesus asserts that the central operating convictions of his ministry stem directly from the Bible. "A lawyer asked him a question to test him. 'Teacher, which commandment in the law is the greatest?' Jesus said to him, 'You shall love the Lord your God with all your heart, and with all your soul, and with all your mind. This is the greatest and first commandment. And a second is like it: You shall love your neighbor as yourself. On these two commandments hang all the law and the prophets'" (Matt 22:35–40).

Jesus and Liberation

Matthew's Gospel first introduces us to Jesus when Joseph learns that Mary's pregnancy will result in the birth of a son to be named Jesus, "for he will save his people from their sins" (Matt 1:21). We see a direct link between Jesus's very name and his saving vocation. Joshua was a common name—Josephus mentions twenty different people with that name in his writings about first-century Judaism. However, surely Joseph and Mary's contemporaries associated this name most of all with one of Israel's most important leaders, Moses's successor who led the people into the promised land. Hence, Jesus's vocation, to "save his people from their sins" has to do with liberation—from idolatry, from passivity, from oppression.

When Jesus begins his ministry in his hometown Nazareth (Luke 4:16–30), he speaks of liberation. He brings "good news to the poor" that they may relate to God directly, even in their poverty. He "proclaims release to the captives"; people will be freed from various sorts of bondage (e.g., economic, physical, and demonic). He lets "the oppressed go free."

---

3. Wright, *Jesus*, 129–30.

These various acts of liberation are caught up in the phrase that Jesus "proclaims the year of the Lord's favor" (Luke 4:19). He evokes the "year of jubilee," the redistribution of wealth every fifty years prescribed in Leviticus (25:8–12). Jesus draws on Torah to transform how people view debt and God's participation among the people. "The elites used debt to press their advantages and to imperil the lives of others. Jesus saw debt differently. Rooted in the prophetic strands of the Torah, Jesus' view was that debt is an opportunity for forgiveness."[4]

God does not demand repayment for every ounce of indebtedness. Rather, God offers abundant mercy. The debts would be released without any kind of payment. Jesus's God "was not a God who maintained debt records for the purpose of foreclosing on the poor, but a God who canceled debt and restored life."[5]

Again, we have an explicit affirmation here against retribution. The nature of the salvation Jesus proclaims turns the debt motif on its head. Jubilee theology does not accept the logic of retribution that portrays God as demanding perfect obedience or a violent sacrifice as a necessary basis for earning God's favor. Jesus began his ministry by proclaiming a word of pure acceptance—the poor, the captives, the oppressed are given a simple word of unilateral welcome by God. "When Jesus said, 'God made the sabbath for people,' he meant that God had liberated the Jews by taking them out of Egypt. The sabbatical year, like the day of the sabbath, must be practiced. They are both meant to liberate people and not to enslave them."[6] Jesus indeed liberates ("saves"), but he does so simply by announcing that it is so. In this way, he is in continuity with the core salvation story of the Old Testament. Nothing has changed in the content of that story.

In Luke 4:24, Jesus speaks of not being accepted in his own hometown. The two object lessons he mentions concerning salvation in the Old Testament both concern people outside the Jewish covenant. He speaks of how the widow at Zaraphath (1 Kgs 17:1–16) and of Naaman the Syrian (2 Kgs 5:1–14) both received God's mercy even though they were not part of the covenant community (Luke 4:25–27). In like manner, Jesus seems to say, the poor, the captives, and the oppressed who receive God's mercy in Jesus's time will include some who are outside the covenant. Jesus sees himself as a light to the nations (Luke 2:32)—and presciently, sees this as a point of offense for his contemporaries.

---

4. Herzog, *Jesus*, 107.
5. Ibid., 132.
6. Yoder, *Politics*, 65–66.

Jesus's Teaching on Salvation

The Presence of the Kingdom

The first part of Mark's gospel briefly introduces John the Baptist and informs of Jesus's wilderness temptations. Then, in the middle of chapter one, Jesus begins to proclaim his message. Mark tells us that Jesus returned to Galilee from the wilderness. After John is arrested, Jesus takes the stage, "proclaiming the good news of God" (Mark 1:14). Jesus begins: "The time is fulfilled, and the kingdom of God has come near; repent, and believe the good news" (1:15).

Does Jesus speak of something brand new or does he offer a renewed reminder of what already is? These words in Mark 1:15 note the beginning of Jesus's ministry. He says them before he does anything. So, he seems to mean, listen to the good news of God's love that has always characterized reality no matter how blind human beings have been to it. The God of Abraham, Moses, and Joshua remains a merciful, saving God.

We may see five key points in Jesus' opening proclamation: (1) "the kingdom of God," (2) that kingdom has "come near" or is "at hand," (3) the call to "repent," (4) the call to "believe," and (5) the description of the message as "good news."

(1) First, the "kingdom of God" is a creative, fluid symbol meant to convey God's participation in human life as creator and savior. The kingdom is about God's rule, God as the ultimate shaper of what is and what will be. For Jesus to link his own presence with God's kingdom speaks about his own identity. Titles such as "Son of God," "Messiah," and "Lord" speak of Jesus's close connection with God's kingdom. This close connection conveys a great deal about God and God's kingdom, too. We know about this God and this kingdom by being attentive to what Jesus said and did.

If Jesus's way defines the kingdom of God, what matters most in this kingdom are right relationships between human beings and God and among human beings. Jesus's way values kindness, respect, care, just love, and shalom—directly in continuity with Torah. In calling what is happening in his life and among his followers the presence of God's kingdom, Jesus means for his hearers to take what he says with utmost seriousness. However, he offers not the king's scepter with which to dominate the members of his kingdom. Rather, he offers an invitation—join with us voluntarily, not out of fear but out of love.

(2) Second, Jesus considers this kingdom to be "near," to be "at hand." He points to God's rule in the present tense. The kingdom of God is not some otherworldly "heaven" or totally future reality present only at the

end of history. A certain tentativeness may be perceived here, too. Jesus does not mean to assert that with him pure perfection will now characterize human life. When he says, "at hand" or "near," he conveys a sense of partialness and fragility. The kingdom is genuine and present, but also incomplete. The kingdom may be resisted; it does not steamroll everyone in its path.

Jesus also expresses with the "at hand" aspect a sense of the direct linkage between his particular presentness and the presence of the kingdom. He says, "I am here and, hence, the kingdom of God is near."

(3) Third, given the presence in Jesus of God's kingdom, what does he ask of his listeners? Two simple responses: "repent" and "believe." This type of reaction closely parallels what God asked of the children of Israel in light of God's earlier saving acts.

The close parallel with the Old Testament story reinforces our sense that Jesus fits within the gift/response dynamics of God's saving efforts there. Jesus presents the kingdom of God as already present. Because it is present, listeners may "repent" and "believe." Jesus offers no hint that repentance and belief are conditions God requires before making the kingdom present. "Jesus does not offer forgiveness to those who repent and promise to do works of restitution. He declares people forgiven before they repent." Jesus reached out to those who were for various reasons unable to do works of restitution (e.g., toll collectors, prostitutes). "To these he declares: Your sins are forgiven (Luke 18:9–14)! Now you can repent!"[7]

The first step toward salvation is repentance, one of John the Baptist's terms, too. Jesus shared John's message that repentance did not involve going to the Temple and offering sacrifice.[8] However, the contrast between "repentance" in the context of Jesus's message and in the context of John's message looms large. John basically presents repentance as an act born out of fear—you will receive God's destroying wrath unless you turn from your sinfulness, submit to the cleansing ritual of baptism, and drastically change your lives in an ascetic direction. Repentance means turn away from "this evil generation" and your complicity in it.

In contrast, Jesus presents repentance in the context not of fear but of joy. He teaches, not, "turn because God is angry and will destroy." He teaches, rather, "turn because God is love." The kingdom's presence means you may enter it just as you are. Jesus spoke nothing of the need

---

7. Wink, *Human*, 78.
8. Wright, *Jesus*, 257.

to start with a cleansing ritual; Jesus sees God as present now, amidst our impurities.

As human beings' main problem, Jesus addresses his listeners' ignorance of the true character of God. "Fear not!" Turn from your quavering in your misconceptions wherein you understand yourself to be destined for punishment. To repent, in Jesus's message, indeed does mean change, a turning from alienation and brokenness. However, the context is different from repentance in John's message. One turns from fear to mercy. One returns to the God who made us and loved us.

(4) The next step, after repentance, is to "believe." "Believe" also may be translated as "trust." Trust in God, trust in the genuine presence of the kingdom of God. Trust that Jesus indeed embodies the character and will of the true God. Recognize that the world as presented in Jesus's message (and in Torah and the prophets) is where we are most at home.

To "repent and believe" means to turn from fear, mistrust, and alienation toward joy, trust, and healing. "Belief" in the way Jesus speaks of it here means to accept, in the core of one's being, that goodness and truth and beauty are genuine and that they are present in the at-hand kingdom of God. God's kingdom may be lived in, right now, by anyone who so chooses.

(5) That the object of trust is the God revealed both in Torah and Jesus constitutes the "good news." God will enter our lives here and now with healing love as we turn toward God. Everything Jesus does after his opening proclamation fleshes his message out. He embodies the kingdom of God and shows its presence via healings, teaching, perseverance in face of suffering, and confrontations with the oppressive Powers. He shows that repentance will be fruitful when it is genuine. He also shows how his way offers possibilities for genuine transformation from violence toward peace, selfishness toward generosity, and isolation toward community.

As we will see, Jesus's embodiment of the gospel message leads directly to his death. However, God does not require this death as the necessary means to effect salvation. Jesus's death does not gain its meaning as an expression of retributive justice where God's need for a sacrifice to satisfy God's holiness or honor or justice. Rather, Jesus's death gains its meaning because it stems from the response of the Powers to the salvation already given by God through straight out mercy and revealed to the world with unprecedented clarity by Jesus.

Jesus's death adds nothing to the means of salvation—God's mercy saves, from the reprieve of Cain and the calling of Abraham in Genesis

1–12 on. Instead, Jesus's death reveals the depth of the Powers' rebellion and the ultimate power of God's love. So Jesus's death indeed profoundly heightens our understanding of salvation. It reveals the logic of retribution as an instrument of evil. It reveals that God's love prevails even over the most extreme expression of (demonic) retribution.

Evidence of Jesus's Identity

Following the first programmatic statements, Jesus went to work to embody the presence of the kingdom with his words and deeds. Matthew gives us a clear portrayal of the basic dynamics in the section beginning at 4:23 and ending at 9:35, introduced and concluded by two identical verses: "Jesus went throughout Galilee, teaching in their synagogues and proclaiming the good news of the kingdom and curing every disease and every sickness among the people."

In between these two verses we read of Jesus's two-pronged ministry—authoritative teaching (including the Sermon on the Mount) and works of healing. Both elements reveal the nature of the present kingdom, and the nature of salvation in relation to this kingdom.

Jesus's mentor, John the Baptist, heard about Jesus's ministry. John's arrest by Herod Antipas had coincided with the beginning of Jesus's public ministry. So John had been unable to see for himself. From the reports he heard, John got the idea that this former disciple had a somewhat different agenda than John's own. So John sends some messengers to question Jesus. "Are you the One who is to come, or are we to wait for another?" (Matt 11:3).

Jesus responds: "Go and tell John what you hear and see: the blind receive their sight, the lame walk, the lepers are cleansed, the deaf hear, the dead are raised, and the poor have good news brought to them" (Matt 11:4–5). Jesus indeed understood himself in messianic terms, but he recognized that his message differed from what John expected. It is a message of welcome, not threat. Jesus contrasted himself to John in this way: "John came neither eating nor drinking . . . ; the Son of Man came eating and drinking" (Matt 11:19).

Jesus's response to John's question serves as a programmatic summary of his message. What shows most of all that he is God's agent? Jesus answers: the "Coming One" heals those who hurt and proclaims the good news of God's love to those who need it most.

Jesus's Teaching on Salvation

Within this Matthew 4:23—9:35 section marked off by the two statements about Jesus's ministry, we find the Sermon on the Mount, chapters 5–7, and a concentrated account of Jesus's healings in chapters 8–9. We gain important insight into Jesus's understanding of his own identity and his own understanding of how salvation may be gained when we note who he healed. Since Jesus himself focused on his healing ministry when he answers John's question about his identity, we should take these stories seriously.

Who gets healed here? A leper, who would have been considered ritually unclean and hence excluded from the community, comes first (Matt 8:1–4). Next follows a centurion (a Roman military leader) who asks Jesus to heal his paralyzed servant. Jesus commends this Gentile's faith ("in no one in Israel have I found such faith" [8:10] and heals the servant [8:5–13]).

For the next recipient of Jesus's healing, his disciple Peter's mother-in-law, he heals a fever that had left her bedridden (Matt 8:14–15). Next, Jesus casts out demons and heals sick people (8:16–18). Jesus's healing moves to Gentile territory on the other side of the Sea of Galilee in the country of the Gadorenes. Here he cast demons out of two people who harassed travelers (8:28–34). Upon returning home, he heals a paralyzed man (9:2–8). Then, a different kind of healing happens when Jesus calls the tax collector Matthew to leave his work and follow him (9:9).

Dramatically, Jesus heals a synagogue leader's daughter who had been pronounced dead and a woman who had been suffering from a continuous menstrual flow for twelve years, rendering her perpetually unclean (Matt 9:18–25). Jesus completes the series of healings by giving sight to two blind men (9:27–31) and voice to a man silenced by demon possession (9:32–33). To cap off the display of Jesus's healing, which reached to such a spectrum of needy people, comes a foreboding commentary by a religious leader: "By the ruler of the demons he casts out the demons" (9:33).

This account of Jesus's healing shows how his welcome extended indiscriminately and unconditionally to an entire spectrum of people. Jesus welcomed those labeled "unclean" such as the leper and chronically menstruating woman, as well as leaders among the occupying Roman army, a tax collector, the child of a leader in the religious structures of Jesus's hometown, Gentiles in Gadara, and Jews in Nazareth. Male and female, old and young, wealthy and poor all received God's healing touch. Jesus's

PART ONE: The Bible's Salvation Story

"healings function in exact parallel with the welcome of sinners, and this, we may be quite sure, was what Jesus himself intended."[9]

Salvation as healing here comes as a gift of a merciful God with no hint of the logic of retribution. Just as God, out of gracious initiative, liberated the Hebrew slaves in days of old, so here, out of gracious initiative, God brings healing to those in Jesus's world enslaved by demons, blindness, sickness, and even the trappings of power.

We do see in this passage a hint of a connection with Jesus's death. Jesus's death will not be necessary as an act of sacred violence required to make salvation possible. However, the Powers (as represented by the religious leader in Matt 9:33) react to the salvation Jesus offers by condemning him. The dark clouds we glimpse here grow bigger and darker before the end. Jesus's message of salvation will not be totally clear until the storm is spent, his persevering love fully surfaces the Powers' hostility, and God's love remains standing.

Jesus's Prescription for Eternal Life

The synoptic Gospels include only two stories of Jesus being asked directly about eternal life. Both stories illumine Jesus's understanding of salvation. One story, that includes the parable of the Good Samaritan, occurs only in Luke's Gospel (10:25–37). All three synoptic Gospels contain the other story, Jesus' encounter with the "rich young ruler" (Matt 19:16–26; Mark 10:17–22; Luke 18:18–25).

The "expert in the law" (Luke 10:25 NIV) asks Jesus about inheriting eternal life right after Jesus blessed the seventy of his followers who returned to him after traveling about sharing his message. The lawyer asks, in effect: What about those of us who are not privileged to be part of this group, how do we enter into God's blessing of salvation?

We best read the lawyer's question as an intellectual challenge. The lawyer has his own ideas and wants to see how Jesus matches up. Jesus, sensing this, turns the tables and asks the lawyer what he thinks. The lawyer answers with his summary of the Tradition, quoting together Deuteronomy 6:5 ("You shall love the Lord your God with all your heart, and with all your soul, and with all your strength") and Leviticus 19:18 ("You shall love your neighbor as yourself").

Jesus affirms this response: "You have given the right answer; do this, and you will live" (Luke 10:28). We see one more explicit statement of

9. Ibid., 191.

Jesus's continuity with the Old Testament understanding of salvation. The lawyer's answer reflects accurately the biblical teaching on salvation, and Jesus gives this teaching his full affirmation.

Granting that the way to salvation includes loving both God and neighbor together, the lawyer asks for clarity concerning the neighbor. Jesus's powerful story underscores "neighbor" as an all-encompassing category. "Neighbor" includes even one's national enemies—the "Samaritan" being a neighbor to the Jew even while one of the Jews' long-time enemies.

In portraying neighborliness in this way—and we must remember that he has just agreed that loving one's neighbor is the key to salvation—Jesus characterizes eternal life in terms of mercy toward the one in need. Jesus unites his own way of life as God's Messiah (as seen in his healing ministry) with the way of life characteristic of those who gain salvation.

The dynamic of salvation is the dynamic of mercy, of love without limit, of welcome and generosity. What the ancient Hebrews learned with God's two central gifts (liberation from slavery in Egypt and Torah to guide their lives of grateful response to that liberation), Jesus's listeners now hear reiterated. Love of God results in love of neighbor.

The second instance of Jesus being asked directly about eternal life may be found in all three synoptic Gospels. In Luke's version, Jesus's encounter with the rich ruler follows immediately after Jesus's assertion that little children, with their open hearts and trusting spirit, show what is needed for entry into God's kingdom.

The ruler, perhaps wondering if Jesus's statement about children leaves him out, asks how he might inherit eternal life. Jesus responds: "You know the commandments: 'You shall not commit adultery, you shall not murder, you shall not steal, you shall not bear false witness, honor your father and mother'" (Luke 18:20).

Again, Jesus understands himself in harmony with the biblical tradition. This time, he links salvation with the Commandments that introduce Torah. The love command from the earlier story and this summary of the Commandments should be seen as equivalent. Implied in any summary of the Commandments are the prelude to the Commandments (because "the Lord your God brought you out of the house of slavery," Exod 20:2) and the first Commandment ("you shall have no other gods before me," Exod 20:3; that is, love God fully).

The rich ruler, like the lawyer, agrees with Jesus concerning this understanding of salvation. And, again as well, Jesus goes on to add depth to the basics, fully in line with biblical teaching. Jesus makes clear that two closely linked elements lie at the heart of the Commandments: (1) do not idolize wealth and (2) to be committed to God means to be committed to care for the vulnerable ones in the community.

When we consider Jesus's two responses to direct questions about salvation, we see something unremarkable if we understand Jesus to be in continuity with the Old Testament. Jesus actually adds nothing to the Old Testament portrayal of salvation. What must one do to be saved? Love God wholeheartedly (Deut 6:5). Love one's neighbor as oneself (Lev 19:18). Follow the Commandments (Exod 20:1–17).

Jesus does challenge assumptions by the lawyer and the ruler about the implications of these convictions. However, first Jesus places himself in the mainstream of the Old Testament teaching about salvation and in the mainstream of how his contemporaries understood salvation. Both stories clearly show how unremarkable Jesus's understanding of salvation would have been.

So, when Jesus goes beyond the simplicity of his agreement with the lawyer and rich ruler we must not forget this fundamental agreement. The "beyond" where Jesus moves—neighborliness as exemplified by the Samaritan, sharing possessions with those in need—does not place Jesus in tension with Torah. Rather, they place him directly in the prophetic stream. He does not innovate here but speaks from the heart of Old Testament salvation teaching.

What gets Jesus in trouble links with what got the prophets in trouble. He makes this connection himself ("Blessed are you when people hate you, and when they exclude you, revile you, and defame you on account of the Son of Man. Rejoice in that day and leap for joy, for surely your reward is great in heaven; for that is what their ancestors did to the prophets," Luke 6:22–23). Love of neighbor means transcending nationalistic barriers. Following Torah means to critique trust in wealth and to care for the needs of those one's culture had impoverished.

We do not see in these two stories any hint that Jesus thinks of salvation in terms of the logic of retribution. In fact, Jesus's message characteristically contrasts with the God-as-wrathful message of John the Baptist.

Jesus's Portrayal of God

When Jesus proclaimed and then enacted the presence of the Kingdom of God he presented two crucial beliefs about God: God initiates salvation

Jesus's Teaching on Salvation

and God welcomes all kinds of people who share the one characteristic of a desire for a relationship with God.

Jesus himself manifested a close relationship with God, as seen by his use of the terminology of "Father." For Jesus, "Father" conveys intimacy and mutuality, not a hierarchical, distant, stern, and punishing sense of God. Besides living in light of this Father-intimacy himself, Jesus also encouraged his followers to think of God in the same way. Jesus taught his followers to pray to "our Father," to think of God as one who loves them like a parent. Salvation has to do with responding with trust to the compassionate care of a loving God. In using the analogy of entering the Kingdom like children (Mark 9:36) Jesus evoked such a sense of intimacy.

Jesus also uses God as his model when he calls upon his followers to take the radical step of loving their enemies. "Love your enemies, do good, and lend, expecting nothing in return. Your reward will be great, and you will be children of the Most High; for he is kind to the ungrateful and the wicked. Be merciful, just as your Father is merciful" (Luke 6:35–36). God is Jesus's paradigmatic model for calling his followers to live by the logic of mercy and to reject the logic of retribution. For the God Jesus calls "Abba," holiness leads to initiating mercy, not to initiating sacred violence in order to punish.

One of the most evocative pictures of God that Jesus gives comes in his famous Prodigal Son parable in Luke 15:11–32. It could just as easily be called the Parable of the Welcoming Father. This parable also contains a third actor, the older brother. This brother's hostility toward the father's welcome forebodes the Powers' hostility toward Jesus's way of welcome.

The father in the parable respects his younger son. The son does not appear to deserve such respect, but the father without quibble acquiesces to his son's request for his inheritance (Luke 15:12). The father contradicts traditional wisdom, as reflected in the Book of Sirach. "To [your] son, . . . do not give power over yourself, as long as you live" (Sir 33:20). "Do not give to the ungodly; hold back their bread, and do not give it to them. . . . For the Most High also hates sinners and will inflict punishment on the ungodly" (Sir 12:4, 6).

Things get worse in Jesus's parable. The son wastes his inheritance, ends up destitute even to the point of shaming himself by working as a tender of pigs (Luke 15:15). The son decides to go back home and serve his father as a hired hand, assuming he can no longer be considered his father's son (15:18–19). However, the father upsets all expectations. As soon as he sees his son in the distance, he is filled with compassion (not offended holiness!) and forgets all decorum expected of a person in his position. The father runs to and embraces his son even before any words of confession are uttered.

The son then does express his regret, that he is no longer worthy to be considered his father's son. But the father brushes his son's words off, calling for a robe and ring that signify the full reinstatement of the son. The older brother protests, and the father respects him too. "Son, you are always with me, and all that is mine is yours" (15:31). The parable ends with the decision of the older son left open. Will he join in his father's incredible mercy or not?

This parable, justly called the "gospel in miniature,"[10] captures Jesus' understanding of God and salvation in a nutshell. As we have seen, this view of God and salvation stands in full continuity with the view of the core Old Testament story.

The "Great Divide"

Matthew concludes his final account of Jesus' teachings in 25:31 with a portrayal of the last judgment. We hear of the division of sheep from goats, the former joining the "kingdom prepared for you" and the latter heading for "the eternal fire prepared for the devil." Those who join the sheep are the ones who ministered to the needy. They actually ministered to God when they offered help to "the least of these who are members of my family" (25:40).

Those who join the goats are convicted because they disregarded "the least of these" and thereby disregarded the Lord (25:45). Jesus mentions only this criterion. He catches up here one of the central motifs we have seen that dates back to Torah and found consistent expression in the prophets and Jesus' own ministry: God has loved you unconditionally and shown that love to you. For that love to be part of your lives, you must respond to it with gratitude.

Faithful people verify their gratitude concretely through care for vulnerable people in their midst. Nothing else embodies so well the divine/human relationship. We are all vulnerable before God. Only God's mercy makes us whole. We become whole as we incarnate that mercy in our treatment of other vulnerable ones.

Jesus expressed this kind of care most overtly, perhaps, in his practice of open table fellowship with many kinds of "unclean," hence vulnerable,

10. Donahue, *Gospel*, ix.

people. "For Jesus, table fellowship with unclean persons was possible because God was compassionate—that is, forgiving, accepting, nourishing of righteous and sinner alike. Because God accepted such as these, God's children were to do so as well."[11]

So, Matthew's account of the "great divide" provides one last statement showing Jesus's continuity with the Old Testament portrayal of salvation. Nothing in this scene of judgment hints at the logic of retribution playing a role in the "sheep" entering the kingdom. It is the logic of mercy. God loves you, trust in that love and share it with others. That's it.

Jesus's Allusions to His Death

According to the Gospels, Jesus did point forward to his own death as a likely possibility containing salvific meaning. From the resistance he received to this idea from his disciples and from their deserting him when he faced arrest, we may suspect that the disciples did not themselves make the link between Jesus's death and salvation until after God raised him.

Jesus most directly linked his death with salvation in Mark 10:45. Mark tells of Jesus predicting his death in 8:31; 9:31; 10:45. In all three, Jesus tied together his identity as Messiah with his suffering and with his call to his followers to share in that suffering. He asks them to join in the overthrow of the values of power politics. As part of this third prediction, Jesus states that his followers are to serve others, not dominate them. In doing so they will follow him, "for the Son of Man came not to be served but to serve, and to give his life a ransom for many."

Ancient Israelites used the term "ransom" (originally a compensation required for the release of slaves) as a metaphor for the liberation of God's people—from slavery in Egypt (Exod 21:8,30; Lev 25:47–52) and from the oppression of exile (Isa 43:1–7; 44:21–23). It need not imply a price paid to someone so much as simply a metaphor for bringing redemption.[12]

Jesus devotes his life to bringing people liberation from the various bondages imposed by the Powers—and calls on his followers to do so as well. They effect liberation by remembering God's previous work of liberating slaves from the Egyptian empire and by trusting in Yahweh instead of kings, horses, chariots, and other elements of power politics (see Mark 10:42–43).

---

11. Borg, *Conflict*, 149.
12. Brondos, *Paul*, 43.

PART ONE: The Bible's Salvation Story

Jesus recognizes that the Powers will fight against his liberating message. He willingly faces their violence. He gives his life to show clearly that the call to serve rather than dominate actually does lead to salvation. "The deaths of Jesus and some of his disciples would 'ransom many' by unmasking the Powers and revealing their defection from their divine vocations. The redemptive suffering of the few would show others a new world of power relations in which 'success' is measured by the capacity to help liberate others."[13]

In the words of John Howard Yoder: "It is precisely in the crucifixion that the true nature of the Powers has come to light. Previously they were accepted as the most basic and ultimate realities, as the gods of the world. Never had it been perceived nor could it have been perceived, that this belief was founded on deception. Now that the true God appears on earth in Christ, it becomes apparent that the Powers are inimical to Him, acting not as his instruments but as His adversaries."[14]

Later on, Jesus shares a final Passover with his closest disciples. Passover, of course, celebrated God's liberation of the Hebrew slaves from their bondage in Egypt. Like the motif of "blood" in Leviticus 17:11, in the celebration of Passover what is in mind is life.[15] Likewise, in Jesus's words, though he alludes to his coming death when he speaks of pouring out his blood: "for many," his point is to assert that he brings life. He brings Exodus-like liberation from the domination of the Powers. He does not die as a sacrifice according to the logic of retribution meant to satisfy the just demands for recompense of a "holy" and "wrathful" God. To the contrary, Jesus willingly gives his life as an expression of God's pure mercy. Only a commitment to the way of love that does not waver even in the face of the Powers' extreme violence opens the way to true life.

JESUS'S "SOTERIOLOGY"

"Jesus" means "savior." From the beginning, the Gospels center on the salvation to which Jesus witnesses. When we read the Gospels against the backdrop of the Old Testament (and not against the backdrop of post-biblical Christian theology) we see complete continuity between the core Old Testament salvation story and Jesus's own teaching about salvation. Jesus follows the prophets and Torah in his basic equation: God initiates

---

13. Wink, *Human*, 94.
14. Yoder, *Politics*, 146.
15. Daly, *Christian*, 119–20; Rogerson, "Sacrifice," 53.

salvation, first, last, and always. God does this out of love and with the intent, reflecting God's total commitment to human beings, to bring healing to the alienated human race.

In other words, nothing needs to happen to change God's disposition toward human beings or to enable God to overcome limitations imposed on God's mercy by "holiness" and "justice." God does not need some sort of sacrificial violence in order to satisfy God's honor or appease God's wrath in order to offer salvation to alienated human beings.

Jesus proclaimed a simple salvation message. Turn to God and trust in the good news of God's love. To make this message perfectly clear, Jesus expressed the good news of God's love in concrete ways. Jesus healed physical damage. Jesus overpowered demonic oppression. Jesus reached out especially to the vulnerable ones, the ones labeled "sinners" and outcastes who were excluded and oppressed due to the sin of the powers-that-be in Israel. Jesus's soteriology contains no hint of salvation according to the logic of retribution.

However, tragically, the logic of retribution does enter into the gospel story in a significant way. Jesus, who followed after the prophets, violated laws and assumptions and expectations and conventional wisdom—out of faithfulness to Torah. Jesus confronted the Powers that dominated his people's culture, the Powers that dominated his people's religious institutions, and the Powers that dominated the "secular" government of first-century Palestine.

As a consequence of Jesus challenge to the status quo, the Powers did follow the logic of retribution—against Jesus. So, the story of Jesus's death does indeed contribute to the New Testament portrayal of salvation. Not, however, because God needed Jesus's death as a violent sacrifice that would enable God to offer forgiveness to humanity.

Rather, Jesus's death as part of the salvation story reveals like nothing else the hostility of the fallen Powers to the social outworking of the logic of mercy. Because of the depths of their hostility, the Powers put Jesus and God to the test. How does love deal with deadly hatred? The basic issue here is whether the logic of mercy may actually make a difference in a world governed by retribution. Does Jesus offer a genuinely different way, an approach to violence that does not merely escalate the violence?

In Part II of this book, I will look much more closely at the story of Jesus's death. I will argue that the story does offer hope. The story unveils the extent of the Powers' hostility toward God. When it does so, it means to heighten our disillusionment with agents of cultural exclusivism, religious institutionalism, and political authoritarianism. The story refutes their claims to be legitimate agents of God. The story also shows how Jesus modeled an appropriate response to the Powers and refused to the very end to add to the spiral of violence.

PART TWO

Jesus's Death and Salvation

IN CONSIDERING JESUS AS Savior, we face a tension between two seemingly incongruous aspects of the story. On the one hand, as we saw in chapter four, Jesus taught and practiced a ministry of love. He demonstrated through his actions and words the reality of mercy and compassion in God's creation. He proclaimed a message of peace. He thereby placed his message squarely in the mainstream of Israel's faith traditions. And yet, on the other hand, Jesus died a criminal's death. The religious authorities and the political authorities joined to sentence him to crucifixion, the most painful and humiliating of executions.

I see three general options for deciding how to interpret the relationship of these two seemingly contradictory elements of the story.

(1) We may think within the logic of retribution and resolve the tension by minimizing the significance of the first element, Jesus's living and teaching a message of love. For salvation's sake, only two points truly matter: (a) that Jesus lived a sinless life and (b) that Jesus died a sacrificial death. Jesus's crucifixion then becomes the means to achieve salvation.

A major problem with this approach is that it brings into play a notion of salvation foreign to Jesus's own thought and foreign to the Old Testament salvation story. We have not been prepared by the story up to now for this kind of innovation. "The scriptures as a whole provide no ground for a portrait of an angry God needing to be appeased in atoning sacrifice."[1] Accepting the logic of retribution as central to God's work of salvation and thereby making Jesus's crucifixion a salvific act, undercuts the meaning of the Bible's salvation story and negates Jesus's own understanding of salvation.

---

1. Green and Baker, *Recovering*, 51.

(2) A second approach goes to the other extreme and argues that all that actually matters is the truthfulness of Jesus's message of love. That he was crucified is tragic, even extraordinarily evil, but that event adds nothing to how we understand salvation. We best simply name the crucifixion as something terrible that should never have happened, see it as the negation of meaning, and then to drop the subject.[2]

This approach is closer to the heart of the story of the Old Testament and Gospels. However, Jesus's execution may have importance for how we understand salvation even if we reject the idea that Jesus's death as a sacrifice was necessary to change God's disposition toward human beings. To minimize the importance of Jesus's crucifixion risks avoiding one of the deepest challenges people of faith face—how do we deal with violence and evil in the world? Simply to name Jesus's crucifixion as violent and then dismiss it as having no relevance for our soteriology may well leave us with a superficial view of salvation.

(3) So, a third approach, taken in this book, proposes that Jesus's crucifixion is crucial for how we understand the Bible's salvation story, though not because it adds a needed element that makes salvation, for the first time, possible. Rather, Jesus's crucifixion illumines what is at stake in God's efforts to bring healing to the world, what forces oppose these efforts, and how those forces may be overcome. Jesus's crucifixion illumines the inherent social dynamic of biblical salvation and the inextricable connection between Jesus's way of life and our possibilities to find healing.

---

2. See, e.g., the discussion by Brock and Parker, *Proverbs*.

FIVE

The Death of Jesus

THE STORY OF JESUS'S death reminds us like nothing else that the healing God offers is not simply spiritual or individualistic or easy. The biblical story tells of salvation as a matter of trusting God's always directly available mercy. However, the simplicity of this story must not blind us to the difficulty of actually accepting, appropriating, and living in light of its message.

So I will consider the story of Jesus's death as a crucial element of my agenda in this book. This story helps us understand the violent dynamics of our world and helps us answer the question of how to respond to violence without adding to the violence. This story helps us understand why the simple message of God's love has not been readily embraced in our world. And this story helps us understand how God works to overcome these problems.

THE POWERS AND THE STORY OF JESUS'S DEATH

In the chapters that follow we will look closely at the story of Jesus's death. By doing so, I will by inference show how using the logic of retribution as the basis for understanding Jesus's death and our salvation actually leads to the opposite conclusion from what the story conveys. The story tells us that the logic of retribution was an instrument of the fallen Powers, not God—and that Jesus's followers should see in the story a direct refutation of that logic.

The story of Jesus's death shows the extent that humanity resists God's saving initiative. More than providing a one-time drama centered on a unique work of redemption, the story reflects the ongoing pattern of

PART TWO: Jesus' Death and Salvation

history. We see this pattern in how Jesus's life evokes resistance from the structures of human culture, leads to suffering, and ends in vindication.

The story of Jesus's death tells of love in the "real world." We have not resolved the issue of salvation until we face the fact that people resist God's love. We may accept the portrayal in the Bible of salvation as pure loving initiative from God; God requires nothing to be made willing to save. Yet we know from the Bible and from human history that this loving initiative meets with resistance. So we must go beyond simply establishing the centrality of love to learn more why this resistance happens and how to respond to it.

Jesus faced resistance from three general types of sources:

(a) *Cultural exclusivism* centered around the legal system that regulated the culture's sense of right and wrong and served as an identity marker (that is, the New Testament's portrayal of the interpretation of Torah practiced by the Pharisees).

(b) *Religious institutionalism* centered around a sacred institution that served as the center of the culture and brooked no opposition to its monopoly on sacred power (that is, the temple in Jerusalem and the priests who supervised the temple's operation and guarded its status).

(c) *Political authoritarianism* in the form of a political kingdom that exercised its control through force and responded quickly and harshly to challenges to its political hegemony (that is, the government of the Roman Empire in Judea in the governorship of Pontius Pilate).

The law, temple, and empire may all be understood in terms of the Powers analysis developed by Walter Wink.[1] Drawing on the imagery of principalities and powers, most explicitly articulated in Pauline writings but implied and assumed throughout the Bible, Wink presents the Powers in terms of the basic social structures of human life (e.g., language; cultural mores; laws; institutions such as governments, schools, and organized religion).

Like humanity, the Powers are created good and are necessary for us to function socially—actually, they inevitably arise among people. An example would be the way language works. Once we begin speaking with others, language comes into existence. We have no language without human beings; at the same time, language exists outside each particular person. Each new person is born into a world shaped by language. So, we are all shaped "from the outside," as it were, by language that exists before

---

1. See Wink's trilogy, *Naming; Unmasking;* and *Engaging*. On Wink's thought, see Gingerich and Grimsrud, *Transforming*.

we exist but would not exist without us. Hence, we can say languages "exist" even if they are completely dependent upon human beings for their existence. We may even speak of languages as "fallen" in the sense, for instance, that languages shape how their users see the world and may perpetuate stereotypes that we share as we learn language.

Other Powers, such as law, temple, and state, may more clearly be seen as fallen. These Powers link with specific structures that inevitably make up human social life—and are necessary for human social life. Yet, these structures may become too important in human beings' eyes; they may become idols. Biblically, the Powers are meant to serve God's purposes by providing structure to social life. The law provides guidance for practical living; the temple provides a center for ordered religious life; the state makes sure material needs of people within it are met and that laws are applied fairly in ways that protect vulnerable people in the nation.

However, the Powers as fallen tend not to be responsive to God's loving initiative. Throughout the Bible we see the Powers causing trouble for those who manifest God's love. It is as if the Powers in their rebellion want to be worshiped and to encourage distorted and harmful inter-human dynamics that enhance their control over human beings.

Precisely in embodying God's love the way he did, Jesus threatened the existing structures of power in his culture. These structures provided substitute forms of meaning and security that exploited human fears and uncertainties. Jesus's way lessened the importance of the Powers linked with the law, the temple, and the state. The Powers did not like that, to say the least.

In what sense does Jesus bring salvation from the dominance of the fallen Powers? The Powers rely on belief. As long as we believe in their ultimacy, trusting in them for security and meaning, the Powers rule. Jesus challenges human beings to change our allegiance. He asks us to trust in God's love and not the sense of superiority over others that legalistic belief in the law provides. He asks us to end our trust in the assured access to God that temple rituals (at a price) provide. He asks us to end our trust in the sense of power over others that being on good terms with the empire provides. In these ways, trust in Jesus breaks the hold of the Powers.

Jesus himself models disillusionment with the claims of the Powers in his own life. However, perhaps more profoundly, when we recognize that these Powers brutally murdered Jesus we will see that they do not possess the truth as they claim. The more one knows of Jesus's way and Jesus's

PART TWO: Jesus' Death and Salvation

close connection with God, the more the treatment he received from the agents of law, temple, and empire will heighten disbelief in their claims.

The story of Jesus's death highlights the bases for our rejection of the logic of retribution. The Powers responded to Jesus retributively. Jesus did violate the rules and values the Powers claimed to be true. The penalty for one who violates those rules and values is punishment—in this case, death. Jesus died according to the logic of retribution. The Powers that killed Jesus were the ones following the logic of retribution, not God. That Jesus died as he did shows that the logic of retribution reflects a rejection of God's will, not its fulfillment.

The Gospels understand Jesus's death as the key event in the story they tell. My question is this: why is Jesus's death so important to this story?

For much of Christian theology, Jesus's death overshadows his life and teaching, provides a notion of salvation via a violent sacrifice, and renders peripheral his teaching concerning salvation summarized above in chapter four. I will argue that, to the contrary, the story of Jesus's death actually confirms what we have already seen. The basic message of salvation throughout is God's unqualified mercy. God's mercy evokes resistance from the Powers, depending as they do upon fearfulness, selfishness, and violence. This resistance, profound and deep, ultimately results in the Powers conspiring to put Jesus to death. They seek retribution for his violation of cultural, religious, and political expectations for humanity subject to the Powers' domination.

The murder of Jesus exposes the consequences of making the Powers into idols. It reveals the logic of retribution as opposed to God. Such a revelation frees those with eyes to see from trust in cultural boundary markers, religious institutions, and governmental structures. Such freedom allows people to recognize and appropriate God's mercy as indeed the central life-enhancing force in the universe. The story of Jesus's death also highlights how he models authentic faith in the true God. Jesus shows courage and love to be sufficient resistance to the incredible violence and hostility of which the Powers are capable. In the face of the worst imaginable torture and humiliation, Jesus remained faithful to the path of loving God and neighbor above all else.

The story concludes by vindicating Jesus's way of life, his approach to the Powers. God raises Jesus from the dead, which emphasizes that the Powers acted in rebellion against God, not as agents of God. Jesus's death and resurrection stand in harmony with the Old Testament salvation story. They clarify that earlier story, reinforce its truthfulness, and heighten disillusionment with the Powers that try to obscure that story.

The Death of Jesus

The Gospels' portrayal of Jesus' death shares with the traditional retributively oriented view of atonement the recognition that retributive justice was responsible for Jesus's death. However, they draw a diametrically opposed conclusion about the legitimacy of such justice.

For substitutionary atonement, God's retributive justice must find an innocent and pure sacrifice in order to balance the scales of the moral universe that have been upset by human sin. Such a sacrifice satisfies the needs of God's holiness and makes salvation possible by meeting the requirements of retributive justice. For the Gospels' portrayal, in contrast, the outworking of the misguided commitment to retributive justice leads the Powers of law, temple, and empire to judge Jesus to be guilty and to punish him with crucifixion. We do need to note that the guardians of the law were not directly involved in the final events leading to Jesus' crucifixion; however, from early on the Gospels' accounts portray them as desiring to destroy Jesus.

Contrary to the substitutionary view, the Gospels portray Jesus's death as part of the salvation story because it (1) exposes the idolatry linked with these Powers, (2) reveals the inherently anti-God stance of the logic of retribution, and (3) profoundly underscores Jesus's stance in responding to the Powers as the kind of persevering love that coheres with God's character and will.

I will focus on these conflicts (over law, temple, and empire) in chapters six through eight. We will see that Jesus was not "innocent." He did violate the rules of the Powers-that-be. The logic of retribution led these Powers to take recourse against this "rebel"; Jesus's execution was "just" according to the regulations of the law, temple, and empire. As William Herzog writes, "In some sense, every charge against Jesus had some basis in reality. He was not crucified by accident, nor was his crucifixion the result of a case of mistaken identity."[2]

However, as the story makes clear, though not "officially" innocent, Jesus was good, godly, and faithful. Hence, Jesus's fate surfaces the injustice of the Powers' regulations. Jesus's fate also exposes the injustice of the logic of retribution. Jesus's death exposes retributive "justice" as unjust. It does not express God's will but expresses rebellion against God.

I will present Jesus's death as "salvific," but not as a God-willed outworking of the logic of retribution. Instead, Jesus's death links with salvation in that: (1) it exposes the fallacy of the logic of retribution, (2) it exposes the direct link between this murderous logic and the institutions

---

2. Herzog, *Jesus*, 240.

PART TWO: Jesus' Death and Salvation

that exploit it, (3) it shows that the spiral of violence that is set loose and ever-deepened by this logic may be broken only by non-retaliation and mercy in the way Jesus embodied them, and (4) it sets the stage for God's act that vindicates how Jesus exposed the Powers and embodied domination-free life when God raises Jesus from the dead.

SETTING THE STAGE: BIRTH NARRATIVES

Matthew and Luke's birth narratives foreshadow the coming conflicts. We see in King Herod's response to Jesus's birth the reception Jesus will receive from people in power. Herod tries to nip in the bud the career of what he feared would be a major threat. Herod's rationale might not have been that different from Pilate's thirty years later (note that Pilate and Antipas, Herod's son, became friends at the time of Jesus' arrest, Luke 23:12). They both feared possible threats so much that they willingly ordered horrendous acts of violence to stop those threats (see also Pilate "mixing the blood of Jewish insurgents with their sacrifices," Luke 13:1).

Herod sets out to have all young children killed "in and around Bethlehem" (Matt 2:16). Herod did not live long enough to learn that his mass murder failed to prevent this new "king" from arising (Matt 2:19). His violence shows how political authoritarianism responds to perceived threats—and how the powerful perceived Jesus's advent as a threat from the start. So, Matthew right away prepares the reader for Jesus's ultimate fate in Jerusalem.[3]

Luke does not tell of Herod. In his story, the intimations of conflict to come actually arise from those on Jesus's side. Mary prophesies prior to Jesus's birth that with her child "the Mighty One . . . has scattered the proud in the thoughts of their hearts. He has brought down the powerful from their thrones. . . . He has . . . sent the rich away empty" (1:49–53). Surely we are to understand that "the proud," "the powerful," and "the rich" will not accept this outcome willingly—and in fact will be quite hostile toward Jesus's message.

INITIAL TENSIONS

In Jesus's temptations at the beginning of his ministry, he rejects the various options Satan lays before him, and sets the stage for ongoing conflicts. Reading the temptations carefully, we see a close link between the Powers

---

3. Carroll and Green, *Death*, 26.

of social structures ("the kingdoms of the world," Luke 4:5 and "the temple in Jerusalem," Luke 4:9) and the spiritual forces of evil. The conflicts Jesus faces have to do with both human structures and spiritual forces. The two often go together, as when Paul writes "none of the rulers of this age understood [that God's wisdom was revealed in Jesus]; for if they had, they would not have crucified the Lord of glory" (1 Cor 2:8).[4]

Luke points to coming conflicts when he concludes after the temptations: "When the devil had finished every test, he departed from [Jesus] until an opportune time" (4:13).

In Luke's account, Jesus begins his public ministry when he speaks in his home congregation (4:16–30). After asserting the presence of God's kingdom (good news to the poor, release to the captives, sight to the blind, and freedom for the oppressed), he hears affirmation. "All spoke well of him and were amazed at the gracious words that came from his mouth" (4:22). However, Jesus senses antipathy, and he asserts right away that he expects not to be accepted in his hometown. He then uses two provocative examples from the Bible of how God's blessing came to Gentiles in the time of past prophets Elijah and Elisha, in part due to the hard hearts of the Hebrews. His use of these stories changed the tenor of Jesus's encounter completely.

"When they heard this, all in the synagogue were filled with rage" (Luke 4:28). Their rage leads them to seek to throw Jesus off a cliff to his death. Jesus slips away, but we now know that his ministry may not have a happy ending. "This confrontation between a prophet and his people is programmatic for the story that ensues. Jesus will embody God's gracious favor for the poor and sick and marginalized—for outsiders. And in doing so, he will make enemies, setting in motion a spiral of conflict that will result in his death."[5]

Luke then tells of Jesus's mighty works, his establishing a community of disciples, and his authoritative teaching. "Pharisees and teachers of the law" came "from every village in Galilee and Judea and from Jerusalem" to observe what Jesus said and did (Luke 5:17). In the presence of these observers, Jesus ministered to a paralyzed man and proclaimed that this man's sins were forgiven due to his friends' strong faith. These acts offend those who investigate Jesus. "Who is this speaking blasphemies? Who can forgive sins but God alone?" (Luke 5:21). The gauntlet is thrown down—and Jesus picks it up. He proceeds, defiantly, to heal the man's paralysis.

---

4. Wink, *Naming*, 45.
5. Carroll and Green, *Death*, 63.

PART TWO: Jesus' Death and Salvation

Jesus spoke of the need for change, using the image of "new wineskins" for the "new wine" he embodied since the old were not adequate. He implicitly critiques the existing structures: Pharisaic cultural exclusivism and temple-centered religious institutionalism. Jesus did not deny that his message would elicit conflict. The old patterns that engendered the blindness and oppression he sought to remedy would not yield to his reforms willingly.

Conflicts Intensify

Luke tells a story highlighting Jesus's relationship with Pharisees (7:36–50). Jesus does seek to connect with them and accepts an invitation to share a meal with one of the Pharisees. The tone of this encounter is positive, not hostile. In the course of the meal, "a woman of the city, who was a sinner" enters and, deeply moved, begins to wash Jesus's feet. Jesus's host is offended, saying to himself, "If this man were a prophet, he would have known who and what kind of woman this is who is touching him—that she is a sinner" (7:39).

Of course, Jesus does know who this woman is. What confirms Jesus as a prophet is precisely his welcome of sinners such as this woman, as Torah had prescribed (see, e.g., Lev 19 with its special concern for vulnerable people). Jesus uses the opportunity to make a point about love and forgiveness. "Her sins, which were many, have been forgiven; hence she has shown great love. But the one to whom little is forgiven, loves little" (Luke 7:47).

This story ends amicably, but nonetheless provides further evidence of the split between Jesus's vision for the renewal of Israel (based on healing love toward vulnerable people in the community) and the Pharisees' (based on clear demarcations between pure and impure people with the intent to strengthen the community's adherence to the way of purity).

Mark's Gospel introduces the conflict in chapter two. Here, we see "a progression of hostility—from scribes 'questioning in their hearts' (Mark 2:6–7), to open queries of the disciples about Jesus' behavior (2:16), to open confrontation with Jesus about his disciples' behavior (2:18, 24), and finally to a collective attempt by the Pharisees to catch Jesus in a religious infraction (3:2). The malevolence reaches its crescendo finally in 3:6: 'Immediately the Pharisees went out and with the Herodians conspired against him, how they might destroy him.' "[6]

6. Ibid., 26.

The Death of Jesus

Luke adds a note bringing a new player to the slowly developing dynamic of hostility toward Jesus when he writes of Herod Antipas, the ruler of Galilee, hearing of Jesus (Luke 9:7–9). At this point, Herod is "perplexed." Later, Herod will join Pilate in Jerusalem to condemn Jesus to death (23:1–12). Herod, who had John the Baptist executed, represents political authoritarianism. Here, he seems to fear that Jesus, like John, will threaten his power. Herod "tried to see him" (9:9). When he does finally succeed in seeing Jesus (23:6–12), it is to play a role in Jesus's execution.

Luke links Jesus's success with his awareness of impending doom. After Peter confesses Jesus as "Messiah" (the king), Jesus accepts the title, but then links his kingship with his death. "The Son of Man must undergo great suffering, and be rejected by the elders, and be killed" (9:22). In light of this outcome, Jesus issues a challenge. "If any want to become my followers, let them deny themselves and take up their cross daily and follow me. For those who want to save their life will lose it, and those who lose their life for my sake will save it. What does it profit them if they gain the whole world, but lose or forfeit themselves?" (9:23–25).

Jesus makes clear an inevitable, unavoidable link between following his way and conflict with the Powers that were so hostile to him. He takes this for granted—not because he romanticizes suffering and sees it as intrinsically redemptive. Rather, the inevitability of conflict reflects the nature of the Powers. They will not relinquish their domination without a fight.

Luke signals Jesus's decisive change in focus: "when the days drew near for him to be taken up, he set his face to go to Jerusalem" (9:51). Quite a bit happens in Luke's story before Jesus arrives for his final week in Jerusalem (19:28). Conflicts with the Pharisees continue. But this turn toward Jerusalem reflects Jesus's choice to take the initiative and move from the outskirts of Israelite culture toward the center. Jerusalem, home of the temple and Roman occupational government, looms as the locus of Jesus's mission to break the hold of the Powers.

In Luke, Jesus often refers to the developing conflict and to the opposition he faces. He speaks of rejection to his followers: "Whoever listens to you listens to me, and whoever rejects you rejects me, and whoever rejects me rejects the one who sent me" (Luke 10:16).

Jesus strongly criticized the Pharisees:

> Now you Pharisees clean the outside of the cup and of the dish, but inside you are full of greed and wickedness. You fools! Did not the one who made the outside make the inside also? So give

for alms those things that are within; and see, everything will be clean for you. But woe to you Pharisees! For you tithe mint and rue and herbs of all kinds, and neglect justice and the love of God; it is these you ought to have practice, without neglecting the others. Woe to you Pharisees! For you love to have the seat of honor in the synagogues and to be greeted with respect in the marketplaces. Woe to you! For you are like unmarked graves, and people walk over them without realizing it. (Luke 11:39–44)

From these words, we see that Jesus did not reject the external details of law observance that the Pharisees strove to uphold. Those should not be neglected (Luke 11:42). However, the heart of the law has to do with "justice and the love of God" (11:42). Jesus affirms the prophets' message, the core content of Torah as seen in Leviticus 19 and the story of the exodus. The law means to cultivate love and justice—the details are secondary, though necessary.

For Jesus, the law, properly understood, seeks love and justice for the entire community. This emphasis focuses on those most likely to be treated unjustly. "Many of the people Jesus healed came into one of the banned categories. These healings, at the deepest level of understanding on the part of Jesus and his contemporaries, would be seen as part of his total ministry, specifically, part of that open welcome that went with the inauguration of the kingdom—and, consequently, part of his subversive work, that was likely to get him into trouble."[7]

When he focused on the vulnerable ones, Jesus exposed the problems of the Pharisees insofar as they focused more on the external details than on love and justice. When they criticize him for welcoming so-called "sinners" and those labeled "unclean," they reveal that their own priorities lay contrary to the actual priorities of God. In exposing this contradiction—both by actions and strong verbal statements—Jesus evoked hostility. "Jesus' table fellowship with toll collectors and sinners was a profanation of the Pharisees' version of the great tradition, and therefore, an offense to Moses. Jesus reclined with the impure and unclean, without apology or hesitation. He turned the meal into a different kind of community."[8]

Jesus recognized the intensity of this hostility, and he suggested that the conflict that emerged here was in continuity with the history of Israel. He joined "lawyers" (or, "scribes," scholars of the law who were responsible for sustaining the written Torah) with Pharisees in his critique:

7. Wright, *Jesus*, 192–93.
8. Herzog, *Jesus*, 153.

> Woe also to you lawyers! For you load people with burdens hard to bear, and you yourselves do not lift a finger to ease them. Woe to you! For you build the tombs of the prophets whom your ancestors killed. So you are witnesses and approve of the deeds of your ancestors; for they killed them, and you build their tombs. Therefore also the Wisdom of God said, 'I will send them prophets and apostles, some of whom they will kill and persecute,' so that this generation may be charged with the blood of Abel to the blood of Zechariah, who perished between the altar and the sanctuary. Yes, I tell you, it will be charged against this generation. Woe to you lawyers! For you have taken away the key of knowledge; you did not enter yourselves, and you hindered those who were entering. (Luke 11:45–52)

Jesus, in keeping with his concern for genuine healing and his belief in Torah as a key element of that healing, has deep concerns about how these experts of the law turn it into a burden that is "hard to bear" (11:45). They do nothing to help people with that burden. They turn what should be a source of healing into a source of hurt and brokenness.

Jesus links himself with the prophets of old who were killed by the lawyers' ancestors in Israel (Luke 11:49). In doing so, he again underscores the inevitable outcome of his ministry. The problems he surfaces—here, the way the law becomes a burden instead of a balm—are deeply entrenched. The only way to make clear how profound the problems are is to make clear without a doubt that the structures that purport to further Torah actually corrupt Torah. This effort requires surfacing for all to see how these structures will turn with deadly violence against the true messenger of Torah.

Jesus critiqued the Pharisees because they focused on tithing provisions and ignored the center of Torah: justice, mercy, and faith (Matt 23:23). "Jesus implies that his reading of the Torah is compatible with the prophets, not opposed to them. Any reading that truly fulfills the Torah must be congruent with the vision of the prophets."[9]

Understandably, given the vehemence of Jesus's critique, Luke reports that the lawyers and Pharisees "began to be very hostile toward him and to cross-examine him about many things, lying in wait for him, to catch him in something he might say" (Luke 11:53–54). The die is cast. Jesus faces deadly foes.

Even as the tensions mount between Jesus and religious leaders, his fame spreads and crowds gather by the thousands. Jesus's popularity,

---

9. Ibid., 168–69.

PART TWO: Jesus' Death and Salvation

ambivalent as he feels about it since he recognizes the mixed motives of many in the crowds, makes him ever more of a problem for the cultural, religious, and political Powers. In this volatile time, having a charismatic prophet such as Jesus in their midst, drawing crowds, challenging the authority of the religious structures and their leaders, increased the leaders' anxiety.

Jesus's message of love and liberation, when presented powerfully in such a context, inevitably heightened stress. The system is corrupt; the hold of the Powers must be broken. And conflict will grow, because the Powers will not surrender. He recognizes his own fate as the catalyst of such conflict—to be "baptized" into violent suffering.

Though the main focus in the story of Jesus's ministry is on conflicts with religious leaders, Luke for a second time alludes to problems political leaders also have with Jesus, serious enough to be life threatening. "Some Pharisees came and said to him, 'Get away from here, for Herod wants to kill you'" (Luke 13:31). Jesus dismissed Herod with a scornful insult, "Go and tell that fox for me" that I must die in Jerusalem, not Galilee (13:31–33).

Jesus links his own fate with murdered prophets (Luke 11:33–34). Like them, when he speaks confrontational words that call Israel back to the living Torah, he will be met with deadly violence. "The Pharisees, and perhaps Herod as well (Luke 13:31–33), wanted to destroy Jesus because he was invading dangerous territory and offering an alternative vision of its meaning. [For example,] the Pharisees saw the possessed as dangerous deviants requiring social ostracism or cure because they were a threat to the social order; Jesus saw the possessed as God's people in need of liberation from alien possession and redemption from evil control."[10]

Luke's story of Jesus's journey from the time he "turns toward Jerusalem" (9:51) to when he arrives (19:28) concludes with a dark parable (19:11–27). Those who invested what they had been given successfully received a reward and those who did not received punishment. The parable challenges Jesus's listeners to commit themselves to the true king, the one who stands in contrast to earthly kings characterized by injustice and oppression. Though the true king (as reflected in Jesus's life of healing and genuine justice) follows the law of love, to refuse to commit to this king will lead to negative consequences. Jesus does offer a genuine choice, and to say no to him leaves one to the fate of those who become like that in which they trust.

10. Ibid., 210.

Jesus's Final Days

The story moves toward its climax when Jesus arrives in Jerusalem to great acclaim. In Luke's version, people "spread their cloaks on the road" (19:36), an act with royal significance (see 2 Kgs 9:13). The other Gospels speak of "leafy branches" (Mark 11:8 and parallels)—an allusion to royal processions (1 Macc 13:51; 2 Macc 10:7). The last week of Jesus's life begins with this scene that identifies him as a kingly personage. The question that remains to be answered is how his kingship will find expression.

Jesus grieves the fate of Jerusalem. The city, whose name means "city of peace," fails to "recognize on this day the things that make for peace" (Luke 19:42). The city and its powerful people are in thrall to the Powers of religious institutionalism and political authoritarianism. The violence at the heart of that thralldom will be fully exposed in the events to come.

The identity of Jesus's opponents changes drastically once he arrives in Jerusalem. The Pharisees mostly depart from the picture, replaced by the chief priests and Sadducees. The law and its application are replaced by the temple as the center of controversy. Now, we no longer have only threats of violence toward Jesus; the threats are acted on.

Just as Jesus had challenged the Pharisees and their scribes head on when he healed in their presence on the Sabbath and forgave the sins of unclean people in their presence, here in Jerusalem Jesus also takes the challenge to the temple authorities. "It is well-nigh certain that the high-priesthood was the moving agent on the Jewish side in the final proceedings against Jesus; and if one has to explain what disturbed that group about Jesus, something that could be interpreted as presenting a danger to the Temple/sanctuary would be the most plausible factor."[11]

When he arrives in Jerusalem, Jesus heads straight to the temple. Mark's version focuses more on the conflict over the temple, so we will follow his account at this point. Mark tells of Jesus confronting people in the temple who sold cultic items and who changed worshipers' money to allow them to buy the cultic items. Jesus "overturned the tables of the money changers and the seats of those who sold doves; and he would not allow anyone to carry anything through the temple" (Mark 11:15–16). This symbolic act, one of several, emphasizes Jesus's challenge to the prevailing understanding of the temple as the heartbeat of Israel's relationship with God.

---

11. Brown, *Death*, 458.

He asserts that God intended the temple to be "a house of prayer for all the nations." He quotes Isaiah 56:7 and alludes to the original call of Abraham and Sarah to be a "light to the nations" (Gen 12:3). Instead, in echo of the charge Jeremiah had levied versus the first temple (Jer 7:1–11), Jesus charges that the temple had become "a den of robbers" (Mark 12:17).

Earlier, Jesus critiqued the problematic uses of the law by the Pharisees with hope for reform. With the temple, however, we get the clear sense that the corruption is fatal. Jesus sided with Torah over against the Pharisees' use. He does not side with the "true" use of Herod's temple. Unlike with the Law, Jesus seems to see the temple as a dead end, not a structure that can be restored to an original, life-enhancing purpose.

The temple scene opens and closes with Jesus's curse of the fig tree. He acts out a condemnation of the temple for being barren. "When Jesus came to Jerusalem, he symbolically and prophetically enacted judgment upon it—a judgment which, both before and after, he announced verbally as well as in action. The Temple, as the central symbol of the whole national life, was under divine threat, and, unless Israel repented, it would fall to the pagans."[12]

After many allusions to Jesus's opponents' hostility toward him and their noises about punishing him, at this point we move close to the time when they will actually carry out the threats. "When the chief priests and the scribes heard [of Jesus driving out the merchants], they kept looking for a way to kill him." At this point, they hesitate, "because the whole crowd was spellbound by his teaching" (Mark 11:18). But they ultimately do not find that problem insurmountable.

The next day, the temple leaders challenge Jesus. "By what authority are you doing these things? Who gave you this authority to do them?" (Mark 11:28). Jesus does not give a straight answer, and the leaders equivocate, still aware (and fearful) of the crowds.

Jesus exacerbates the confrontation and tells a provocative parable. He speaks of a vineyard (the temple) whose owner (God) leases it to tenants (the religious leaders). When the owner sent a servant (the prophets) to collect the rent (to hold the leaders accountable to Torah), the tenants beat the servant and sent him back empty-handed. Another servant is sent—and murdered. And again. Finally, the owner sends his own son (Jesus), who the tenants also murder. At this point, the owner himself comes to destroy the tenants and give the vineyard to others. "When [the leaders] realized that he had told this parable against them, they wanted

---

12. Wright, *Jesus*, 417.

The Death of Jesus

to arrest him, but they feared the crowd. So they left him and went away" (Mark 12:1-12).

The debates continue, with strong hostility in the air. Jesus takes one more shot at the temple. "One of the disciples said to him, 'Look, Teacher, what large stones and large buildings!' Then Jesus asked him, 'Do you see these great buildings? Not one stone will be left there upon another; all will be thrown down'" (Mark 13:1-2).

So, when he curses the fig tree, drives out the merchants, tells the parable of the vineyard, and predicts the actual physical destruction of the temple, Jesus sets himself firmly against the religious structures that dominated his culture. In doing so at a time of such volatility, with the highly controversial Roman occupation forces seeking to maintain their dominance over Judea, Jesus exposes the collaboration of religious institutionalism with political authoritarianism—and thereby makes clear that both stand in opposition to Israel's true God.

Jesus's enemies, still concerned about the crowds, wait until the cover of darkness to strike. "The chief priests and the scribes were looking for a way to arrest Jesus by stealth and kill him; for they said, 'Not during the festival or there may be a riot among the people'" (Mark 14:1-2). After Jesus shares a Passover meal with his disciples, he takes them to "a place called Gethsemane" for a time of prayer. It is late, and Jesus's friends fall asleep. He awakens them; at that moment "a crowd with swords and clubs, from the chief priests, the scribes, and the elders" arrive and after a brief clash arrest Jesus (Mark 14:32-50).

Since the temple leaders ordered Jesus's arrest, he was taken to them that same night. "All the chief priests, the elders, and the scribes were assembled" (Mark 14:53). These officials made up the temple's governing council, the Sanhedrin. At this point, they were ready to end Jesus's life. He seemed like too much of a threat to their top-down order and the uneasy stability they had attained in relation to the Roman occupation leaders.

As Mark tells the story, this impromptu trial made little progress because the various witnesses that came forward to testify against Jesus did not agree with one another; hence, they did not provide the required proof to convict Jesus of the capital offense of blasphemy. Jesus remained silent until finally the high priest challenged him directly: "Are you the Messiah, the Son of the Blessed One?" Jesus finally speaks: "I am," he admits, and then—once more—adds to the conflict here by quoting Psalm 110:1 and Daniel 7:13-14: "You will see the Son of Man seated at the right hand of the Power and coming with the clouds of heaven" (Mark 14:61-62).

PART TWO: Jesus' Death and Salvation

This settles the Sanhedrin's case, in their mind. "The high priest tore his clothes and said, 'Why do we still need witnesses? You have heard his blasphemy! What is your decision?' All of them condemned him as deserving death" (14:63–64). The precise nature of the blasphemy here remains unclear. However, we do know that if Jesus claimed to be Messiah (i.e., king), the Romans would be alarmed. They would be sure to react harshly to any hint of a new political leader among the Judeans who would be hostile to Roman occupation.

John's Gospel voices this fear of a Roman reaction most clearly. The chief priests, prior to arresting Jesus, met to discuss what kind of threat he posed. They said, "What are we to do? This man is performing many signs. If we let him go on like this, everyone will believe in him, and the Romans will come and destroy both our holy place and our nation." The chief priest, Caiaphas, then asserted "it is better for you to have one man die for the people than to have the whole nation destroyed.... From that day on they planned to put him to death" (John 11:45–53).

N. T. Wright summarizes the main bases for the conviction on the part of the religious leaders at the end of the "trial" that Jesus deserved his execution:

> He was sent to the Roman governor on a capital charge (1) because many (not least many Pharisees, but also, probably, the chief priests) saw him as "a false prophet, leading Israel astray"; (2) because, as one aspect of this, they saw his Temple-action as a blow against the central symbol not only of national life but also of Yahweh's presence with his people; (3) because, though he was clearly not leading a real or organized military revolt, he saw himself as in some sense Messiah, and could thus become a focus of serious revolutionary activity; (4) because, as the pragmatic focus of these three points, they saw him as a dangerous political nuisance, whose actions might well call down the wrath of Rome upon Temple and nation alike; (5) because, at a crucial moment in the hearing, he not only (as far as they were concerned) pleaded guilty to the above charges, but also did so in such a way as to place himself, blasphemously, alongside the God of Israel.
>
> The leaders of the Jewish people were thus able to present Jesus to Pilate as a seditious troublemaker; to their Jewish contemporaries as a false prophet and a blasphemer, leading Israel astray; and to themselves as a dangerous political nuisance. On all counts, he had to die.[13]

13. Ibid., 551–52.

The Death of Jesus

After Jesus's night trial before the Sanhedrin, his captors take him to Pontius Pilate, the Roman governor of Judea. According to John's version of the story, the Sanhedrin did not have the authority to execute Jesus (John 18:31), but needed to turn him over to Pilate for the final decision for condemnation and the actual execution.

Only Luke adds a brief encounter between Jesus and Herod Antipas, the ruler of Jesus' home region of Galilee. As Luke had noted earlier (9:9), Herod had wanted to see Jesus, "hoping to see him perform some sign" (23:8). Herod ends up disappointed. "He questioned him at some length, but Jesus gave him no answer" (23:9). So Herod sends Jesus back to Pilate. "That same day, Herod and Pilate became friends with each other; before this they had been enemies" (23:12). The Powers of political authoritarianism unite in putting an end to the life of this Nazarene prophet.

The various Gospels differ in how they present Jesus' time with Pilate. Only John gives detail to the obvious political agenda that this ruthless representative of the Roman Empire seems to have pursued.[14] John highlights the significance of Jesus's messianic claims—that is, that he could be perceived to claim to be a king, in opposition to the emperor and in opposition to the Roman occupation of Judea. "The charge against Jesus in the [Sanhedrin] trial is that he claimed to be King of the Jews. Under Roman law that might seem to be sedition: those who are authors of sedition or move the people to upheaval are liable to crucifixion."[15]

Pilate mostly, though, treats Jesus as a tool to manipulate the Jewish leaders and to transfer the crowd's support for Jesus into support for Rome. "Pilate's intention is not to placate 'the Jews' but to humiliate them."[16] He talks with Jesus, asks him if he is indeed the king of the Jews. Jesus responds by trying to explain that his "kingship," his messiahship, is not "from this world." By this, Jesus means that he is not a king like Caesar seeking to gain power through brute force. "If my kingdom were from this world [that is, if my kingdom were of the worldly realm of power politics like Caesar's], my followers would be fighting to keep me from being handed over to the [Jewish leaders, and, ultimately, the Romans]" (John 18:33–36).

When Pilate persists, "So you are a king?" (John 18:37), Jesus does not deny his identity but again tries to help Pilate see that he is concerned not about power politics, but about truth—the truth of God's kingdom that

---

14. Rensberger, *Johannine*, 87.
15. Brown, *Death*, 717.
16. Rensberger, *Johannine*, 94.

PART TWO: Jesus' Death and Salvation

rejects fighting for power with violence. Pilate has no interest, though. He acts bored with the conversation and asks, rhetorically, "What is truth?" Without waiting for an answer (that is, without listening to Jesus' voice [18:37]), he walks away to face the religious leaders.

What follows is a masterful piece of manipulation by Pilate. He tells the religious leaders he sees no case against Jesus. Noting the custom of the Romans to release a political prisoner on Passover (John 18:39), he gives the Sanhedrin the choice, Jesus or Barabbas, a violent revolutionary. The leaders are so wrought up in their anger towards Jesus that they call for Barabbas to be released, though he presented way more of a violent threat to society than Jesus.

Pilate next tortures and ridicules Jesus, then places a crown of thorns on his head to reflect his "ridiculous" claim to be king. This agitates the religious leaders all the more. "Crucify him!" the chief priests cry (John 19:6). Pilate makes as if to release Jesus. This elicits bitter protests from the leaders: "If you release this man, you are no friend of the emperor. Everyone who claims to be a king sets himself against the emperor" (John 19:12).

Pilate is closer to getting what he wants. The religious leaders, speaking as people on the top of the hierarchy of the Jewish people, move ever closer to a public affirmation of the current arrangement. They argue for the inviolability of the emperor's status. They do not say Jesus should die because his claims to be God's emissary violate Jewish law; they say Jesus should die because his claims threaten the emperor's status.

Pilate takes one last step. "Here is your king!" he cries as he brought Jesus before the crowd. "Crucify him!" the crowd responds. "Shall I crucify your king?" Pilate asks. Now comes the denouement: "The chief priests answered, 'We have no king but the emperor'" (19:15). We have no king but the emperor; this directly contrasts with the Passover hymn that declares to God, "We have no king but you."

Pilate gets what he wanted, a public confession from the chief priests of the emperor's sovereignty.[17] Jesus served Pilate's purpose. Then, immediately Pilate ends his charade of trying to release Jesus and "hands him over to be crucified" (John 19:16).

The style of execution the Romans used for political criminals, crucifixion, gained notoriety both for the profound physical suffering it caused those executed, and for its public nature. Those Rome executed served as

---

17. Ibid., 95.

examples, communicating to all who watched them the folly and costliness of resisting Roman dominance.[18]

Regardless of Jesus's own statement to Pilate that his kingdom differed from the worldly empires, Pilate had him executed as a political criminal, one convicted of an offense against the state. "Crucifixion has a political and military purpose: to silence and deter rebels. Jesus was one of those thousands of Jews executed publicly on crosses, because what they represented had to be suppressed in order to safeguard law and order in the Roman state."[19]

As a part of this execution, Jesus suffered a long stream of humiliations, from being mocked and tortured, to be being hung, naked, to die in broad daylight. "Crucifixion was dreaded first and foremost because of its shameful character. It was designed to be an instrument of contempt and public ridicule. The victim died naked, in blood sweat, helpless to control body excretions. The cross epitomizes human concepts of defilement and exclusion."[20]

According to Mark, Jesus spent six hours on the cross from the time the nails were driven in until his death (15:25–34). As extraordinarily brutal as that experience would have been, Jesus actually suffered a shorter time on the cross than many others. Sometimes, crucifixions took days before death released the victim. The message of Jesus's crucifixion, though, would have been one of unsurpassing disgrace—as seen by Jews and Romans alike.[21]

Mark tells of several women remaining nearby as Jesus died. They watched Joseph of Arimathea, a dissenting member of the Sanhedrin who opposed Jesus's condemnation (Luke 23:50–51) and had gained Pilate's permission, retrieve Jesus's body. "Then Joseph bought a linen cloth, and taking down the body, wrapped it in the linen cloth, and laid it in a tomb that had been hewn out of rock. He then rolled a stone against the door of the tomb. Mary Magalene and Mary the mother of Joses saw where the body was laid" (Mark 15:46–47).

I will pick up the story after this point in chapter nine below. Before that, though, I will look more closely at the meaning of the story of Jesus's death. How is the story of Jesus's death related to the Bible's portrayal of

---

18. Green and Baker, *Recovering*, 26; Wright, *Jesus*, 543; Carroll and Green, *Death*, 169–70.

19. Douglass, *Nonviolent*, 7.

20. Green and Baker, *Recovering*, 163.

21. Goergen, *Death*, 34.

PART TWO: Jesus' Death and Salvation

salvation? I believe that at the heart of the saving relevance of the story we find an exposure of the Powers of cultural exclusivism, religious institutionalism, and political authoritarianism as responsible for Jesus's death. They too easily become idols that claim trust that is due God alone. As such, they become the very forces from which God's saving work means to liberate human beings.

Jesus's resurrection will prove to be much more than an appendix to the basic salvation story originating in the call of Abraham and Sarah. The resurrection adds a profound message of vindication to the entire story. Jesus's ministry sought not to present some discontinuous message of salvation that supercedes the Old Testament salvation story. From start to finish, Jesus's message totally reinforced the original story. His resurrection vindicates this message.

Jesus died, not to fulfill the logic of retribution's need for some heretofore missing ultimate sacrifice that will finally satisfy the demands of God's holiness. Rather, Jesus died to illumine the ages-old truth—God's mercy seeks healing for all who trust in it. This mercy perseveres even in the face of the powerful violence of its enemies.

SIX

Jesus's Death and the Powers
Cultural Exclusivism (Law)

WHY DID JESUS GET killed? What meaning does his death have in relation to salvation? These two questions are closely related; neither may be answered without reference to the other. In the following three chapters, I will focus on the first question (why did Jesus get killed?) in order ultimately to answer the second question (what meaning does Jesus's death have in relation to salvation?).

In brief, I will argue that Jesus died because he challenged the main cultural and political Powers of his day—the law, the temple, and the empire. He challenged these Powers when he exposed them as oppressive and idolatrous in their contemporary forms. This exposure took two forms: (1) he overtly critiqued the Powers and (2) he established alternative social practices that bypassed the Powers' domination. These Powers reacted to Jesus's challenge by deadly retribution. They executed him in the most shameful and painful way possible.

As Walter Wink writes: "The death of Jesus was not 'necessary' because God needed Jesus killed in order to save the world. Rather, Jesus was killed because the Powers are in rebellion against God and are determined to silence anyone who slips through their barbed-wire perimeter with a message from the sovereign of the universe."[1]

Jesus's death had meaning for salvation, then, primarily (1) as a public demonstration of the Powers' true character in their fallen state; (2) as a witness to Jesus's own freedom from the Powers' domination; and,

---

1. Wink, *Human*, 102.

PART TWO: Jesus' Death and Salvation

(3) when God vindicated Jesus on Easter, as a testimony to God's endorsement of Jesus's way as true faithfulness.

We may find meaning in Jesus's death in relation to the continuity of his life and teaching with the Old Testament salvation story. Jesus lived and taught a vision of Torah in line with Moses and the prophets. A merciful God gave the commands for the sake of human well-being. As with the prophets of old, Jesus's vision brought him into conflict with those who sought to dominate others when they twisted Torah and made human beings subservient to rules and regulations.

Jesus reiterated the Old Testament message that God loves human beings, that salvation follows from simply trusting in that love, and that the social life that follows from centering life on God's love takes the form of mutual regard and service, not domination and exploitation. That such a message led to conflict with the cultural, religious, and political leaders delegitimizes those leaders and their structures. Such a public delegitimizing frees people with eyes to see from the bondage born of inappropriate trust in the dominators. Such liberation makes up a major part of the salvation Jesus brought, made startlingly clear when he faced the death-dealing retribution of the Powers.

The three conflicts I will examine differed in significant ways from each other. In the first, the conflict related to the law, the Gospels tell us that Jesus debated with the leaders (the Pharisees) over the best appropriation of the law. Jesus affirmed the law, but he disagreed with the Pharisees over how best to understand and apply its teachings. This disagreement became intense; we are told that some Pharisees sought to destroy Jesus. We should note, though, that in the story of Jesus's actual arrest and crucifixion, the Pharisees play no role. At that point the combined efforts of the religious and political Powers centered in Jerusalem exacted the deadly price of Jesus's resistance to their domination.

The Gospels portray Jesus as having a respect for the temple as it should function, but unlike with the law he does not convey the message of affirming the "true temple." The temple ultimately seems to play no intrinsic role in Jesus's portrayal of the salvation story. Jesus apparently recognized that the temple had not been part of Moses's original mediation of God's will for God's people. He also recognized the role the temple played in exploiting Hebrew people and in hiding God's intent for the Hebrews to be a light to the nations.

The third conflict, with the empire, seems somewhat indirect in the Gospels. Jesus does not overtly challenge Rome's rule in Palestine.

However, on the one hand, the Roman government, embodied in Pontius Pilate, obviously saw Jesus as enough of a threat to crucify him. On the other hand, if we take seriously Jesus's message of God's kingdom, we will recognize that he articulated a vision for social life that overturned the values of empire ("the rulers of the Gentiles lord it over their subjects; it shall not be so among you," Mark 10:42–43).

In all three cases, though, we see that the conflict centered on Jesus offering an alternative vision—for how Torah might be applied, for how communal worship might be understood, and for how social life might be ordered. His message of salvation included both a critique and delegitimization of the structures that dominated life and an articulation of a vision for how the Powers might be transformed (not simply rejected).

In looking more closely, first at the conflict concerning the law, we must begin by looking back at the role Torah plays in the Old Testament salvation story and how its role in the life of the Hebrew community became complicated—and, hence, how Jesus's message led to intense quarrels.

Torah and God's Mercy

In my discussion above of the Old Testament salvation story and of Jesus's own teaching concerning salvation, I portrayed Torah as an expression of God's mercy. The Old Testament story recounts how God brought healing to the ancient Hebrews by acting graciously to liberate them from slavery in Egypt.

The next step in the outworking of this mercy was for God to reveal to the Hebrews an outline for their communal life that would solidify the gift of liberation they had been given. This outline for communal life, the law (Torah) came to the Hebrews as a gift. They sought to live according to its dictates as a grateful response to God's freely given favor, not as a means to gain that favor. "Obedience to the commands of God is not submission to the divine fiat but response to the divine grace. The community structured by the effort to discern God's covenantal will is to be in harmony with the qualities revealed in God's graceful activity to bring the community into being."[2]

However, the story also emphasizes that lack of gratitude signifies an inability appropriately to appreciate God's mercy—with hurtful consequences for the community. As we saw in the eighth-century prophets

2. Birch, *Let Justice*, 126.

PART TWO: Jesus' Death and Salvation

(Amos, Hosea, and Micah), the Hebrews' inability to appreciate God's mercy—with its implication that mercy for us means mercy for everyone—led to a transformation in the society. Injustice (the failure to recognize that the one true sign of the Hebrews' appreciation of God's mercy is their treatment of vulnerable people in their midst) and idolatry (trusting in sources other than God's mercy for their identity and security) had become widespread. As a consequence, chaos threatened to return to the community.

The prophets, reinforcing the original message of the meaning of Torah, saw the answer for the Hebrews' problems in the "conservative" direction of a return to Torah. Such a return involved a renewed appreciation of this merciful God alone as worthy of their trust. It also involved shaping their common life according to God's directives for how liberated people are to live in order to sustain their liberation and genuinely leave Egypt behind.

The prophets' words did not successfully effect a social transformation. As portrayed by prophets of the exile, the northern kingdom of Israel first, then the southern kingdom of Judah, fell to outside forces because both rotted internally due to continued tolerance for injustice and idolatry. The terrible fate of the Hebrews' two nation states vindicated the prophets' words.

The survival of these prophecies assured that within the Hebrew peoplehood, the prophets' ideals remained available. Generations later, Jesus of Nazareth drank deeply from the wells of ancient Hebrew prophecy and Torah. He reiterated the same basic message: God loves the world; trust in that love; shape your lives by it. According to the story, Jesus understood himself in continuity with the Old Testament message of salvation.

Matthew's Gospel gives this account of how Jesus answered a question concerning what he understood to be the greatest commandment. "You shall love the Lord your God with all your heart, and with all your soul, and with all your mind. This is the greatest and first commandment. And a second is like it: You shall love your neighbor as yourself. On these two commandments hang all the law and the prophets" (Matt 22:37–40; also parallels).

Matthew also reports how Jesus reiterated the main message of Torah in his Sermon on the Mount and characterized his relationship with the law as follows: "Do not think I have come to abolish the law or the prophets; I have come not to abolish but to fulfill" (Matthew 5:17).

We have seen as well that both Luke and Matthew make it clear in their two accounts of Jesus's birth how observant Jesus's family was, as well

Jesus's Death and the Powers

as his relatives, the family of John the Baptist. These birth stories set the stage for the emphasis throughout all four Gospels on Jesus's continuity with the Old Testament, Jesus as the fulfillment of Israel's hopes. And yet, the first intimations of profound conflict in Jesus's ministry come from those who considered themselves as the guardians of Torah, the Pharisees.

Torah and Cultural Exclusivism

The roots of Jesus's conflict with the Pharisees go back to post-exilic Israel. The story tells how not long after Judah's King Josiah was killed, the Babylonian Empire conquered Judah and destroyed the temple and the king's palace. Babylon took the Judean ruling class into exile. Eventually, in a battle of empires, the Persian Empire defeated Babylon and allowed Jewish exiles to return to their homeland. The earlier prophetic warnings of likely disaster should Israel and Judah not more faithfully order their lives according to Torah remained in the people's memories. Many committed themselves to avoid repeating the past transgressions, to work harder to shape Jewish life in Israel according to the dictates of the law.

The post-exilic existence of the Jewish people was always uneasy, a struggle to sustain their identity without being a nation-state. The community bounced from the domination of one empire to another—Babylon to Persia down to Rome in Jesus's day. Out of this struggle to survive as a people, the Israelites developed strategies to maintain their identity. At the core of these efforts we find the establishment of "boundary markers" that provided for ways to make it clear who was a part of the community and who was not. Key markers included the practice of male circumcision, following kosher eating habits, observing the Sabbath, and prohibiting marriages between people within the community and those outside the community.

Such strategies should not be seen as inherently regressive, but rather as creative means to sustain peoplehood in a hostile environment.[3] These external and enforceable practices served as ways for the Hebrew people to keep alive their community's traditions and understandings of themselves as Yahweh's people. Surely, the emergence of a strong commitment to revitalize the observance of Torah did much to sustain Jewish identity as a peoplehood without a nation-state.

During this period of the late sixth and fifth centuries BCE, the writings that eventually joined together to make the Hebrew scriptures were

---

3. Ibid., 308–9.

PART TWO: Jesus' Death and Salvation

gathered, edited, and organized. Concerns for making Torah central for the identity of the people greatly shaped how the Bible was formed.

From the point of view of the vision of Abraham's children blessing the nations by showing the world God's liberating mercy, the dynamics around the quest for preservation of the community created tensions. The identity markers could become absolutized. The order of the Bible's salvation story—first liberating mercy that indicates God's favor, then the response of obeying the law or offering sacrifice—may be forgotten. Then we have the problematic view that to obey the law or to offer sacrifice became the means to obtain God's mercy.

The same type of problem attends to the establishing of boundary markers. In the Hebrews' social context—precarious, dominated by foreign empires (or, for those diasporic Jews who did not return to Palestine, seeking to sustain their community as a minority culture)—the establishment of clear distinguishing practices helped maintain their identity. However, the purpose for which they maintained the identity remained potentially elusive.

In the prophets' view, when boundary markers reminded the people of God's already-given mercy and their calling to bless the nations, they would be creative and life-sustaining. Yet, the boundary markers could convey the wrong message. They could be absolutized, seen to provide a sense that our community's survival in and of itself matters most. In such circumstances, any threat to its survival (equated with any threat to the boundary markers) must be stopped.

The Bible, though formed to help the community survive in the colonial context and though its editors and shapers surely affirmed strong boundary markers, nonetheless allows for warning voices that keep the prophetic impulse alive in Israel.

The books of Ezra and Nehemiah portray sympathetically the necessary and creative efforts to sustain peoplehood in the context of colonialism. They provide the rationale for the boundary markers. However, along with Ezra and Nehemiah, we also find the little book of Jonah. The tensions between Ezra and Nehemiah versus Jonah prefigure the tensions we see in the Gospels between Jesus, representing the prophetic impulse of the book of Jonah, and the Pharisees, representing the great priest Ezra's concern for community sustenance through the maintenance of boundary markers such as circumcision, kosher eating, and sabbath observance. Though we cannot date Jonah precisely, many commentators place it roughly at the time of Ezra.[4] If so, the book likely intended to challenge an uncritical

---

4. Fretheim, *Message*, 34–37.

Jesus's Death and the Powers

tendency to absolutize the boundary markers and institutionalize religion among the Hebrews.

The character Jonah echoes the mindset of Hebrews who think only of their internal life when he rejects the call to share the word of God with outsiders. And these were not just any outsiders. The Ninevites lived in the capital city of Assyria, the great empire that plagued Israel and Judah. As such, they represent people from all the empires that sought to crush Israelite traditions and distinctiveness. After he fled the call to go to Nineveh, Jonah discovered first through trauma then through miraculous rescue that God is way bigger than the boundaries of Israel. After being saved from drowning, Jonah does go to Nineveh and successfully witnesses to them. God responds to the Ninevites with mercy because, as Jonah fears, God is "a gracious and compassionate God" (4:2).

This story reiterates the "light-to-the-nations" calling and implies that efforts to sustain the community still need to keep that calling in mind. The book concludes with an open question: "Should I not be concerned about that great city?" We are not given Jonah's answer, implying that this question needs continual reflection among the Hebrews.

The Traditions of the Pharisees

Jonah provides a witness to the impulse that Jesus sought to embody in first-century Jewish Palestine. When Jesus did so, he almost immediately came into conflict with a group of Ezra's spiritual descendants known as the Pharisees. Though Jesus understood himself as living fully in the tradition of Moses, he did not share the Pharisaic understanding of that tradition. Most centrally, Jesus did not affirm the Pharisees' use of the oral law. Jesus shared an affirmation of the written law, Torah—the five books of Moses—as God's directives for life. The Pharisees, though, gave much more authority to traditional interpretations that sought to apply Torah more widely. Jesus, like the Pharisees, was a partisan in a debate among Jews—how best to carry on the traditions of Israel.

After the Babylonian exile, when the restored Palestinian Jewish community sought more faithfulness to Torah, teachers produced verse-by-verse commentary of Torah known, as Midrash. Midrash applied specific laws more directly. The extensive commentary was passed on by word of mouth over the generations, hence the term "oral law."[5]

---

5. Evans, "Midrash," 544–48.

PART TWO: Jesus' Death and Salvation

A second type of oral law began to emerge about two hundred years before Jesus. If the Midrash was a commentary on Torah, interpreting and applying the actual writings of the Bible, this second type of tradition, the Mishnah, concerned itself with applying Torah to circumstances not spoken of in the biblical writings. The written version of the Mishnah, called the Talmud, was not produced until the 4th century CE.[6]

The Mishnah also came to be called the oral law, or, as in Mark 7:5, the "tradition of the elders." It gave community people guidance on how to live Torah, recognizing that the words of Torah did not always speak directly to issues of daily living. When the oral law began to develop, it was understood to be secondary to written Torah. Over time the authority of the oral law grew. The Pharisees probably emerged around the same time as the beginnings of the Mishnah, and may have understood their role to be the main guardians and appliers of these teachings. "Theologically, the Pharisees shared common Jewish orthodoxy (they believed in one God, the election of Israel, the divine origin of the law, and repentance and forgiveness). They developed a substantial body of non-biblical 'traditions' [oral law] about how to observe the law."[7]

The oral law developed into an extensive and detailed system of practical law, much more extensive than Torah itself.[8] The Mishnah guided religious practice among Palestinian Jews, attempting to speak to all kinds of religious issues that might arise. These are a tiny sampling of the kinds of questions the Mishnah spoke to: "Can laborers on top of a tree or wall offer a prayer? Can one open up quarries or wells during a sabbatical year? If one is naked and makes a dough offering from barley in one's house, does that make the offering unclean? Is tying a knot considered work that violates the Sabbath? Can a man divorce his wife for burning a meal? What is the proper death penalty for someone who blasphemes—burning, stoning, beheading, or strangling? Is a man ceremonially unclean if he touches a mouse? If an unclean bird sits on the eggs of a clean bird do the eggs remain ceremonially clean?"[9]

As the ones overseeing the application of the oral law, the Pharisees echoed the motivation from hundreds of years before when Ezra oversaw the implementation of the boundary marker-oriented approach to strengthening Israel's identity. Ezra sought to sustain the people of Yahweh

---

6. Brooks, "Mishnah," 871–73.
7. Sanders, *Historical*, 44.
8. Avery-Peck, "Oral," 34–37.
9. Kraybill, *Upside-Down*, 153.

as a distinct community in the face of great pressures to assimilate and lose their identity. The Pharisees reflected that same impulse.[10] They hoped to shape the entirety of the Israelite people. They did not seek simply to be one party among many. They led a quest for holiness (as they understood it) as public policy and played a central role in shaping the Jewish peoplehood in the generations after the exile.[11]

The Pharisees sought to give clear direction to observant Jews concerning how to apply Torah to concrete living. They presented it as living and relevant, a life-enhancing source of clarity for living as a distinct community that would honor God. They called for a holy nation in the face of great pressure from the outside world to conform uncritically to the all-powerful Roman Empire. "The Pharisees sought to extend or at least live out the holiness required in the Temple more widely in the holy land."[12]

The Pharisees carried forward a centuries-long concern to avoid the crises that had shaken Israel through an emphasis on Sabbath observance, proper tithing, prohibition of marriage with non-Jews. "Theologically, the calamity of 586 BCE was seen as God's judgment upon Israel because of its corruption by the practices of the nations"[13]—hence, the ongoing need to remain separate from surrounding cultures. In the Gospels, Pharisees concerned themselves with three central boundary markers from the time of Ezra: circumcision, kosher eating, and Sabbath observance.[14] "Precisely those regulations of the Torah that marked the distinctiveness of the Jewish people . . . were the ones to be developed in greater detail as defenses against the temptations to assimilation in the sea of Hellenism."[15]

The law of Moses clearly forbade working on the Sabbath. Descendants of the Hebrews liberated from Egypt must remember that they were no longer slaves; they could rest one day a week. The detail the Mishnah went into considering Sabbath observance reflects how seriously the command to honor it was taken. In its written form, the Mishnah devotes 240 paragraphs to Sabbath behavior, outlining in detailed specificity what could and could not be done.

In practice, such a detailed focus seemed to change people's emphases concerning the Sabbath from an affirmation and celebration of God's

---

10. Dunn, *Jesus Remembered*, 269–70.
11. Borg, *Conflict*, 74.
12. Dunn, *Jesus Remembered*, 288. Cf. also Herzog, *Jesus*, 148.
13. Borg, *Conflict*, 67.
14. Dunn, *Jesus, Mark*, 193.
15. Van Buren, *Theology*, 191.

PART TWO: Jesus' Death and Salvation

mercy and the value God has placed on human beings (such that slavery is rejected). When the central concern became to sustain boundary markers more than to celebrate God's mercy, the tone of Sabbath legislation changed.

For one thing, legalism easily reared its head. Ingenious devices evolved that allowed people to finesse (or get around altogether) restrictive legislation. Donald Kraybill gives an example. The law dictated that people were not allowed to walk more than 3,000 feet on the Sabbath. However, to circumvent this, they could "establish residence" at the end of their Sabbath day's walk, a day in advance. They established residence by carrying two meals to a place 3,000 feet from their home. One meal they ate there and another they buried—thereby "establishing residence." On the Sabbath day, people could travel the 3,000 feet from their permanent home to their "newly established residence" and then go an additional 3,000 feet. This legal detour doubled the length of the Sabbath-day journeys.[16]

Another even more serious problem for Jesus resulted because the Sabbath had been established as a central boundary marker. Anyone guilty of violating the Sabbath (and of hence violating a central boundary marker) threatened the entire community. The Sabbath had become crucial for a sense of community identity. Those who adhered to the oral law's Sabbath regulations thereby validated their identity as community members; those who did not would be excluded. And, as enforcers of the oral law, the Pharisees took on the role of keeper of valid membership in the community. Anyone who threatened their practice of boundary maintenance threatened the Pharisees' status head on.

The concern for kosher eating practices also stemmed from a concern about maintaining purity—they again reflected the post-exilic desire to avoid a repeat of the judgment that had befallen "impure" Judah and Israel. In this purity-conscious context, table-fellowship carried much weight. To invite a person to share a meal showed great respect for that person; conversely, one would never share a meal with those outside one's community's boundaries. Those considered dirty and polluted must be avoided. To eat with another indicated acceptance.

Should a pure person share a meal with an impure person, the latter's pollution was understood to be contagious. Thus, table fellowship with unclean people violated purity regulations. So, too, did failure to engage in ritual cleansing prior to eating. This washing purified one from any "dirt" inadvertently obtained in one's daily life.

16. Kraybill, *Upside-Down*, 157.

In order to help people differentiate between clean and unclean, the oral law provided detailed specifics. "Camels, badgers, swine, vultures, eagles, and winged insects, to name a few, were all considered unclean. Cemeteries were taboo. Contact with a contaminated person or animal polluted a clean object. The Mishnah devoted 185 pages to laws of defilement and purity. Ceremonial washing before each meal marked conscientious Pharisees." They exerted great effort to maintain ritual purity, hoping to contribute thereby to Israel's faithfulness.[17]

Of the various means Israelites used to distinguish themselves from the surrounding world, circumcision went back the farthest—even to the story of Abraham (Gen 17). The Abraham story portrays circumcision as a sign of the covenant. It signified one's close connection with Yahweh—both the promises and expectations. By the time of exile in the 6th century BCE, with its inevitable mixing of Hebrews with Gentiles, circumcision served as the definitive sign of Jewishness.

During the exile, Jews sought mightily to retain their distinctiveness in relation to the surrounding world. Doing so required explicit self-consciousness. The sustenance of their Jewish identity depended, among other things, upon the practice of circumcision. Israel clarified its own identity in relation to uncircumcised others.

The practice of circumcision stood as a central externally apparent boundary marker for the Hebrews throughout the biblical period. However, already for the prophets circumcision had become an ambiguous symbol. Jeremiah 9:25–26, for example, speaks of the standard distinction between the circumcised (Israel) and the uncircumcised. Jeremiah, however, makes this distinction in order to criticize Israel, said to be "circumcised only in the foreskin" but "uncircumcised in heart."

Other passages reflect the same concern when they link circumcision with other parts of the body, such as the heart (Lev 26:41; Deut 10:16; 30:6; Jer 4:4), the ears (Jer 6:10), and the lips (Exod 6:12, 30). These texts use the notion of circumcision metaphorically to refer to organs (other than the penis) that are to function freshly in obedient responsiveness to the demands of Yahweh's covenant. The usage suggests a means of making the organ more sensitive and responsive, so that "circumcision" moves from literalness to theological commitment.[18]

Throughout the biblical tradition we see tensions concerning the use of these boundary markers. On the one hand, we see a strong impulse

---

17. Ibid., 158–59.
18. Brueggemann, *Reverberations*, 33.

for community preservation and to find security via close adherence to regulations that reflect God's will. On the other hand, we see prophetic concern for the problem of externalization of religion that leads to a loss of emphasis on core prophetic themes such as liberation, compassion, and living justice.

These tensions clearly shaped the Pharisees' reaction to Jesus. "The conflict between Jesus and the Pharisees is to a considerable extent about the social vision that flows from taking the traditions of Israel seriously. For the Pharisees, the core value of their social vision was holiness/ purity; the core value of Jesus' social vision was compassion."[19]

JESUS AND THE PHARISEES

As the Gospel of Matthew tells of the early period after Jesus begins his ministry, its allusions to religious leaders are innocuous, even positive. Directly after returning "from the mountain" where he gave his great Sermon, Jesus heals a leper and instructs him to "go show yourself to the priest, and offer the gift that Moses commanded, as a testimony to them," an allusion to Leviticus 14 and the procedure outlined there for the ritual healing of leprosy (Matt 8:1–4). A little later, a scribe approaches Jesus wanting to follow him (Matt 8:19).[20] At this point in the story, we see no hint of conflict.

However, the storm clouds soon begin to gather. Jesus journeys to Gentile territory and heals two demoniacs (Matt 8:28–34). When he returns home, he immediately tells a paralyzed man that his sins are forgiven. "Then some of the scribes said to themselves, 'This man is blaspheming'" (9:3). Jesus catches wind of the criticism, and immediately intensifies the tension when he heals the man and asserts directly that he has the power both to forgive sins and heal paralytics (9:6).

Matthew first mentions the Pharisees by name in the next episode when Jesus calls a tax collector to follow him and then joins with "many tax collectors and sinners" to sit at dinner. "When the Pharisees saw this, they said to his disciples, 'Why does your teacher eat with tax collectors and sinners?'" (Matt 9:10–11).

---

19. Borg, *Conflict*, 7–8.

20. The Gospels are somewhat ambiguous in their use of "scribe." They are most generally portrayed as "bureaucrats and experts on Jewish life," affiliated both with the temple and the Pharisees. Matthew links them more closely with the Pharisees than Luke or Mark (Salderini, "Scribes," 1015).

From now on, tensions escalate. A paradigmatic account of the growing conflict and a sense of what is at stake may be found at Matthew 12:1–14 (and parallels: Mark 2:23–28, 3:1–6; and Luke 6:1–11). Because the Pharisees went out among the people and encouraged adherence to the dictates of the oral Torah, Jesus encountered them often. "The similarity between Jesus and the Pharisees—sharing the same tradition, struggling with the same questions, competing for the allegiance of the same people—accounts for the depth of the conflict between them."[21]

To argue that Jesus was close to the Pharisees leads to a recognition that this closeness would actually heighten the possibilities of conflict. For Jesus to enter the scene as one who rigorously observed Torah and gained a public following but did not join the Pharisees meant he would be seen as a direct rival. "A Jesus who was as loyal to the covenant but who had different ideas of what covenant loyalty involved would almost certainly pose a threat to Pharisaic self-understanding and identity."[22]

The Matthew 12 passage contains two stories that illustrate Jesus's contrast with the Pharisees. For Jesus, here, immediate human well-being takes precedence over strict adherence to the letter of the law concerning Sabbath regulations. This choice of priorities reflects Jesus's understanding of salvation as a matter of God's free mercy rather than human beings finding a way to cohere with God's "holiness."

The first story in Matthew 12 tells of Jesus's allowing his disciples to gather grain and eat on a Sabbath day because they were so hungry. The Pharisees who learned of this confronted Jesus. "Look, your disciples are doing what is not lawful to do on the Sabbath" (12:2).

Jesus responds with a couple of biblical examples of how the Sabbath laws are not absolute. "Have you not read what David did when he and his companions were hungry? He entered the house of God and ate the bread of the Presence, which was not lawful for his or his companions to eat, but only for the priests" (Matt 12:3; for David's acts see 1 Sam 21:1–6; the legislation concerning the bread of the Presence may be found at Lev 24:5–9). So, even though the letter of the Law asserts that this bread was only for priests, a "higher law," that of giving food to hungry people, allowed for an exception.

The second example comes with the question, "have you not read in the law that on the Sabbath the priests in the Temple break the Sabbath and yet are guiltless?" (Matt 12:5). The Sabbath law makes exceptions for

21. Borg, *Conflict*, 153.
22. Dunn, *Jesus, Mark*, 73.

PART TWO: Jesus' Death and Salvation

priests (see Num 28:9-10), allowing them to do work that exceeds strict adherence to the letter of the Law in importance. Jesus's example implies that the temple must take priority over strict adherence to Sabbath legislation. Jesus then asserts, "something greater than the temple is here" (12:6). Hence, what is present (the kingdom of God as represented in Jesus's ministry) must certainly take priority over strict adherence to the Sabbath regulations.

What "is here" is characterized by the quote from Hosea 6:6 that Jesus uses to cement his point: "If you had known what this means, 'I desire mercy and not sacrifice,' you would not have condemned the guiltless" (Matt 12:7). So, what actually stands as greater than the temple (the place where "sacrifice" happens) is the central characteristic of God's kingdom: mercy. Jesus contrasts this mercy with the Pharisees' condemnatory attitude toward needy people getting something to eat. These are two different notions of religious priorities.

Mark's version tells of Jesus summarizing the issues in this way: "the Sabbath was made for humankind, not humankind for the Sabbath" (Mark 2:27). This saying makes it clear that the basic issue is not that the Pharisees believed in the law and Jesus did not. Rather, we have a contrast between two concepts of the purpose of the law. One emphasizes that the deeper meaning of the law (i.e., mercy) allows for flexibility in how the details are practiced, as long as we are serving human well-being. The other points more to strict consistency, assuming that each piece of the regulations carries equal weight and that to violate one is to violate the whole.

The second altercation in our Matthew 12 passage escalates the conflict. Jesus moves on to a synagogue, it still being the Sabbath. The Pharisees set Jesus up for criticism when they point to a man with a withered hand and ask, "Is it lawful to cure on the Sabbath?" (12:10).

Jesus answers their question with a parallel type of logic to what he used in the first encounter. Here, he starts with the example of a sheep that falls into a pit on the Sabbath. "Will you not lay hold of it and lift it out?" (Matt 12:11). He assumes anyone would say, "of course." Then he makes his point. "How much more valuable is a human being than a sheep!" (12:12). That is to say, of course it is lawful to heal on the Sabbath. As central as Sabbath observance is to living in harmony with God, one must realize that all the regulations are meant to foster human wholeness, not to be ends in themselves. To underscore his point, and to defy the apparent assumptions of the Pharisees that the letter of the law matters the most, Jesus concludes the encounter by healing the man's withered hand.

Jesus makes it clear here, with his assertion that "it is lawful to do good on the Sabbath," that his conflict with the Pharisees is about who best understands the purpose of the Law. Healing a person is within what the Sabbath law allows. Jesus does not reject the law but sets observance of it in the context of the wider meaning of the law. Mercy comes first. The issue is not law or no law; the issue is how the law is interpreted.

So, Jesus rejected the tendency to see Sabbath observance itself as the key basis for evaluating faithfulness. He goes deeper: "The Sabbath was made for human beings, not human beings for the Sabbath, and that at no time, however sacred, can it be wrong to do good or save life." To make the specific observation absolute creates a "fence round the Torah" that endangers "what the fence was intended to protect."[23]

We have here a deadly serious set of differences, made clear by the Pharisees' response. "The Pharisees went out and conspired against him, how to destroy him" (Matt 12:14). Refusing to be intimidated, though, Jesus, after he becomes aware of the Pharisees' plans, leaves the synagogue, is followed by many people, "and he cured all of them" (12:15). He reiterates what he understands to be appropriate for the Sabbath—to bring healing to those in need.

What is at stake in this conflict? Why would the Pharisees conspire to destroy Jesus because of these altercations? We may see at the heart of the Pharisees' response, according to these stories, the conviction that the integrity of their purity project might require the use of violence to be sustained. That is, they would follow the logic of retribution in responding to someone who violates their understanding of God's will for their society. "The Pharisees' core is purity, because they wish to replicate in their social life the holiness of God by maintaining the holiness to which God has called the people (Lev 19:2). Jesus's core value is forgiveness, because he views God as a God of mercy (Luke 6:36)."[24]

The Pharisees committed themselves to the survival of the covenant community. This survival required strict adherence to the Law as they interpreted it. Violations of the law, if left uncorrected, threatened the community's survival. For the Pharisees the covenant community was the central structure that demanded their loyalty. This loyalty required strict cultural exclusivism, with clear lines of demarcation between insiders and outsiders.

---

23. Dunn, *Jesus Remembered*, 569.
24. Herzog, *Jesus*, 177; see also Borg, *Conflict*, 7–8 and Dunn, *Jesus, Mark*, 79–80.

PART TWO: Jesus' Death and Salvation

Jesus moves among them, ministers within the same community, and shows apparent slackness in relation to sustaining the boundaries (such as when he eats with tax collectors and sinners and thereby violates the eating purity codes; or when he heals Gentiles and thereby disregards the clear separation reflected in the practice of circumcision; or when he allows his followers to eat freshly picked grain on the Sabbath and then, himself, heals on the Sabbath and thereby disregards the Sabbath regulations). Jesus thus threatens the very existence of this Power that had become an absolute for these Pharisees. Hence, from the Pharisees' perspective, Jesus deserves vengeance.

For many Pharisees, table fellowship had been elevated to be a central element of Israel as set apart to Yahweh. To work in this way, it required the faithful to practice strict separation "from the impure, the non-observant, the sinner, precisely at and by means of the meal table." Jesus directly challenged that approach. He practiced table fellowship that crossed boundary lines rather than reinforced them. He "was open to invitations from a wide range of people; he was notorious for eating with tax collectors and sinners. Holiness for Jesus, we might say, was not a negative excluding force, but a positive including force."[25]

Jesus also challenges the Pharisees' authority as interpreters of Torah. He debates scripture with them and dares to make a flat assertion concerning that content of the Law codes that goes against what they taught. Jesus does not reject the law; rather, he "claimed to defend its intent against interpretations that would destroy its meaning or dull its edge."[26]

When Jesus de-emphasizes external markers for purity he also undercuts Pharisaic authority by depriving them of their bases to determine who would be in good standing within the covenant community and who would not. "Jesus objected against a boundary-drawing within Israel which treated some Israelites as outside the covenant beyond the grace of God. Such attempts to erect internal boundaries within Israel, creating internal divisions within Israel, were contrary to the will of God. Jesus was more critical of those who dismissively condemned 'sinners' than of 'sinners' themselves. Just as the poor were God's special concern, so the excluded and marginalized were of special concern for Jesus' mission."[27]

The Apostle Paul's writings, especially his letters to the Galatians and the Romans, help clarify why this conflict over the law would have been

---

25. Dunn, *Jesus Remembered*, 603.
26. Yoder, *Jewish-Christian*, 49.
27. Dunn, *Jesus Remembered*, 532.

so volatile. The basic problem, in Paul's perspective, was that the law had become for many in the covenant community not so much practical guidance for how to live faithfully in light of God's mercy and saving work for Israel—as it was in the books of Moses. Instead, for many, including the Pharisees as presented in the Gospels, the law had become their community's badge of cultural exclusivism.

In line with the cultural exclusivists, people within the covenant community understood their adherence to the regulations, both the written Torah and the oral Torah, as the basis to sustain their identity as God's specially chosen people. Doing rituals that marked them as different from those outside their community (what Paul termed "works of the Law," Rom 3:20) sustained this sense of difference.

In three key areas, the laws had special importance for identity sustenance: food laws (kosher food, ritual cleansing), Sabbath observance, and the circumcision of males. Faithfulness to these practices was absolutely necessary to Israel's identity; it showed that these practices signified God's special connection with the covenant community.

For Jesus to challenge reliance on these practices as the center of religious life threatened the entire system at its core. These practices were "sacred." They were absolutely necessary, since Israel's distinctiveness from the Gentiles stood at the heart of her identity as envisioned by the Pharisees. For example, "Jesus' table companionship with toll collectors and sinners was a profanation of the Pharisees' version of the great tradition, and therefore, an offense to Moses. Jesus reclined with the impure and the unclean, without apology or hesitation."[28]

This focus on the law as identity guarantor fostered a very brittle social dynamic, as seen in the conflict between Jesus and the Pharisees as presented in the Gospels. The Pharisees became convinced that they determined who did and who did not have the possibility of gaining God's favor. They surely saw the actual arbiter of such a possibility being the law itself, not themselves as human beings. However, the law always requires human interpreters. Because of the Pharisees' bias toward ritual purity, they erected high and rigid standards for access to God—and perceived Jesus's challenge to those standards as a direct threat.[29]

When such identity markers have a determinative role for the community's self-understanding, a large part of the value the community gives itself will tend to be based on the existence of outsiders. To soften the clear

---

28. Herzog, *Jesus*, 153.
29. Borg, *Conflict*, 100.

PART TWO: Jesus' Death and Salvation

lines of exclusion would threaten the community's sense of its value. In Jesus's context, for him to claim on the one hand to be an emissary of God and authoritative interpreter of the law (seen in his powerful acts) and, on the other hand, to extend welcome to outsiders also would have been perceived as a terrible contradiction and a direct threat.

With the covenant community so concerned with its own survival, the original vocation given this community—to be a light to the nations (Gen 12:3)—may be pushed to the side. For Jesus to remind the community of this vocation, both by his openness to Gentiles and by his emphasis on the community being attractive to outsiders due to its practice of mercy and justice, would also likely to be perceived as a direct threat.

The Law and Retribution toward Jesus

Jesus and the Pharisees differed sharply over the relative weight to be given to strict adherence to the regulations as compared to mercy-oriented flexibility. If one sees the strict adherence as essential to the sustenance of the community, an emphasis on the need for flexibility would easily be perceived as a direct threat.

The basic dynamic may be understood as one of placing loyalty to the covenant community's survival as the highest loyalty. For those who understood this survival to depend on strict legalism within the community, strict and harsh treatment of those whose slackness threatens the community's survival becomes necessary.

Jesus did not accept the Pharisees' sense of loyalty to the covenant community as they defined that community. In his view, the quest for a "pure" community insofar as it led to harshness, violence, and hurtful exclusivism, misguidedly violated—rather than upheld—Torah. So he acted to embody a different vision of the community characterized by inclusiveness even toward those the Pharisees considered unclean.

Jesus did violate the community standards established by the Pharisees and transgress the law—as interpreted by the Pharisees. In their opposition to Jesus and their desire "to destroy him" (Matt 12:14), they simply enforced what they saw as God-ordained retributive justice against one who broke the law. This one threatened the work God sought to do through Israel.

However, as the Gospels tell the story, Jesus actually represented the true God—shown by his remarkable deeds, such as when he healed disease, overpowered Satan and demons, and taught authoritatively. Jesus,

Jesus's Death and the Powers

though a genuinely good and faithful person, nonetheless deserved punishment according to the dictates of the religious leaders. The Gospels present us with a direct conflict between the forces of cultural exclusivism and the true God. Cultural exclusivism and its attendant reliance on the law understood in a legalistic way proves itself to be a Power in rebellion against the true God.

Jesus did not flinch from conflicts with the Powers of cultural exclusivism. We saw that in Matthew 12:1-14 when he debates with the Pharisees and openly violates their view of the law and heals on the Sabbath, again and again. He intended to make it clear for those with eyes to see that the true God values mercy and healing above cultural exclusivism. By his own freedom in the face of hostility from the defenders of cultural exclusivism, Jesus offers the way to salvation from bondage to those Powers.

As portrayed in the Gospels, those Powers responded to Jesus's display of powerful healing love by seeking to destroy him. Such an act would, for those with eyes to see, actually delegitimize the Powers and their claims to represent God. For people with such sight, simply to turn to God as shown in Jesus provides all that is needed to gain salvation.

As it turns out, the Pharisees fade into the background when the actual arrest and execution of Jesus occurs. It would appear that other Powers essentially pushed them aside—and the Pharisees remained unwilling to ally themselves with the Powers linked with the temple and the Roman Empire.

That the Pharisees were not complicit in the actual killing of Jesus must, on the one hand, be remembered. The relationship between the Pharisees and the message of Jesus should be recognized as being more complex than texts such as Matthew 12:1-14 might indicate. Jesus had significantly more in common with the Pharisees than with the temple and the empire.

Yet, on the other hand, we should not diminish the conflict either. According to the story, in the years immediately following Jesus's death, the Pharisees led violent opposition to Jesus's followers. That opposition did result in executions, most famously the stoning to death of the Christian leader named Stephen recounted in the Book of Acts.

The conflicts with the Pharisees continued. They focused, as the Gospels portray the conflict between Jesus and the Pharisees, on the issue of the interpretation of the law. The early Jesus movement rejected cultural exclusivism. This rejection led to the inclusion of Gentiles as Gentiles into their version of the covenant community—and ongoing conflicts.

SEVEN

Jesus's Death and the Powers
Religious Exclusivism (Temple)

THE OLD TESTAMENT SALVATION story as interpreted by the eighth-century prophets and then reiterated in Jesus's life and teaching centers around God's liberating acts in the exodus and Torah's provisions for social life meant to sustain that liberating work. This version of the story minimizes the role of the temple. It understands the temple to be secondary, even extraneous, to the core salvation dynamic. At most the temple plays a role as the scene for sacrificial acts that convey the community's commitment to God.

However, other strands of biblical tradition see the temple more positively. And, in the Gospel accounts even if Jesus himself does not orient salvation around the temple, it plays a central role in how the drama unfolds. As Mark tells the story, Jesus's altercation with the temple leaders in Jerusalem became the final catalyst that triggered his arrest and led to his execution.

THE LEGACY OF SOLOMON'S TEMPLE

Before Solomon built the temple at Jerusalem, the tribes of Israel had worshiped in a number of sanctuaries, most prominently Shiloh. The Philistines destroyed Shiloh in the battle recounted in 1 Samuel 4. The Philistines took from the Hebrews the Ark of the Covenant at that time. The Hebrews eventually regained the ark and established it in Jerusalem. King David and his successor, King Solomon, used the desire to have a place where the Ark would be housed as the basis for constructing a temple. God did not allow David to build the temple himself. However, Solomon did build the temple, as described in 1 Kings 6–7.

Solomon constructed the temple as a central element of his successful efforts to centralize the power of the kingly office in Israel. Among other elements, these efforts included Solomon's gathering an extraordinarily large collection of wives. Besides serving apparent political benefits gained through marrying women from other countries and thus establishing alliances, this gathering of such a harem also served Solomon's hopes to ensure a large progeny of heirs and to establish his own potent fertility.

Solomon also oversaw a rationalized system of tax districts to take the place of the traditional clans and tribes. In so doing, he furthered the power of the centralized state by deliberately eliminating the tribal system of decentralized power. "Under Solomon's administrative policies the concern for equitable distribution of economic resources reflected in the covenant law codes is displaced by an economics of privilege that begins to create sharp class divisions of wealthy and poor within Israel."[1]

Solomon also developed a large and elaborate bureaucracy. This bureaucracy reflected Solomon's effort to imitate larger empires by institutionalizing technical reason and pushing Israel's Torah-based communal dynamics to the margins. Solomon established an extensive standing army. This development created a permanent military class with centralized authority. It also meant that the gathering of armaments and possibilities of engaging in warfare would not require a broadly based sense of community support, but rather would be an ever-present reality.

The temple provided the central symbol holding together various elements that reflected Israel's political transformation. The temple reflected Israel's conformity with surrounding nations. Solomon, when he created the centralized king-dominated religious institution centered in the temple, returned Israel to a style of social organizing more similar the Egyptian empire than the covenant community established by exodus and Torah. Reflecting this transformation, we see no prophetic figures such as Moses or Samuel at the center of social discernment processes in Israel. When prophets emerge in Solomon's time, he shunts them to the edges for private conversations—and they play no role in the official religious life of the community.

---

1. Birch, et al., *Theological*, 248.

PART TWO: Jesus' Death and Salvation

The temple in Solomonic Israel encouraged a hierarchical, static, king-controlled style of religion.[2] Religion's subordination to the king may be seen even in the timing of construction. The king's palace comes first; "God's temple" comes second. Israel's understanding of God undergoes a corresponding shift in light of the temple's emergence. God is now fully accessible to the king. No longer wild and free, God is contained within "God's house" and, in effect, available to the king at all times. "Now there is no notion that God is free and that [God] may act apart from and even against this regime. Now God is totally and unquestionably accessible to the king and those to who whom the king grants access (cf. 1 Kings 8:12–13)."[3]

The construction of the temple on "Mount Zion" creates in Israel a tradition in tension with the prophetic/Torah tradition. These two traditions often compete; the later prophets drew on the Mosaic tradition, the defenders of the king-centered status quo drew on the Davidic/Solomonic tradition. These two traditions present reality in significantly different ways.[4]

Though Solomon borrowed from other nations to transform Israel, he sought not so much to imitate per se as to strengthen his own power and that of his heirs. "The temple served, more than anything possibly could have done, to gain for the distinctive theology of Jerusalem and of the Davidic covenant, a firm and enduring place in Israel's religion."[5] Hence, the temple should not be seen first of all as an example of religious syncretism, though it did have that element, but first of all as part of a strategy to centralize power politics.

For Mosaic faith, Israel serves a transcendent God, not simply a God who supports Israel's interests whatever they might be. This faith provides bases for prophetic critiques that continued to challenge Israel's public life. The prophets, who affirmed God's freedom, called Israel to serve God's purposes or suffer consequences. The God of the kings and the temple, on the other hand, existed to serve the state. After Solomon, it was not thinkable in establishment Israel that God would act apart from or even against the king's agenda (see 1 Kgs 8:12–13).[6]

---

2. Brueggemann, *Prophetic*, 34.

3. Ibid., 35.

4. Levenson, in *Sinai*, writing from a Jewish perspective, draws a contrast between these two traditions; he, though, argues ultimately for their compatibility.

5. Clements, *God*, 64.

6. Brueggemann, *Prophetic*, 34–35.

With Solomon, God enters Israel's life at the beck and call of the king and his minions. The king's servants control access to God. This new approach to religious faith and practice in Israel serves a useful function (for the king). It severely limits the possibility of resistance to the king's policies that would be based on God's transcendent will that exists in freedom from the will of the king. No longer may one approach God formally apart from doing so on the king's terms. So no word from God that would stand against the king's will could be heard. "In many ways [the temple] represents the danger of the domestication of the radically free God of Israel's covenant tradition."[7]

As events unfolded, prophets did arise among the Israelites who did not accept the Solomonic arrangement. However, for most of the major pre-exilic prophets, we have little evidence that the community respected their words or give them a widespread hearing. They, indeed, were mostly "voices crying in the wilderness." Their access to the public was greatly limited because, as a rule, the religious institutions remained the monopoly of the king.

In the time before Solomon, the shrines and sanctuaries that provided the context for Israel's worship were quite simple in both their construction and function. They were decentralized and impermanent. With Solomon, this changes drastically. Solomon's temple was far from simple. It was large, elaborate, and ornate rather than functional. Solomon gathered materials for the construction of the temple from many foreign sources. The structure he created differed qualitatively from what had existed before.

Solomon's temple appears to have echoed other neighboring structures. "The various features find parallels from Egypt to Mesopotamia. This is what one would expect, of course, for a sacred precinct constructed and decorated by Phoenician craftsmen."[8] A crucial expression of this departure from the sensibility of Torah may be seen in the floor plan for the temple that provided for three separate areas including an outer court, a holy place, and a "Holy of Holies." Likely Israel borrowed this plan from other nations. It reflects a quite different set of theological assumptions from Israel's prior understandings. Having separate areas provides for different levels of holiness. The closer one moved to the Holy of Holies the more authorization one required. This dynamic enhanced distinctions among the people and a loss of direct access for the vast majority.

7. Birch, et al., *Theological*, 248.
8. Miller and Hayes, *History*, 203.

PART TWO: Jesus' Death and Salvation

Along with the loss of access, the temple also fueled the development of an elite class of those few who could gain the authorization to move to the inner sanctums of the temple where, supposedly, access to God was possible. These religious elites, of course, served at the pleasure of the king. In this way, access to God came to be thoroughly politicized, and God came ever more to be the tool of human leaders. So long as the people accepted these arrangements, the religion served as a powerful tool to sustain social control. The temple played an important role for those with political power. Religious institutionalism served political authoritarianism.

Another reflection of Solomon's agenda to transform Israel via the religious institution, along with the floor plan of the temple, may be seen in the exotic nature of the materials used for its construction. Many of the these materials (e.g., the cedars of Lebanon) came from far away. This also reflected Solomon's willingness to depart from Israel's old traditions of suspicion toward foreign alliances. The use of much gold along with cedars and other expensive materials made a strong statement about Solomon's desire to lift up wealth as a prime attribute. Again, the contrast with the simplicity of the Mosaic tradition's cultic practices that encouraged access across the community and highlighted communal sharing could not be much greater.

The temple that Solomon had constructed surely exacerbated the distance between the wealthy and powerful in relation to the vulnerable and dispossessed. These socio-economic tendencies reflected the increased priority placed on wealth accumulation and display by the powerful people in Israel. The temple indeed communicated the centrality of Yahweh for Israel's faith—over and above other gods. Yet it also glorified Solomon himself and witnessed to his achievements. It reflected the social evolution of Israel away from the central priorities of Torah toward the power- and wealth-enhancing practices of Israel's neighbors, thereby signaling also the theological evolution Israel had undergone.

In contrast to the God of Moses, who liberates slaves and acts dynamically in the world, free from control by human power blocs, the God of the temple reinforces the power and order of Israel's political hierarchy. Israel under Solomon, centered on the temple, differs greatly from Israel under Moses, centered on Torah. Consequently, Israel's view of God changes, too.

The temple presented itself as centered on worship of Yahweh. In practice, though, the worship of Yahweh in this context also added to the legitimacy and prestige of the king and his supporters. Under Solomon, and for the generations that follow until the temple was destroyed, the temple played the role of "royal chapel" much more than of a community sanctuary.

Though its builders structured the temple so as to evoke a sense of awe at God's power and holiness, the temple's close ties with the ruling elite subordinated the transcendence and freedom of God to the will of the governing authorities in practice. The temple centralized worship under the auspices of the state and rendered virtually impossible a word of prophetic challenge. As the temple displaced Torah, God's demands for the practice of shalom lost their status as the core of the life of the community, equally applicable to king and ordinary citizen alike.

As the story—to its undying credit—nonetheless tells us, the emergence of temple-religion as officially dominant among the Hebrews did not eliminate prophetic challenges. In many famous cases, the prophetic word pitted the actual will of Yahweh over against the message (implicit as much as explicit) of the temple and its leaders. The prophets, at their most intense, portray the temple as being opposed to God.

Israelites came to see the temple as evidence for God's support of Israel—in effect, support that they assumed continued regardless of how closely the community followed Torah. The rituals could easily be delinked from covenant faithfulness. "Israel could feel itself so sure of the immanent presence of Yahweh that it forgot his transcendent lordship. That this danger did in fact have a deep and harmful effect on the popular attitude of Israel is evidenced by the criticism of Israel's worship made by the prophets."[9]

Most famously, Jeremiah 7 contains harsh words for the temple and its leaders. Jeremiah linked loyalty to the temple with injustice. "Will you steal, murder, commit adultery, swear falsely, make offerings to Baal, and go after other gods that you have not known, and then come and stand before me in this house, which is called by my name, and say, 'We are safe!'—only to go on doing all these abominations? Has this house, which is called by my name, become a den of robbers in your sight?" (Jer 7:9–11).

Jeremiah insisted that the temple did not ensure that Yahweh would bless the community. Just as Yahweh had earlier reacted to unfaithfulness by taking away Israel's worship center, so too again in Jeremiah's day. "Yahweh's presence was holy, and was set in Jerusalem as an act of grace, but in the face of Judah's sins [Yahweh] would no longer continue in the midst of

---

9. Clements, *God*, 79.

an unholy people. A performance of a cultic act, however conscientious, could be no substitute for obedience to the covenant."[10]

Ezekiel, in chapters 8 through 11, also portrays the temple in negative terms, the sight of many "abominations" from which God's presence will surely depart. Ezekiel shared Jeremiah's critique of the false security based on assumptions that Yahweh would protect the Israelite kingdom regardless of its faithfulness. "In violent and daring ways, Ezekiel makes clear that all to which Yahweh has been committed is revocable and is now being revoked. It is not possible for Judah or its religious establishment to hold Yahweh in thrall to its own interests."[11]

So, this temple, constructed at great cost and with great fanfare by Solomon and meant to be "God's house," led to a great deal of ambivalence among the Hebrew prophets. The image of "God's house" had a mixed meaning—"God's house" provided a sense of God's presence among the people, a place for worship and renewal of commitment and "God's house" provided a way for the powers-that-be to domesticate God, to keep God under their thumb.

The Second Temple

In the end, the Babylonian armies in 587 BCE (2 Kgs 25:1–22) reduced Solomon's temple to rubble. Israel's institutions—Davidic kingship and the temple—were not permanent. They could not prevent the destruction the prophets understood to be an expression of God's judgment. "The temple was in ruins, and with it many of the people had been driven out from Yahweh's land. The idea of any kind of permanent bond between Yahweh and the land of Judah with its temple was completely discredited."[12]

Babylon deported most of the Judean ruling class from Jerusalem to Babylon (see Jer 52:28–30). After the Persian Empire gained ascendancy over Babylon, many of the Jewish exiles returned to Palestine. The Persians then allowed the Israelites to rebuild the temple on a much more modest scale (see Ezra 1–2). This "second temple," constructed under the leadership of Zerubbabel in the years 520–516 BCE, provided for a restoration of a religiously oriented structured social life for Israelites.

As Walter Brueggemann summarizes:

---

10. Ibid., 85–86.
11. Birch, et al., *Theological*, 340–41.
12. Clements, *God*, 98–99.

The devastating Babylonian conquest, the destruction of the Temple, and the exiles of Judeans to Babylonia were followed by an unparalleled phenomenon—a miracle wrought by the Judeans themselves. They were the only people in antiquity exiled from the homeland and national religion who maintained their religious and social identity in captivity. All other exiled people assimilated, as did the "Ten Lost Tribes of Israel." Then, still another miracle: in response to King Cyrus's edict, a substantial number of Judeans, though established now in Babylonia, did return and erect the Second Temple.[13]

The books of Haggai and Zechariah tell how this reconstruction happened under the auspices of the new dominant empire in the Middle East, Persia. The construction of the rebuilt temple and later efforts under Ezra and Nehemiah to re-establish the Hebrew community in Jerusalem, were not, as in Solomon's time, linked directly with a Jewish nation-state. Nonetheless, they still served the purposes of the dominant political powers.

The Persian authorities gave permission for these renewal efforts (see Ezra 7:11–26; Neh 2:1–8). That the elite of the empire approved the rebuilding of Israel's temple and its faith community indicates that they saw such efforts to serve the empire's purposes. The renewal, then, "must be understood not just in terms of the religious conditions and needs of the Jewish community in Palestine but in terms of the political interests of the Persians."[14]

Though the prophet Ezekiel had envisioned a rebuilt temple that would provide a powerful symbol for Jewish independence and legitimacy (see Ezek 40–48), the actual rebuilding occurred in the context of continued Persian domination—possibly even depending upon Persian financing. Hence, the actual second temple not only provided a center for the reconstruction of Israel's life of worship but also provided an instrument for the Persian Empire's collection of taxes and a symbol of the Jewish leaders' dependence upon the Persians for their legitimacy. This rebuilt temple made it clear that Israel functioned independently in its religious life only at the prerogative of the empire.[15]

In the years that followed, Jews exhibited various attitudes toward the second temple. For many, the beliefs linked with the first temple remained viable—the temple as the dwelling place of God, unique in all the earth.

---

13. Brueggemann, *Introduction*, 365. See also Miller and Hayes, *History*, 458.
14. Miller and Hayes, *History*, 462.
15. Brueggemann, *Introduction*, 365; Miller and Hayes, *History*, 445.

A post-587 BCE prophet such as Ezekiel, though critical of the religious practices in the temple, nonetheless still saw it as God's dwelling place—at least the promised new temple. The prophet Zechariah also held out the hope that God's promises to Israel would still be fulfilled—including God's return to Jerusalem (Zech 1:17).

On the other hand, others also with roots in the story expressed more hostility toward the temple. This more negative viewpoint found expression in the emergent apocalyptic expressions of faith that arose during the inter-testamental period.

This tradition drew on Ezekiel's hopes for a new temple—which ultimately contrasted with the actual reality of the second temple. For some, then, Ezekiel pointed toward the structure constructed under the Persians while for others, that actual second temple failed to be a genuine replacement. The temple that was built under Haggai and Zechariah paled in relation to Solomon's temple. It was smaller, less physically impressive. As well, for some, the actual religious practices in the second temple fell short of what was needed. Debates swirled continually over how these practices should be implemented. Finally, many critics believed that the second temple had not been built in the way God had specified the temple should be built.

Regardless of the ambivalence many Israelites felt about the second temple, it remained at the center of Jewish life—down through the days of Jesus in the first century CE.

THE TEMPLE IN JESUS'S TIME

The temple housed the one Jewish altar on which the high priest performed the sacrificial rites of atonement once a year for the entire Jewish world. The temple provided the location that made possible the forgiveness for the people's sins. Here, through entering the Holy of the Holies, the high priest entered the presence of God on behalf of all Jews.

The importance of the temple for Jewish identity only increased over time. It served as God's dwelling place, "the only place where God's relations with human beings could be mediated through the sacrificial system. The temple claimed a monopoly on sacrifice and forgiveness." As a consequence, "the traditions limiting the power of monarchy and subjecting the ruler to the justice of Torah were minimized as were the prophetic critiques of the temple."[16]

16. Herzog, *Jesus*, 121.

Jesus's Death and the Powers

After the Romans gained control of Palestine, they established Herod as their client king, beginning in 37 BCE. Herod understood that to link the temple with his authority would enhance his power. So he embarked on an ambitious building project, expanded the temple greatly, and sought to approach the splendor of Solomon's temple.

The temple had grown to be a majestic symbol of power and might again. It stood at the heart of Judaism—both politically and religiously. Certainly, for most Israelites it fulfilled Yahweh's promise to dwell with the people and deal with their sins and their exile. As well, the temple embodied Yahweh's "legitimation of the rulers who built, rebuilt, or ran it. It was bound up inextricably with the royal house, and with royal aspirations."[17]

The temple also served as an economic center. As many as 18,000 priests participated in the temple activities. Many lived in the countryside and served at the temple for a week-long period twice a year. A number, though, remained on permanent assignment in Jerusalem.[18] An elite group of chief priests managed the operation. The temple treasury functioned as a huge national bank. It held the tithes and offerings required of Jews throughout the world. The elaborate temple operation generated the major source of revenue for the city of Jerusalem, and its tentacles stretched into the countryside where it owned large estates farmed by poor peasants.

Devout Jews living beyond Palestine came to the temple three times a year to celebrate religious festivities. In springtime the Feast of the Passover chronicled the deliverance from Egypt. About fifty days later the Feast of Pentecost offered thanks for the first fruits of the harvest. In the fall the Feast of Tabernacles included a solemn march around the altar in gratitude to God for the completed harvest. Most importantly, Jews celebrated the great Day of Atonement holiday in autumn. On that day, the high priest sacrificed a goat for his own sins and sent another one into the desert for the sins of the people. During these pilgrim festivals, Jerusalem's normal population of about 25,000 grew to as many as 180,000 people.

The temple stood as a monumental reminder that God's people of the promise had direct access to the divine through their rituals. Each morning and each afternoon, day after day, the "continual" burnt offering of an unblemished lamb was sacrificed on behalf of the community. These perpetual offerings likely required about 1,200 animals each year. As well, an offering of incense mixed with spices burned daily. Devout Jews also

---

17. Wright, *Jesus*, 411.
18. Herzog, *Jesus*, 138.

offered private sacrifices. The smell of smoke and burning flesh filled the air of the temple.

The priests held various duties in the sacrificial system. They removed ashes from the altar, prepared firewood, killed the lamb, sprinkled blood on the altar, cleaned the lampstand, and prepared the meal and drink offering. At least twenty priests, chosen by lot each day, performed the regular sacrifices while others attended to the special offerings.

The temple stood at the center of Jewish faith. For many, it symbolized God's living presence on earth. Believers came to the temple to pray, believing that from this site their prayers went directly to God. Here converts offered sacrifices. Here mothers presented purification offerings at the birth of each child.

Jewish taxes arrived from far and wide to support the temple. The Sanhedrin, the final Jewish authority in religious, political, and civil matters, made their home here along with the high priest. The high priest, priest of all priests, symbolically headed both faith and nation. Only the high priest, in purity, could part the curtains and enter the holy of holies in the very presence of God once a year on the Day of Atonement. He officiated at sacrifices on the Sabbath and during pilgrim festivals. The high priest was required to have direct ties to the family of Aaron.

The high priest wielded considerable power as the president of the Sanhedrin. This supreme council had judicial and administrative authority in religious and civil matters. It was a self-perpetuating body composed of chief priests, scribes (usually, though not always, from the Pharisee party), and nobility, and operated as the supreme court of Jewish authority.[19]

The high priest became the most powerful Jewish leader in relation to the occupying Roman leaders. He negotiated ceremonial and political matters with the Romans. The office of high priest fell generally to a member of just a few Jerusalem families. "Eventually, four high-priestly families virtually monopolized appointments to the high-priestly office."[20]

The high priest and Sanhedrin stood at the top of a network of thousands of lesser priests who lived in the countryside and regularly participated in temple ritual. High priests generally collaborated closely with the Roman government. Because they lacked support from their supposed leaders, the general population took organized resistance to Roman oppression into their own hands on several occasions. "These factors left the

---

19. Much of my summary of the temple here is drawn from Kraybill, *Upside-Down*, 60–73.

20. Herzog, *Jesus*, 91.

province of Judea in a precarious position. It was a powder keg waiting to explode.... Any prophet, like Jesus, who criticized the temple, could expect to receive prompt attention and a hostile response from a ruling class already stretched to its limit."[21]

The religious party that centered in Jerusalem and made up most of the Sanhedrin was known as the Sadducees. The Sadducees, in contrast to the Pharisees, rejected the oral tradition and professed skepticism concerning personal immortality (including resurrection) and the existence of demons and angels. They generally came from Jerusalem's wealthy upper class. They accepted the Roman occupation and cooperated with the Romans in order to keep the temple viable.[22]

The role of the Sadducees, and, in fact, the role of the second temple following Herod's expansion, in many ways harkened back to the first temple under Solomon. It provided for centralized religion, enhancing centralized political authority. The leaders of the temple in Jesus's day, as back in Solomon's day, supported the political and religious hierarchies in Jerusalem. They practiced a kind of sacrifice that inverted the theology presented in Leviticus. Unlike with Leviticus, for the temple in the first century sacrifice served as a means to connect with God that required the mediation of the religious institution whose wealth and power served the king's interests. "The religion of the temple was always political religion with economic consequences, because the temple was an instrument of the policies of the ruler and the ruling class."[23]

In contrast to this hierarchical religion and its service to hierarchical politics, the Old Testament portrays the original theological rationale for sacrifice as a basis for encouraging gratitude toward God and justice for all in the community, especially the vulnerable ones. Sacrifice in Leviticus stems from an experience of God's mercy and serves the community as a whole, not only the power elite.

As a "conservative," that is, one who drew directly from the tradition of Moses as filtered through prophetic critique, Jesus ended up on a collision course with the temple hierarchy—a course that exposed the true nature of religious institutionalism, its violence and subservience to political authoritarianism.

Jesus was not alone in being unhappy with the temple. The separatist Essenes rejected the legitimacy of the temple as it was operated because it

---

21. Ibid., 105.
22. Dunn, *Jesus Remembered*, 270–71.
23. Herzog, *Jesus*, 113.

was not led by the right people. The Torah-centered Pharisees worked at a theology that would make the blessings bestowed by the temple available through rigorous adherence to Torah. For the large group of non-elite Jews, the temple seems to have symbolized the elite's oppressive practices. When revolutionaries temporarily took over the temple in 66 CE, they right away burned the records of debts. "The unpopularity of the ruling class at this time is well documented, and the widespread dislike of them meant that the first-century temple, and particularly the way in which it was being run, came in for regular criticism."[24]

JESUS AND THE TEMPLE

As sharp as the conflict becomes between Jesus and the temple leadership was, the gospels do not present Jesus as a pure rejectionist. Jesus had a nuanced attitude toward the temple and its sacrificial system—though ultimately he rejected the actual practices of the temple in Jerusalem. More significantly, in harmony with the Old Testament salvation story and prophetic critique, he understood the sacrificial system as peripheral to the dynamics of salvation ("I desire mercy, not sacrifice," Matt 9:13 and 12:7, quoting Hos 6:6).

The two birth accounts, in Matthew and in Luke, give a mixed perspective on Jesus's relation with the temple. Luke presents a more positive view. His story begins with the birth of Jesus's distant cousin John (the Baptist), the son of a priest (Zechariah). While Zechariah was a rural priest not closely associated with the temple (and John certainly does not end up as a temple supporter), simply by being a priest he had some temple connection—rural priests were required to attend temple services several times a year. Zechariah's presence in the story implies at least some sort of continuity between the religious institutions of the time and Jesus's birth.

After Jesus's birth, Luke tells of his parents dedicating him in the temple (2:21–40). Their dedication of Jesus is framed as adherence "to the law of Moses" (2:22), and the sacrifice clearly expresses their gratitude for God's gift of their son (2:24). While at the temple, Jesus's family also encounters two old "saints," Simeon and Anna, who both praise God when they see Jesus for God's work of salvation.

Significantly, Simeon expresses his praise for God's work of salvation that will be "a light for revelation to the Gentiles" (Luke 2:32). Much later, when Jesus returns to the temple he harshly critiques it for not being "a

24. Wright, *Jesus*, 412.

house of prayer for all peoples" (see Mark 11:17: "a house of prayer for all the nations"). Luke also includes the story of Jesus at age twelve visiting the temple and engaging in theological discussions "among the teachers" (2:46). Here Jesus speaks his first words in this Gospel and refers to the temple as "my Father's house" (2:49).

So, Luke presents Jesus coming from a devout family that observed temple rituals, and he shows that in the temple itself people are found who understand Jesus as an agent of God's saving work for the whole world. While these incidents reflect a positive view of the temple, they also provide hints for the bases of critique—insofar as the temple is in harmony with the law of Moses and fosters revelation to the Gentiles, then it may be respected. However, should it depart from those conditions . . .

The impression in Matthew's birth story is subtler. For one thing, Matthew does not actually mention the temple. Matthew gives the picture of a new expression of God's saving work that bypasses the temple. If we associate the temple with King Herod, remembering the extensive resources he used to expand the temple buildings, we get a negative impression. Herod, according to Matthew's story, with the complicity of "all the chief priests [i.e., the temple officials] and scribes of the people" (Matt 2:4), sought to destroy this rumored newly born "king of the Jews." When Herod heard of Jesus' birth, "he was frightened, and all Jerusalem with him" (2:3). "All Jerusalem" likely alludes to the ruling classes, most obviously including the temple leaders.

Up until Jesus's final entry into Jerusalem, the temple plays a peripheral role in stories of Jesus's ministry. The Gospels do portray Jesus as spending his time in the countryside and not in close proximity to the temple. However, that he does so must be seen as significant. Jesus presents his program as something entirely independent of temple religion. For the kind of faith he encourages, the temple and religious institutionalism are irrelevant.

In particular, when Jesus pronounced people forgiven, he circumvented the temple's role in the process of dealing with sins. Temple priests claimed to provide exclusive access to Yahweh. To benefit from a relationship with Yahweh—say, in regard to agricultural success—one needed to go through the priests and temple. When, for example, "Jesus declares God's forgiveness of the paralytic's debts, he steps into the role of a reliable broker of God's forgiveness, and by simply assuming this role, challenges the brokerage house in Jerusalem called the temple."[25]

25. Herzog, *Jesus*, 128.

PART TWO: Jesus' Death and Salvation

Much of the early part of Mark's Gospel conveys this circumvention of the temple and its role as the center of purity concerns by recounting a series of encounters where Jesus ministers without concern for ritual impurity. He heals a man with skin disease (Mark 1:40-45), casts out "unclean spirits" (3:30), eats with "sinners" (2:16), exorcises a man possessed of a legion of unclean spirits (5:1-17), heals a bleeding woman (5:24-34), and touches a girl already dead.[26]

JESUS'S CONFLICT WITH RELIGIOUS INSTITUTIONALISM

The stories in the latter part of Mark's Gospel leading up to Jesus's crucifixion highlight how Jesus's conflict with the religious institution of the temple became overt—and fatal.[27]

The temple was absolutely essential to established life in Jerusalem and Judea. It was the economic center of Jerusalem. An estimated eighty percent of Jerusalem's employment was dependent on the temple.[28] The temple was the political center. Since Israel was a religious state, its religious code was also its state and civil code. The leadership organ of the temple, the Sanhedrin, also carried legislative and executive power. This power was heightened due to the Sanhedrin's cooperation with Roman rule. However, most of all, the temple was the religious center. The temple was where God was present on earth. It was "a religious center and theological symbol of tremendous emotive power."[29]

As Mark's drama approaches its climax, Jesus enters Jerusalem (Mark 11:1). This begins the final stage, Jesus's last week. First thing (11:11), Jesus visits the temple. The conflict is established: Jesus versus the religious leaders, the temple authorities. Things escalate when Jesus returns to the temple a second time and proceeds to "drive out those who were selling and those who were buying in the temple, and he overturned the tables of the money changers and the seats of those who sold doves; and he would not allow anyone to carry anything through the temple" (11:15). With these actions, Jesus expresses his hostility toward the temple ritual.

Mark brackets this confrontation in the temple with a two-part account of Jesus cursing a fig tree and causing it to wither (Mark 11:12-14, 20-21). Mark links Jesus's action in the temple with the fate of the fig tree.

26. Dunn, *Jesus Remembered*, 789.
27. Yoder Neufeld, *Killing*, 77.
28. Dunn, *Partings*, 32.
29. Dunn, *Partings*, 33.

Jesus "came seeking fruit, and finding none, he is announcing the Temple's doom."[30] The fig tree symbolizes Israel and its fate reflects the fate of the temple. Jesus, with his challenge, actually acts out God's judgment on the temple. The problem with the temple is that it has failed to be "a house of prayer for all the nations." Instead, the temple had become a center for religious exclusivism and economic exploitation.[31]

Jesus quotes two Old Testament prophets: Isaiah 56:7 ("My house shall be called a house of prayer for all the nations") and Jeremiah 7:11 ("You have made it a den of robbers"). Isaiah 56 portrays hope that foreigners would flock to Jerusalem. Jeremiah 7 condemns the people of Judea for presuming that God would continue to sustain the temple even in the face of their sinful living.[32] Jesus uses Israel's prophets to challenge temple practices, which he asserts are corrupt and counter to God's intentions. "Isaiah 56:7 stands as the climax to an oracle that is perhaps the fullest Old Testament vision of an inclusive Israel. It also fits the shape and themes of Jesus' ministry to the outcasts and the marginal, those who because of their uncleanness and cultic impurity were either banned from the community or pushed to its very edge."[33]

We are told that in response to this "cleansing" of the temple, "the chief priests and scribes . . . kept looking for a way to kill [Jesus]" (Mark 11:18). These religious leaders were, for a time, restrained by the popularity Jesus had with the crowds. But they intended to do away with Jesus. He threatened their purity-based system of religious control. He not only showed himself to be cavalier towards the purity regulations, but he also gained wide popularity. These factors caused alarm, exacerbated by his direct confrontation with the temple.

The parable of the vineyard immediately follows (Mark 12:1–12). Jesus likens the vineyard to the people of Israel, the watchtower to the temple, and the tenants to the religious leaders. God intended the temple to be a center for justice in Israel, but it instead became a center for injustice. God sent messengers to restore the vineyard to its intended purposes. But the tenants murdered those messengers—the historical fate of prophets in Israel. Finally, the master sends his "beloved son," who the tenants also murder. This final murder ends the owner's patience, and he promises to come to "destroy the tenants and give the vineyard to others."

30. Wright, *Jesus*, 421.
31. Swartley, *Israel's*, 159–60.
32. Ibid., 161.
33. Herzog, *Jesus*, 141.

These tenants (the religious leaders) have shown that they are rivals to the owner (God). The practices of the temple are not faithful to God's wishes but rather usurp God's place as Israel's object of worship.[34] Jesus patterned the parable after Isaiah's Song of the Vineyard (Isa 5:1–7), itself a strong critique of unfaithful eighth-century Israel. The parable ends with a quote from Psalm 118:22–23, a temple Psalm. Temple imagery pervades the parable. That the parable critiqued current temple practices and the religious leaders may be seen in their response. "When [the chief priests and scribes of Mark 11:18 and 11:27] realized that [Jesus] had told this parable against them, they wanted to arrest him" (12:12).

Jesus speaks in Mark 13 of the destruction of the temple. One of the disciples exclaims regarding the greatness of the temple: "Look, Teacher, what large stones and what large buildings!" The temple, reconstructed by Herod, was famous for its splendor. This exclamation likely reflects a sense of security about the temple guaranteeing God's ongoing protection for the chosen people similar to what Jeremiah critiqued in the text Jesus earlier quoted. These "wonderful buildings" symbolized God's presence with Israel.[35]

Jesus, however, was not impressed. "Do you see those great buildings?" he replied. "Not one stone will be left here upon another. All will be thrown down" (Mark 13:2). He alludes to impending physical destruction. Perhaps, too, he refers to the collapse of the spiritual authority of this institution. Immediately after the discourse of chapter 13, we read again, "the chief priests and the scribes were looking for a way to arrest Jesus by stealth and kill him" (14:1).

Finally, they do arrest him and bring him to trial. One of the main charges against Jesus is that he allegedly said he would destroy the temple (Mark 14:58). This charge is false on the surface. Jesus did not say that he would destroy the temple. Yet, ironically, the charge is true in the sense that Jesus's actions and words render the temple's functions meaningless.[36] Mark's gospel does not picture Jesus as actually threatening to destroy the temple. However, the centrality of the accusation that he did (Mark 15:29 indicates that the accusation stayed with Jesus) shows that Jesus's enemies understood him to be a threat to the temple.

Mark's treatment of the temple concludes in Mark 15:38. When Jesus died, "the curtain of the temple was torn in two, from top to bottom." This

---

34. Schwager, "Christ's Death," 114.
35. Hooker, *Mark*, 304.
36. Swartley, *Israel's*, 165.

final event links with what immediately follows, the Roman centurion's confession that "truly this man was God's Son" (15:39). The torn "curtain of the temple" juxtaposes Jesus and the temple as alternative places of divine presence. It provides perspective on what follows, the centurion's confession. The death of the Servant opens the way to God for all the world when it exposes sacred violence and deprives the temple of its mystique.[37] The self-proclaimed locus of God's presence on earth is revealed actually to be an institution that responds to the true revelation of God on earth with violence.

Jesus seems to regard the temple as peripheral to God's work in the world (Mark 11:7). What God wanted to be a house of prayer for the nations was now seen to be a center for robbers. "It excluded potential Gentile believers and expanded the exploitative power of religious leaders—even as they, for example, take away a poor widow's livelihood—cf. Mark 12:41–44."[38]

For Mark's Gospel, there is a clear connection between Jesus being put to death and Jesus's conflict with the temple, Jerusalem's center of religious institutionalism. In several cases—the cleansing of the temple, the parable of the vineyard, the apocalyptic vision, and the accusation before the tribunal—we see a connection between Jesus being perceived as a threat to the institution and the promise that he will be killed for this.

We may follow James Dunn's portrayal of the situation:

> Most likely it was because Jesus was seen as a threat to the status quo, a threat to the power brokers within Israel's social-religious-political system, that they decided to move decisively against him. In the event, it would seem that they were able to portray the decision to hand Jesus over to Pilate for summary execution as a purely religious one (Jesus guilty of "blasphemy"—Mark 14:63–64). In the event, too, Pilate took not very much persuasion to condemn Jesus as a political challenge to Roman power. Jesus was executed in the final analysis, because he had become too much of a thorn in the side of the religious-political establishment.[39]

In the end, though, Jesus's death does not signal that the religious authorities were victorious. Jesus's death actually signifies the opposite. The temple curtain is torn. Jesus, even on the cross, fulfills what the temple

---

37. Ibid., 168.
38. Carroll and Green, *Death*, 32.
39. Dunn, *Jesus Remembered*, 786.

PART TWO: Jesus' Death and Salvation

was meant to and did not—he engendered worship of God by Gentiles as well as Jews. The Gentile centurion confesses, "surely this was God's Son" (15:39).

Jesus, as interpreted by Mark, challenged the dynamics of religious institutionalism head on. He did so when he denied the ultimate legitimacy of his culture's central religious institution. He did not answer the religious leaders when they had him on trial (14:61). By refusing to answer, he, in effect, stated that he rejected their legitimacy as representatives of God.

Mark contains several references to Jesus's mission to the nations in the context of the conflicts in the temple. The temple in Jerusalem, in its cold institutionalism, had lost touch with God's will that the word of mercy be expressed to all peoples. Jesus came to express that word and met only with hostility from the religious leaders. So, in effect, the old temple must be torn down, and a new, open and inclusive temple based on Jesus himself must take its place (as Rev 21:22 states a few decades later: "I saw no temple in the city, for its Temple is the Lord God the Almighty and the Lamb").

Jesus critiqued the temple system. That system originally had a mission to help facilitate creative, communally faithful ways of living for all of the people in the society. But, in ultimately placing its priority on survival and supporting a static, unjust status quo, the temple left its original mission far behind.

Institutionalism stifles creativity. When institutional survival takes priority, then order, security, peace at all costs take precedence. Few risks can be taken. Few new thoughts can be pursued. The people who thrive are not visionaries or prophets, but bureaucrats and yes-sayers. The institution will not welcome a prophet such as Jesus as a messenger from God, nor see him as one sent to provide much-needed light into new ways to respond faithfully to the great crises faced by first-century Judaism. Rather, the institution sees him as a threat, an upsetter of the applecart, a voice to be stilled, rather than a voice to be responded to.

Jesus's conflict with the temple was costly. Many forces in his world benefited from people being subservient to institutions. When he sought to help people to break free from that subservience, he provoked resistance. However, Jesus did witness that such freedom may be attained.

Jesus's witness led to his death. In facing death as he did, though—fully committed to the life of the Spirit and free from dominance by spirit-denying hierarchies and religious ideologies—Jesus's life of freedom amidst the struggle points to an alternative to life lived in obeisance to the sacred violence of religious institutionalism.

EIGHT

Jesus's Death and the Powers
Political Authoritarianism (Empire)

FROM GENESIS THROUGH REVELATION, all the biblical stories take place in the shadow of some sort of empire.[1] Many interpreters believe that Genesis one self-consciously articulates Israel's alternative to the Babylonian cosmology during the sixth-century exile following Babylon's crushing the Judean state.[2] The Book of Revelation contains a thinly veiled critique of the Roman Empire, offering a call for followers of the Lamb to choose loyalty to his way rather than accept empire domination, portrayed in part in terms of the blasphemous city of "Babylon."[3]

In between, various other empires also shape biblical faith—Egypt, Assyria, Persia, and Greece. As well, the political elite within Israel itself tended toward empire-like political authoritarianism. Biblical prophets voice sharp critiques of power politics within their communities because such politics echo the practices of the world's empires. So, it comes as no surprise to find Jesus enmeshed in issues related to the empire of his day—to the point that he gets executed by the empire using the form of killing, crucifixion, that was Rome's tool for retribution against political criminals.

---

1. Howard-Brook, *Come Out*.
2. Cf. Brueggemann, *Genesis*.
3. Cf. Kraybill, *Apocalypse*.

PART TWO: Jesus' Death and Salvation

Contra Egypt

Ironically, the first overt mention in the Bible of a great empire, Egypt, occurs in a story that presents the Hebrew patriarch, Joseph, helping expand the empire's power (Gen 37–50). Joseph brilliantly advises the Pharaoh during famine to provide for stores of food that would be gathered during times of plenty and sold during the hard times—for Pharaoh's great benefit.

The Bible's attitude toward Egypt, and the other empires that follow, takes a decisive turn toward the negative with the beginning of the Book of Exodus. We learn right away how empires work. Joseph had been of service to Pharaoh, and he and his extended family prospered. In time, though, the empire found it more useful to enslave Joseph's people. "Now a new king arose over Egypt who did not know Joseph" (Exod 1:8). Out of fear of the proliferating Hebrew people who had resisted fully assimilating into Egyptian society and its empire state-ideology, the Pharaoh acts against them. He orders "his people" to "set taskmasters over [the Hebrews] to oppress them with forced labor" (Exod 1:10–11).

The text does not actually name this specific Pharaoh, perhaps at least in part because "Pharaoh" came to be used in the tradition as "the personification of earthly oppressive power, cloaked in its own claims to divinity, yet brought low by the power of Israel's God, whose power is exercised in behalf of 'the least of these.'"[4]

Pharaoh's strategy did not work; "the more [the Israelites] were oppressed, the more the Egyptians came to dread them" (Exod 1:13–15). The story of the exodus exposes how Pharaoh clung to power. He refused to relent in his oppressive policies even when things fell apart for him. In the end, Pharaoh's stubbornness led to disaster for his empire and liberation for the Hebrew slaves. Pharaoh's retributive practices turn back on himself and his empire.

The Hebrews' experience of oppressive empire domination fed into a counter-cultural religious and political vision. In contrast to the gods of the empire, who serve the will of the king, the Hebrews worshiped Yahweh, the critic of kings and the advocate of vulnerable, oppressed people. In contrast to the social structure of the empire, with its great disparities of wealth between the elite and the masses, the Hebrews followed a law code (Torah) that emphasized decentralized political power and economic self-sufficiency for all in the community. Torah established strong inheritance

---

4. Birch, *Let Justice*, 123.

laws that intended to prevent economic stratification and the disenfranchisement of vulnerable people and their descendants.

When the Hebrews leave Egypt, they take with them not only a new faith centered on the ideal of freedom, but also take a call to embody this faith as "a new social community in history." This community received guidance through Torah to make concrete in history a people that would "match the vision of God's freedom. That new social reality was utterly discontinuous with Egypt."[5]

In contrast to the militarized culture of the empire, with its permanent standing army, professionalized military elite, and large stores of horses, chariots, and other instruments of war, the Hebrews eschewed being a warrior culture. Their national defense needs would be met by ad hoc coalitions of tribes joining in temporary militias and by trust in their God. "Early Israel rejected entirely the idea that God had delegated to some autocrat the legitimate power to put human beings to death. Early Israel rejected entirely the idea that God was merely the Ground of Being for some political monopoly of force."[6]

In all these ways, Israel defined itself over against the Egyptian empire. The exodus testimony, "this most radical of all of Israel's testimony about Yahweh, verifies that the God of Israel is a relentless opponent of human oppression, even when oppression is undertaken and sponsored by what appear to be legitimated powers."[7]

ISRAEL'S MONARCHY AND THE CRITIQUE OF EMPIRE

The tradition's hostility toward empire, reflected implicitly in the law codes' providing for a decidedly non-empire-like social order, found overt expressions at a major crossroads in the story of the Hebrew community. In the face of bloody internal conflict among the tribes recounted in Judges 20, we read, at the conclusion of the Book of Judges, "in those days there was no king in Israel; all the people did what was right in their own eyes" (Judg 21:25). Then First Samuel tells what happens near the end of the career of Israel's last great judge. "When Samuel became old, he made his sons judges over Israel. . . . Yet his sons did not follow in his ways, but turned aside after gain: they took bribes and perverted justice" (1 Sam 8:1, 3).

5. Brueggemann, *Prophetic*, 16–17.
6. Mendenhall, *Tenth*, 21.
7. Brueggemann, *Theology*, 180.

On top of these internal problems of chaos and corruption, the Hebrews also faced a major external threat. The emerging regional empire of the Philistines sought to overrun the Hebrews. As a consequence of these problems, the elders of Israel sought a human king, like other nations (1 Sam 8:5).

On the one hand, the Hebrews fear losing their identity by being conquered by the Philistines; perhaps the covenant community would thereby be eliminated from the face of the earth. On the other hand, to become "like other nations" could also lead to the elimination of the covenant community should it lose its distinctive character.

Samuel argued, in vain as it turned out, for a third option: continue to trust in Yahweh as your only king, maintain a distinct identity oriented around exodus and Torah, and Yahweh will see that the covenant promises will remain viable. In the course of making his case for sustaining the Yahweh-as-king model, Samuel articulated a powerful anti-empire argument and a strong concern that should Israel take the human king route it would also become empire-like.

This is what kings are like, Samuel asserts (1 Sam 8:10–18). Kings take the people's sons and force them into the military. Kings establish standing armies and pour the nation's resources into sustaining and arming those armies. Kings take the people's daughters. Kings take the best farmland and enrich their courtiers with the people's property. Kings take a tithe of the people's produce, and the people's servants and livestock. In the end, kings enslave the people (as did to the Hebrews' previous human "king," Egypt's Pharaoh).

Samuel warned the people that taking the wrong turn at this crossroads would return them to their status in the Egyptian empire, but he added that this time Yahweh would not respond to their cries amidst their oppression (1 Sam 8:18; cf. Exod 2:23).

Samuel argued in vain. "The people refused to listen to the voice of Samuel; they said, 'No! But we are determined to have a king over us, so that we also may be like other nations, and that our king may govern us and go out before us and fight our battles' " (1 Sam 8:19–20). Yahweh instructs Samuel to relent and "set a king over them" (8:22).

As the story continues, Israel's second king, David, grows in power and seems to head in a direction that would not result in Samuel's warnings being fulfilled. In David's successful early years as he gained and exercised power, and in the provisions for the eventuality of the Hebrews turning toward kingship provided in Deuteronomy 17, the story gives the impression that human kingship did not inevitably have to betray the anti-empire vision of exodus and Torah.

The kingship allowed for in Deuteronomy would still be subordinate to Torah and would serve the anti-hierarchical provisions of the covenant. The king was to come from within the Israelite community and not be a foreigner. That is, the king was to be one who had grown up observing Torah. The King must not take: "not acquire more horses" (that is, no standing army), "not acquire many wives, or else his heart will turn away; also silver and gold, he must not acquire in great quantity for himself" (Deut 17:14–17).

This Deuteronomy text places the king in a subordinate position to Torah. "When he has taken the throne of his kingdom, he shall have a copy of this law written for him in the presence of the Levitical priests. It shall remain with him and he shall read it in all the days of his life, so that he may learn to fear the Lord his God, diligently observing all the words of this law and these statutes, neither exalting himself above other members of the community nor turning aside from the commandment, either to the right or to the left, so that he and his descendants may reign long over his kingdom in Israel" (Deut 17:18–20).

This ideal in Deuteronomy emphasizes two points. First, the king is to be subordinate to and dependent upon Yahweh and the covenant the people had made with Yahweh that was the basis for their hope for shalom. And second, "the king's essential task is to be the instrument of Yahweh's justice and covenant blessing among people (see, for example, royal psalms such as Pss 72 and 101)."[8]

The accounts that follow in 1 and 2 Kings almost all reflect the kings' unwillingness to submit to Torah in this way. King David violates commandments against adultery and murder in his affair with Bathsheba. King Solomon evinces the change from Torah-oriented kingship in his ruthless efforts to gain and consolidate his power (cf. 1 Kings 1–11).

Solomon expanded the king's authority. He reorganized social structures toward much greater centralized control. He instituted rigorous taxation to expand his treasury. He drafted soldiers and expanded the collection of horses and chariots into a large, permanent army with career military leaders. And he also decreed a policy of forced labor for his twenty-year building project of constructing first his palace and then the temple.[9]

---

8. Birch, *Let Justice*, 219–20.
9. Brueggemann, *Prophetic*, 21–38.

PART TWO: Jesus' Death and Salvation

Deuteronomy 17 explicitly stated that kings must not gather horses, gold, or silver for themselves. Solomon did all these things, gaining renown for his wealth. Solomon also cultivated ties with other countries. He had hundreds of wives from many nations. Through his wives, Solomon gained international status. Again, this is precisely what Deuteronomy tells the king not to do. "He must not acquire many wives for himself, or else his heart will turn away" (17:17). We read in 1 Kings 11 that indeed Solomon's heart did turn away. His many wives influenced him to worship other gods. "His wives turned away his heart after other gods; his heart was not true to the Lord his God" (1 Kgs 11:4).

God warns Solomon in First Kings 9:6-8: "If you turn aside from following me... and do not keep my commandments... but go and serve other gods and worship them, then I will cut Israel off from the land... and [the temple] I will cast out of my sight.... This [temple] will become a heap of ruins."

Solomon's turn from Torah-oriented kingship toward political authoritarianism finds further expression with his son, King Rehoboam. Solomon's practices of forced labor elicited resistance and led at one point to a rebellion headed by one of his top officials, Jeroboam. Solomon forced Jeroboam into exile, but the latter returned to Israel after Solomon's death. Jeroboam spoke to King Rehoboam, asking for some changes. Rehoboam rejected Jeroboam's demands, choosing for political authoritarianism. He stated, "My father made your yoke heavy, but I will add to your yoke; my father disciplined you with whips, but I will discipline you with scorpions" (1 Kgs 12:14). So Jeroboam led a secessionist movement that resulted in a split between the northern kingdom, Israel, and the southern kingdom, Judah. Retributive justice severely damaged the covenant community as the king followed the empire way rather than the Torah way.

Kings in both Judah and Israel turn toward idolatry, authoritarianism, corruption, and injustice. As the two Hebrew nations continue to trust in the sword rather than in Yahweh and Yahweh's Torah, they meet the fate of the nations. The northern kingdom falls at the hands of the great Assyrian empire near the end of the eighth century, and a little over one hundred years later, the Babylonian Empire puts an end to Judah.

Prophets emerge in the context of Israel's movement away from Torah. They utter words of sharp critique toward the Hebrew community's increasing conformity with the ways of Empire. However, they also critique the outside empires. In fact, throughout the Bible we find sharp critiques of kings, including, for example, Pharaoh (Exod 1-15), Sennacherib of

Assyria (Isa 37:23–29), the king of Babylon (Isa 14:4–21) and the prince and king of Tyre (Ezek 28:1–19). "Outside of Israel, kingship was considered as 'let down from heaven,' a blessing of the gods. Within Israel, kingship was regarded as human rebellion, a rejection of the rule of Yahweh (whose will was communicated not through the king, but through his prophets)."[10]

The Hebrews among the Empires

Four large empires figure prominently in the Old Testament story—Egypt, Assyria, Babylon, and Persia. A fifth, Greece, plays a large role during the inter-testamental period. And a sixth, Rome, dominates the New Testament.

Egypt

As we have seen, the Egyptian empire looms large over the emergence of the Hebrews as a people. The exodus from slavery in Egypt and the formulation of the law as a counter-testimony to the ideology of Egypt's empire, show how Israel defined itself over against Egypt. "Egypt has become, from the outset of Israel's memory, a defining image of hostility to Yahweh's governance."[11]

The story of Solomon includes several allusions to Egypt. "Solomon made a marriage alliance with Pharaoh, king of Egypt; he took Pharaoh's daughter and brought her into the city of David" (1 Kgs 3:1; see also 1 Kgs 7:8; 9:24; 11:1). While on the surface, these references reflect Solomon's renown and significance in his day, in the context of the traditions of Israel, especially Deuteronomy 17, we may see this alliance as a key indication of Solomon's violating Torah's opposition to foreign influences.[12]

The irony that Solomon would marry into the Egyptian Empire's leadership class rings loudly when we remember Samuel's warning about the people, under their desired king, returning to slavery. Deuteronomy 28:68 also made this connection. The final threatened curse, should Israel not remain faithful to the covenant, reads as follows: "The Lord will bring you back in ships to Egypt, by a route that I promised you would never see

---

10. Lind, *Monotheism*, 18.
11. Brueggemann, *Reverberations*, 60.
12. Ibid.

again; and there you shall offer yourselves for sale to your enemies as male and female slaves, but there will be no buyer."

Egypt surfaces several times as representative of the nations in rebellion versus God (e.g., Ezek 29–32; Isa 19; Jer 46; Ps 87). Egypt bears responsibility for the death of King Josiah, one of the few kings in Judah the Bible portrays as seeking to let Torah govern the kingdom. Josiah goes out to confront Pharaoh Neco and is slain in battle (2 Kgs 23:28–29).

Poignantly, the prophet Jeremiah, at the time of Babylon's destruction of Judah, wrote that he accompanied Jewish exiles into Egypt (Jer 43–44). He critiqued those exiles as idolaters. It is as if the entire history following the exodus has been for naught as people of the covenant return to trusting in power politics and turning from Torah and toward Empire faith.

Assyria

From its northern location, the Assyrian Empire threateningly hovered over Israel. The kings of the northern kingdom, in alliance with other nearby smaller nations, successfully resisted Assyria's imperialism for many years. Eventually, though, as recounted in 2 Kings 17:5–23, Assyria utterly destroyed Israel and moved on to attack Judah. Isaiah 36–39 and 2 Kings 18–20 tell how Assyria besieged Jerusalem. The Judeans staved off Assyrian conquest. Isaiah portrays this event, wherein Assyria withdraws from the attempt to conquer Judah, as evidence of Yahweh's power over against the brutal superpower. Not coincidentally, the books of the Kings portray Judah's king of the time, Hezekiah, as one of only two kings who remained consistently faithful to Yahweh (the other being Josiah).[13]

The antipathy many in Israel felt toward Assyria received voice in the prophecy of Nahum. Nahum joyfully proclaims the impending doom of Nineveh, the capital of Assyria, as due to Assyria's injustice and brutality. Nahum portrays Yahweh as the author of this doom. "Your shepherds are asleep, O king of Assyria; your nobles slumber. Your people are scattered on the mountains with no one to gather them. There is no assuaging your hurt, your wound is mortal. All who hear the news about you clap their hands over you. For who has ever escaped your endless cruelty?" (Nah 3:18–19).

Much later, the book of Jonah uses Israel's antipathy toward Assyria and Nineveh to much different effect. This book critiques Israel's insular

13. Gerbrandt, *Kingship*, 50.

perspective in post-exilic Palestine. To do so, the writer draws on the assumed hostility toward Nineveh and Assyria that would have remained alive in the people's memories. Nineveh plays a rhetorical role in Jonah, and stands as the last place the Hebrews would ever want God's mercy to be expressed. This symbolic use of Nineveh indicates how terrible the actual Assyrian empire had been in the eyes of Israel.

Babylon

During the seventh century BCE, Assyria met its match in the resurgent Babylonian Empire. Babylon succeeded where earlier Assyria had failed—it conquered Judah and destroyed the temple and much of the rest of Jerusalem, and took the ruling class who survived into exile.

Nebuchadnezzar emerged as the ruler of the Babylonian Empire in 605 BCE and remained in power until his death in 562 BCE. Not long after Nebuchadnezzar's death, the Persians under Cyrus replaced Babylon as the dominant Ancient Near Eastern empire. So, Babylon reigned only briefly. However, those were extraordinarily eventful years for the Hebrews, and the Babylonian Empire and Nebuchadnezzar loom large in biblical writings, down through the final book of the New Testament.

Over several invasions and deportations in a couple of decades, Nebuchadnezzar, according to the Old Testament, ended Judah as a nation-state and left the covenant community a small, scattered remnant that barely sustained its consciousness as people of the promise. Because Israel's prophets critiqued their nation for its unfaithfulness, they interpreted the acts of Nebuchadnezzar as expressions of God's judgment on God's people. Nonetheless, this theological assertion did not lessen the evil in the Babylonian Empire's merciless actions.[14] The prophet in Isaiah 47 speaks of God's judgment toward Babylon:

> Sit in silence, and go into darkness, daughter Chaldea [i.e., Babylon]! For you shall no more be called the mistress of kingdoms. I was angry with my people, I profaned my heritage; I gave them into your hand, you showed them no mercy.... You felt secure in your wickedness; you said, "No one sees me." Your wisdom and your knowledge led you astray, and you said in your heart, "I am, and there is no one besides me." But evil shall come upon you, which you cannot charm away; disaster shall fall upon you,

---

14. Brueggemann, *Reverberations*, 18.

PART TWO: Jesus' Death and Salvation

which you will not be able to ward off; and ruin shall come upon you suddenly, of which you know nothing. (Isa 47:5-7, 10-11)

The role of Babylon in Israel's consciousness as the paradigmatic example of political authoritarianism may be seen in the use of "Babylon" in symbolic ways down through the writings of the New Testament—most famously the Book of Revelation, where "Babylon" symbolizes the brutalities and blasphemies of the Roman Empire.

Several hundred years after Babylon fell to Persia and ceased to exist as an empire, the imagery remained vital as seen in the portrayal of Nebuchadnezzar in Daniel 2-4. Nebuchadnezzar's craziness and power worship likely represent Daniel's take on Antiochus IV, the Syrian ruler who oppressed the Jews in the second century BCE. The only redemption possible for this idolatrous ruler is to submit to the ultimate rule of God (Dan 4:34-37). "Nebuchadnezzar—and Babylon—take on a remarkably generative role in the imagination of Israel, and become a metaphor for arrogant, autonomous power that does evil in the world in opposition to Yahweh's will."[15]

Persia

The Persian Empire emerged in the mid-sixth century BCE under the leadership of Cyrus. The Old Testament presents it in a more positive light than the other empires. Several factors likely account for this. Persia defeated the terrible Babylonians, the destroyers of Judah and the temple. Israel's joy at this action is reflected in Isaiah identifying Cyrus as God's "shepherd" (Isa 44:28) and, even, God's "anointed one" (45:1). Persia's victory indeed did serve Israel's purposes. It is hard to imagine the covenant community surviving otherwise. Whatever Cyrus's own motivations, from the Israelites' perspective his actions did look like a saving act of God.[16]

The Persians evidently concluded that their purposes would be better served if they permitted their conquered nations a measure of self-determination.[17] Perhaps this would provide for greater tax revenue and overall productivity in the occupied territories. So, Cyrus allowed the exiled ruling class Hebrews to return to Palestine. Though it provided for

---

15. Ibid.
16. Ibid., 144.
17. Howard-Brook, *Come Out*, 261.

profound challenges as the exiles struggled to reintegrate with those who had remained in Palestine, this return allowed the community to survive.

In addition, Persia not only allowed the Hebrews to build a temple but actually helped finance it. This temple, like its predecessor constructed by Solomon, served people in power by playing an important role is sustaining social order. It served as a tax-collecting center for the Persians but also undeniably played a crucial role in providing a locus for Israel's ongoing identity as people of the covenant.[18] The Persians allowed important Jewish leaders such as Nehemiah and especially Ezra to reshape Judaism and to build viable religious and cultural structures in the fifth century BCE that proved to be essential for the sustenance of the tradition.[19]

The positive impression the Old Testament gives of the Persian Empire in part stems from the likelihood that during this time most of the Hebrew Bible reached its final form. Those responsible for that work may well have avoided producing materials that would alienate their Persian benefactors.

The portrayal of the Persian Empire provides a bit of a counterweight to the otherwise critical spirit of the Old Testament concerning the great empires. Perhaps these ambiguities may actually reinforce our understanding of the Powers as not inherently evil. As Walter Wink writes, they are simultaneously good creations, fallen entities with a proclivity for usurping God's supremacy, and potentially redeemable.[20] The Persian experience provides a sense that empires need not be as brutally oppressive as many are.

The Persian period provides evidence that the covenant community was capable of survival apart from operating its own nation-state and capable of sustaining its particular identity in the context of a dominating empire not committed to the covenant.

ROMAN DOMINATION

The greatest empire of the ancient world emerged in the second century BCE, eventually defeating the remnants of Alexander's empire in Syria, Macedonia, and Greece. The Romans established a relationship with the various provinces in Palestine in which Judea, Galilee, Idumea, and Perea all were ruled by Jewish governments who served as Roman clients.

---

18. Brueggemann, *Reverberations*, 144.
19. Ibid.
20. Wink, *Engaging*.

Herod, originally governor of Galilee, gained power over all the provinces. He was entitled "king of the Jews" by Rome, but had to consolidate his control through his own military prowess. Herod ruled, at the behest of the Romans, from 37 BCE until his death in 4 BCE.

Herod was a typical Roman client-ruler. Rome created mutually beneficial relationships with local elites, especially in the economic arena. "Roman peace guaranteed the preservation of the existing order and therefore the continuation of the status of the indigenous upper classes. On the other hand, Rome guaranteed a peace in the province or in the allied kingdom which was the presupposition for the money and offerings in kind which had to flow to Rome as duties and taxes."[21]

After Herod's death, Rome divided his kingdom into thirds among his sons. Herod Antipas ruled Galilee and Perea for over 40 years and Philip ruled Trachonitis and Iturea for nearly 40 years. The third unit, Judea, though, soon came under the direct control of the Romans due to the failure of Herod's third son, Archelaus, to maintain his authority.

In general, the Roman leadership tolerated the strict monotheism of the Jews and only required that Rome be recognized as the ultimate political authority and be paid taxes. If those conditions were met, Rome allowed some self-governance—with the reality still being one of ultimate Roman dominance. This power found expression in the Roman governor's holding the capability of appointing or dismissing the temple's high priest. The governor "retained stewardship over the high priestly garments, thus effectively controlling its functioning. In classic colonial fashion, Rome maintained exclusive authority over matters of foreign policy and serious domestic dissent (e.g., capital punishment)."[22]

In time, Pontius Pilate became governor of Judea. Contemporary Jewish writers Josephus and Philo portrayed Pilate's governorship as bloody and violent. Luke 13:1 alludes to Pilate's responsibility for the deaths of a group of Galileans. Later on, after the slaughter of a large number of Samaritans, Rome recalled Pilate. Church historian Eusebius wrote that Pilate eventually committed suicide.

JESUS AND EMPIRE

In the Palestine of Jesus's day, society could be divided into two main groups. The ruling class included representatives of the Roman Empire.

21. Wengst, *Pax Romana*, 25.
22. Myers, *Binding*, 56–57.

As well, those government officials who served as clients of Rome, in particular the descendants of King Herod, must be included. A third element of the ruling class included the religious leaders associated with the temple in Jerusalem.

The second group, much larger, included most everybody else: peasants in the countryside and the vast majority of the population of Jerusalem and the other cities. "As in other areas of the Roman Empire, a huge chasm separated those of wealth, privilege, and power from those who produced for and otherwise served the desires of the ruling groups."[23]

Jesus came from this second group and oriented his ministry toward it. Insofar as he encountered people in the first group, he tended to treat them respectfully. He also challenged them, though, to be responsive to the needs of all people and to do away with the cultural dynamics that made the few wealthy and powerful and disenfranchised the many.

Jesus expanded the scope (contra the Pharisees) of who would be included among people of the covenant. Hence, he came into conflict with guardians of the law and guardians of the temple, as we have seen in our previous two chapters. A significant part of Jesus's message, though, also included a critique of the dominant forces from outside Israel's religious structures—the political rulers, the Roman Empire.

Jesus understood himself as linked with earlier biblical leaders, especially Moses, Jesus's own namesake Joshua, and later prophets. These leaders each energetically rejected political authoritarianism. Moses, most foundationally, led the people out of the Egyptian Empire and exposed Pharaoh's corruption and reliance upon oppression and brutality.[24]

Matthew's birth story presents Jesus as born to carry on the tradition of Moses, down to the parallel between Pharaoh's violence and the violence of King Herod. From the beginning of Jesus's ministry, he acts and speaks in defiance of the ruling class's assumptions about their dominance and control over the people. His healing and exorcisms led the Pharisees to make common cause with political leaders (the Herodians) who desire to kill Jesus (Mark 3:1–5). Jesus triggered the rulers' retributive inclinations when he violated their policies of control.

When Jesus proclaimed the kingdom of God, he challenged the Pax Romana. He prayed for the coming of God's kingdom and expected it soon. He believed his own work would inaugurate this kingdom. He

---

23. Horsley, *Jesus and Empire*, 59.
24. Ibid., 81.

PART TWO: Jesus' Death and Salvation

did not accept the empire's claims to be bring the "gospel" (good news) of peace. And he rejected the claim that the empire acts on behalf of God.[25]

The stories of Jesus's exorcisms evoke the sensibility of Moses and Elijah. They too crossed the sea, healed, fed the multitudes in the wilderness, and preached the law. They also evoke memories of Moses's resistance to Pharaoh and Elijah's resistance to King Ahab. Jesus's power over demons (linked on occasion with Roman legions—Mark 5:9; Luke 8:30) symbolized his rejection of Roman power.[26] Remember Jesus's encounter with Satan in the wilderness at the beginning of his ministry. Satan offers Jesus political power as if it belongs to Satan. Jesus later displays his continued rejection of Satan's presence in and among the people when he casts demons out.

Jesus's condemnation of authoritarian types of leadership also reflects his rejection of Rome's power politics: "You know that among the Gentiles (i.e., the Romans) those whom they recognize as their rulers lord it over them, and their great ones are tyrants over them" (Mark 10:42). With this statement, he offers a sharp critique of imperial politics. The "peace of Rome" rests upon the dynamics of oppressive domination. Jesus's "you know" reflects a sense that both he and his listeners knew Roman domination quite well. Jesus presents a different way for political life, not an ethic of withdrawal and resignation. "Peace based on oppressive force is not what Jesus wants."[27]

Jesus's famous confrontation concerning the payment of taxes, when properly understood, presents his listeners with a choice between two competing claimants for his listeners' loyalties. God or Caesar; it has to be one or the other. Those who trust in the true God will deny Caesar's claims for their loyalty. "If God is the exclusive lord and Master, if the people of Israel live under the exclusive kingship of God, then all things belong to God, the implications for Caesar being fairly obvious. . . . Caesar, or any other imperial ruler, has no claim on the Israelite people, since God is their actual king and master."[28]

When given the opportunity in the wilderness prior to the beginning of his public ministry to overthrow the Romans with force, Jesus turned Satan down. And, at the end, when face to face with Pilate, Jesus asserted, "My kingdom is not of this world." However, neither of these

25. Wengst, *Pax*, 55.
26. Horsley, *Jesus and Empire*.
27. Wengst, *Pax*, 55–56.
28. Horsley, *Jesus and Empire*, 99. See also Wengst, *Pax*, 59–60.

points portrays Jesus as apolitical or indifferent to the Roman Empire. Rather, when seen in conjunction with his ministry as a whole, Jesus is in both cases presenting his politics as an alternative to Roman political authoritarianism in the here and now.[29]

Jesus's alternative politics did threaten Roman authoritarianism. So it was the logical consequence that such a threat would be brutally punished. Public crucifixion served most of all as a means to intimidate subject peoples—retribution for the sake of social control.

The language of "kingdom" (the Greek word, *basilea*, may also be translated "empire"—see Dan 1:20; 2:37–45; 4:31, 36, in relation to Babylon) itself indicates that Jesus saw himself posing a contrast between his community and Rome.[30] Jesus's vision reflected the heart of Torah. That such a Torah-oriented vision was revolutionary in first-century Palestine only underscores that the spirit of Empire embodied in ancient Egypt remained alive and well in the time of the Romans. Just as Torah originally countered the empire-consciousness of Egypt, so its renewal in Jesus's ministry countered the empire-consciousness of Rome.

Jesus showed how the original vision for salvation in the Old Testament remained viable. And, in doing so, he directly challenged Rome's hegemony. This challenge meant, according to the logic of retribution, that he must be punished. Due to his agenda, Jesus indeed was a revolutionary. Hence, that he died a revolutionary's death was not a miscarriage of justice in the sense that he truly was seditious in relation to the state's values. In fact, he was more of a threat to these values than the agents of Empire even realized. With Jesus's execution, two contradictory notions of peace meet head on. The Pax Romana ("peace of Rome") relies on violence to maintain its hegemonic order. "On the other hand, Jesus interrupts violence. He creates genuine 'Pax' (peace) by abolishing the notion of enmity altogether."[31]

The Death of a Political Criminal

The central conflicts in Jesus's career occurred with the Jewish religious leaders, not the representatives of the Roman Empire. Nonetheless, Rome

---

29. John Howard Yoder argues persuasively that Jesus self-consciously understood his message to be about creating such an alternative politics in *Politics*.

30. Carter, *Matthew*, 62.

31. Wengst, *Pax*, 4.

PART TWO: Jesus' Death and Salvation

crucified Jesus, using the methods employed on political offenders. And they crucified him with the title "King of the Jews" attached to his cross.

Crucifixion carried enormous symbolic weight. It was more than simply a form of execution. In using it, Roman leaders sought to humiliate those executed as fully as possible in order to emphasize their control over the people in the empire. Crucifixion "insisted, coldly and brutally, on the absolute sovereignty of Rome, and of Caesar. It told an implicit story, of the uselessness of rebel recalcitrance and the ruthlessness of imperial power. It said, in particular, this is what happens to rebel leaders."[32]

We saw above in chapter five some of the key elements in the story of Jesus's execution.[33] Jesus allegedly called himself the "king of the Jews"—a possible conclusion drawn from the use of messianic language of Jesus ("messiah" = "anointed one" = "king"). For Jesus to claim to be "king" would have been a political problem, something that would have put him on a collision course with the putative political leaders, who, of course, would have been highly sensitive to such claims as a threat to their authority.

Jesus as a political problem had the ironic impact of bringing together Pilate and Herod, as they are said previously to have been enemies (Luke 23:12). But they united in their hostility toward this feared usurper. John 19:12 reflects the general sense that Jesus threatened the political leaders with his alleged claims to be king of the Jews: the crowd cries in opposition to Jesus that "every one who makes himself a king sets himself against Caesar."

The allegations of Jesus claiming to be king stand at the center of Pilate's concern when he faces Jesus. His first question focuses the issues: "Are you king of the Jews?" Significantly, Jesus does not answer with a simple denial, even as he also makes it clear that he does not seek to be the kind of "king" who rules the Roman Empire by brute force (or the kind of client king like Herod the Great who ruled Palestine with brute force). "My kingdom is not of this world," Jesus replied to Pilate.

What might Jesus' words here have meant? Traditionally, many have read this as a statement that Jesus has no concern with the politics of the material world but advocates a purely spiritual, "otherworldly" kingdom. However, the evidence indicates otherwise. People perceived Jesus to have this-worldly political significance when he fed the multitude. They

---

32. Wright, *Jesus*, 543.
33. I am especially indebted to the provocative analysis by Rensberger, *Johannine*, 87–106.

sought him afterwards and desired to make him king (John 6). Jesus, of course, disappeared from the scene because he did not trust their motives. However, he acted so as to make people think of him as a political leader. The religious leaders feared that Jesus's activities might have enough this-worldly political significance to make the Romans intervene with the full force of the Empire and impose a military solution to the problem (John 11:45–53).

In the end, Rome executed Jesus as a political criminal.[34] Pilate's decision to crucify him reveals Jesus's death to be linked with the order the empire sought, the Pax Romana. Pilate sought a form of "peace" with this violent act. Only political offenders faced crucifixion. "In the eyes of the Roman provincial administration Jesus was a rebel who endangered the existing peace. A disturber of the peace was done away with, by legal means, by the power responsible for peace."[35]

Jesus was apolitical only if we understand "politics" strictly as power politics, the politics of the sword. However, if we understand politics more generally to mean the way human beings order their social world, Jesus was political. In fact, in this sense, just about everything he taught (e.g., turn the other cheek, don't lord it over others, share with those in need) was political. Jesus offered a political alternative to power politics directly relevant for life in the here and now.

So, when Jesus says "my kingdom is not of this world," he means "my way of ordering human social life is not of the order of political authoritarianism." Jesus still leads a kingdom, a social order in history, but one that structures social life a different way. "It is not a question of whether Jesus' kingship exists in this world but of how it exists; not a certification that the characteristics of Jesus' kingdom are 'otherworldly' and so do not impinge on this world's affairs but a declaration that his kingship has its source outside this world and so is established by methods other than those of this world."[36]

In this sense, then, Jesus did offer a direct challenge to the hegemony of the Roman Empire. According to the values of the empire, its agents were justified in deciding to punish this so-called "king." "For Pilate, to call Jesus 'the one called Christ' (Matt 27:17, 22) expresses Jesus' political threat of sedition, of claiming power without Rome's approval. And

---

34. Horsley, *Jesus and the Powers*, 187–94.
35. Wengst, *Pax*, 1–2.
36. Rensberger, *Johannine*, 97.

PART TWO: Jesus' Death and Salvation

Pilate is right. He correctly understands that the term denotes opposition to Rome's rule and so Jesus must be resisted."[37]

In a broader sense, as well, when Jesus challenged cultural exclusivism (the Pharisees) and religious institutionalism (the temple), he offered a political (not only religious) challenge. The religious leaders, as we have seen, also acted as political leaders who oversaw the social lives of the Jewish people.

Pilate, the political leader who directly represents the empire, plays a crucial role in the events surrounding Jesus's condemnation and execution. Jesus's death reflects on Pilate's practice of political authoritarianism, and as such offers insight into the Powers connected with the state. Pilate "represents and protects Rome's political, economic, military, and legal interests in an exploitative, oppressive and largely unaccountable relationship with those he governs, and as the one who has the almost untouchable power to execute Jesus."[38]

Pilate mostly wants to heap scorn on the Jews' nationalistic aspirations and thereby to solidify the standing of the Romans in their occupation of Palestine. "Pilate's intention is not to placate 'the Jews' but to humiliate them."[39] When the chief priests cry out, "We have no king but Caesar!" (John 19:15), Pilate gets what he had been waiting for. Pilate simply wanted an admission from the Jewish leaders of the supremacy of Caesar.

Pilate seems to assume that he knows the only truth that matters: "There is no king but Caesar." Maybe he did not actively desire Jesus' death. He probably simply did not care about Jesus one way or another. He, perhaps, may be seen as being deeply cynical—and close-minded—and perfectly willing to sacrifice a life such as Jesus' in order to further his own ends. In this case, Pilate's ends would seem to have been to strengthen his position in relation to the Jewish leaders.[40]

Jesus's death, then, did have significance in relation to empire's political authoritarianism. As we have seen with regard to the conflicts over the law and over the temple, Jesus directly threatened the present status quo. He provided an alternative political approach to the temple-centered and law-centered politics enforced by the power elite of his day. The

---

37. Carter, *Matthew*, 163.
38. Ibid., 157.
39. Rensberger, *Johannine*, 94.
40. Ibid., 95.

powers-that-be logically sought to make a public example of how one who advocated such an alternative would face deadly retribution.

Jesus asserted the possibility of direct access to God, not mediated by the temple. In doing so, he undercut the authority of the temple. The power of the temple establishment rested in its monopoly in providing access to God. Because people believed they had to go through the temple, they paid the temple taxes that enriched its treasury and accepted the requirements placed on them. Without that belief, the authority of the temple would collapse.

Jesus also challenged the interpretation of the law that empowered the Pharisees. He advocated an approach to the law that placed the priority on mercy and justice, not on the legalistic focus on external regulations that required experts to interpret and enforce. Just as the temple stood as a mediator between people and God, so, too, the enforcers of the law also stood as required mediators. Jesus repudiated that need.

In his openness to outsiders and welcome to those typically excluded by the guardians of the religious and cultural Powers, Jesus undercut the power of the structures that relied on strong boundary lines for their status. When Jesus did this, the leaders recognized what was at stake, and opposed him vehemently. In their opposition to Jesus, though, according to the Gospels, they reveal their opposition to God.

The "trial" before Pilate reveals the political authority's profound cynicism, close-mindedness, disinterest in the truth, and the deep-seated violence of both Pilate and the empire in general. Pilate begins the encounter when he asks Jesus if he is "the king of the Jews." As Jesus tries to explain how he understands his "kingship," and the role of seeking the truth as at the heart of the genuine kingdom of God, Pilate simply quips, "what is truth?" and then leaves, not interested in listening to Jesus. He has Jesus tortured; then uses Jesus as a pawn as he manipulates the religious leaders, and in the end sends Jesus to the most terrible of executions.

Jesus rejected the Roman Empire at a basic level. He replaced a violent, debt-oriented way of seeing with a way that started with God's mercy. Jesus presented a God "who extends grace even to the ungrateful and wicked. Jesus' message thus crossed the grain of the Roman political order not only at the level of practices and attitudes but also with respect to the most basic questions about 'how the world works.'"[41]

In the end, the largest political significance of the story of Jesus's death may be seen in how he offers a fundamental alternative to political

---

41. Green and Baker, *Recovering*, 40.

PART TWO: Jesus' Death and Salvation

authoritarianism. Jesus exposes it as a kind of anti-politics, a dis-order that gains people's trust as an idol that actually separates them from God. "There is no doubt that by Rome's rules Jesus deserves to die." But the story of Jesus' death, when read in light of his life, invalidates those rules.[42]

At the heart of Jesus's teaching in the final months of his life he instructed his followers, "take up your cross and follow me." He called them to live free from political authoritarianism, to recognize that discipleship puts them directly in opposition to the Powers of empire. That the authorities (human and spiritual) would put Jesus to death proves their idolatrous nature—and the need for people of faith to *dis*trust them.[43]

---

42. Carter, *Matthew*, 167.
43. Yoder Neufeld, *Killing*, 90–91.

NINE

Jesus Brings Salvation

THE EFFORTS OF THE various Powers coalesce in the events leading to Jesus's death.

Some religious leaders initially seek to destroy him because of his perceived threat to the Pharisees' project. They sought a higher level of holiness among the covenant community in order to sustain Jewish identity in face of pressures from the Roman Empire and other syncretistic forces.

Their hostility toward Jesus emerged in part because he entered the scene from outside the official channels. He took upon himself the authority to challenge pharisaic interpretations and standards. Even worse, he violated the holiness regulations of the oral Torah when he welcomed into his fellowship people considered by the strict interpretation to be unclean. Jesus scorned public expressions of commitment to holiness regulations such as ritual cleansing and separation from unclean persons.

Jesus also violated the Pharisees' understanding of Sabbath regulations when he healed on the Sabbath. Besides operating outside the official channels with his public ministry, claiming to operate according to a higher authority outside the Pharisees' circle, Jesus also weakened the strictness of one of the major boundary markers that the Pharisees believed separated Judaism from the threatening outside world.

To exacerbate the tensions, Jesus openly acted in ways that infuriated the Pharisees. He became more of a threat as he gained notoriety. As his following increased, the sense that he might severely undercut the whole Pharisaic project grew more acute.

Jesus did directly threaten the Pharisees' belief about the best approach Palestinian Jews should take toward life in order for their identity as people of God's promise to remain intact. Hence, the Pharisees only

PART TWO: Jesus' Death and Salvation

naturally concluded that they needed to act against this threat. Jesus threatened their ideals—strict adherence to the Sabbath laws, clear separation from unclean people, to follow cleansing rituals closely, and to submit to the oral Torah. Jesus made himself worthy of punishment because of his actions and the way his actions threatened the covenant community.

From the stories in the gospels, it seems the Pharisees may not have been in a position politically to carry out their punitive response to Jesus beyond simply heightening the level of tension. We are nonetheless made to understand that the Pharisaic response to Jesus was governed by the logic of retribution—an understanding that those who violate God's holiness deserve violence, a violence seen to be God's will.

Jesus apparently understood early on that his conflict with the religious leaders would move beyond the "on the ground" differences with the Pharisees. Luke tells us that he purposed to "turn to Jerusalem" (Luke 9:51), and that as he did so his language took on a more ominous tone. He began to speak of suffering and being killed, and to instruct his followers on their calling to take up their crosses and follow him on the same path.

This move toward Jerusalem meant a move toward a conflict with the leaders who ran the Jewish temple. The actual events that led directly to Jesus's arrest and ultimate execution were initiated by Jesus when he confronted those who exploited temple attenders for economic gain in the "cleansing of the temple" incident. Jesus joined the temple incident with other provocative acts, including a direct challenge to the temple leaders with his parable that portrayed them as rebels against God.

If Jesus's challenge to the Pharisees' cultural exclusivism threatened their project, his taking the challenge to the very heart of the Jewish religious and political establishment when he confronted the temple stood as an even bigger threat. As voiced by the chief priest, Caiaphas in John 11, Jesus's actions promised to ignite a firestorm of Roman violence should the occupiers perceive that he was gaining a following that would heighten resistance to tenuous and unpopular Roman control.

Perhaps even more seriously, Jesus's words and actions, given the popular support he gathered, threatened to undercut the legitimacy of the temple among the Jewish population. On one level, this threat challenged the power, wealth, and prestige of the ruling elite. On a deeper level, for many Jews the temple did serve as the locus for God's presence among the people.

A great deal was at stake in Judea as the leaders walked a fine line. They sought to sustain the temple traditions and also remain in good graces with the Roman occupiers. Jesus, when he challenged the legitimacy of the temple, and, more directly, its present leadership and exploitative economic policies, jeopardized the order of the entire Jerusalem culture.

So, Jesus threatened the status quo in relation to the temple and its leadership, the religious insititutionalism of the time, in parallel ways to how he threatened the status quo in relation to the cultural exclusivism of the Pharisees. In doing so, he did violate the peace surrounding the temple establishment. And, as when challenged by the Pharisees, he openly defied their authority to determine God's will, so also with the temple leaders. After he drove out the moneychangers and merchants, he told a parable that directly referred to the temple leaders as enemies of God.

So, here again we see how the logic of retribution enters the picture. Jesus violates the assumptions temple leaders would have had about how to ensure the security of the religious institution in the face of the Roman threat. He also undermines the dynamics whereby the Jewish people continue to seek God through temple processes. This violation threatens the community and its faith-system. Consequently, the violator deserves to be punished—partly to satisfy the requirements of the God of the religious institution, partly to deter others from trying to follow that path, partly (in all likelihood) to mollify the concerns of the Romans.

After the temple leaders pass their judgment on Jesus and ascertain that "justice" would require his punishment, they turn the case over to the governing officials—first (according to Luke's unique version) to the Roman client-king of Jesus' home area, Herod Antipas. Herod then sends Jesus on to the governor of the occupying Romans, Pontius Pilate.

The story that tells of Jesus before Pilate comes down to us in subtle shades. From hints in the Gospels and other sources, we know that Pilate was an ambitious official who, with little reluctance, exercised massive punitive bloodletting force. In the Gospel accounts, Pilate does not display strong antipathy toward Jesus. More, he displays disinterest and scorn. He utilizes the opportunity to use Jesus as a means to make political points over against the religious leaders. When the time comes, after Pilate has made his points, he simply orders Jesus away to be executed.

However, the broader phenomenon of crucifixion, when linked with the stated charges that Jesus claimed to be "king of the Jews" (= Messiah), points toward a direct application of the logic of retribution on the empire's part.

Jesus, when he organized a social movement with a messianic consciousness, did indeed violate the standards of order adhered to by Rome

PART TWO: Jesus' Death and Salvation

in its policies over occupied territories. Jesus posed a threat to Roman hegemony, even as he refused to take the expected path of violent insurrection. Jesus pointed to an alternative political consciousness that chose to give ultimate loyalty to Yahweh's kingship over Caesar's (the meaning of his saying to give to God that which is God's and to Caesar that which is Caesar's).

Because of Jesus's commitment to obey God, obedience that included powerful efforts to make life humane in face of all too common inhumanity, he posed a threat to the religious and political status quo. The leaders of the establishment failed to recognize the validity of Jesus's vision of the God's authentic kingdom. They served their own interests and obeyed what they understood to be God's will when they condemned Jesus to death.[1]

The logic of retribution led the Powers of cultural exclusivism to seek to destroy Jesus (even if they ultimately were unable to do so). It, in turn, led the Powers of religious institutionalism actually to take steps to arrest Jesus, try him, and turn him over to the state for punishment. However, the Powers of political authoritarianism actually took the final step and used the state's ultimate tool of punishment to execute Jesus.

The collaborative work of the Powers did eliminate Jesus. His countercultural movement that had sought a Torah-centered renewal of the way of mercy and shalom in Israel lay in ruins. We are told in general terms that Jesus's followers deserted him in his time of crisis. The representative, and deeply tragic, example of Peter drives home the depths of these ruins. Peter, who generally stood most closely with Jesus through the teachings and mighty works, and who joined Jesus on the Mount of Transfiguration, seeks desperately to separate himself from the whirlpool of retribution that swept Jesus up. Peter's denial of "ever knowing Jesus" underscores vividly that Jesus's movement approached its death as he neared his.

It would appear at this moment, also illumined by the crowds' turning from support of Jesus to cry for his death, that the Powers of death had overwhelmed the Powers of life. We do read of a tiny spark of life that remains for Jesus's community—though not so much a spark of hope for a future as simply a spark of loyalty. Several women stayed in Jesus's vicinity and remained nearby as he suffered his final breaths. They then attend to his burial.

As we know, though, death does not have the final word in this story.

---

1. Lorenzen, *Resurrection*, 244.

God Vindicates Jesus

Jesus's followers experienced his arrest and crucifixion as a devastating blow to their hopes and beliefs. As reported by Luke, they "had hoped he was the one to redeem Israel" (24:21); in the days that followed the shattering of those hopes they scattered and wandered around Judea.

Jesus's most prominent disciple, Peter, led the desertion by Jesus's followers during his trial and before his crucifixion. The followers fled Jerusalem, returning to their homes in Galilee. They concluded by the nature of his fate that God had abandoned their leader—in line with Deuteronomy 21:23: "For a hanged man is accursed by God." Jesus's mission ended up for naught. His message about God's mercy proved to be no match to the forces of true power in their society. Whatever they may have thought about resurrection, they clearly seemed not to have imagined that it would apply to Jesus.[2]

We are not told about Peter's internal processes in the time that followed his denials that he knew Jesus, but we may assume he was especially devastated—both at Jesus's apparent failure to carry through on the promise to bring a new order into being and at his own failure to stand with Jesus when everything came crashing down. The few of Jesus's followers who remained close to him—Jesus's mother Mary, Mary Magdalene, a couple of others—seem to have remained simply out of love for him and as an expression of solidarity in their grief.

Though the story tells that Jesus alluded to resurrection when he discussed his likely death, it seems clear that no one actually understood him to mean his personal resurrection prior to the general resurrection at the end of time. Even if his followers did understand him, in some sense, to have been the Messiah in the days before his execution, we have no clear evidence that anyone would have associated a messianic identity with personal resurrection. That is, the events of Easter Sunday took everyone by surprise.

After Jesus breathed his last, according to Luke's account (23:50–56), a member of the temple leadership (the Sanhedrin) named Joseph, from the nearby town of Arimathea, managed to get permission from Pilate to remove Jesus's body from the cross and bury it in a tomb he owned. The two Marys learned where the tomb was and planned, following the Sabbath, to go to it with spices and ointments to anoint Jesus's body for burial.

---

2. Ibid., 184.

PART TWO: Jesus' Death and Salvation

However, when they arrived on Sunday morning to do their work, they discovered that the stone that sealed the tomb was rolled aside and the tomb was empty. To underscore that no one expected Jesus's personal resurrection at this point, we read of the women's absolute terror. Mark's gospel ends with this terror, as they flee from the empty tomb (Mark 16:8).

Luke also tells of the women's terror, but continues to tell that the women encounter "two men in dazzling clothes" who tell them that Jesus has risen (Luke 24:5). The women then tell the other disciples what they had seen. Again, to underscore the lack of expectation of Jesus's personal resurrection, the disciples treat the women's report scornfully—"these words seemed to them an idle tale, and [the disciples] did not believe [the women]" (24:11). However, Peter does take the story seriously enough to go to the tomb himself to investigate. He finds "the linen clothes [that Jesus had worn] by themselves" but no body. He returns home, amazed (24:12).

After this, Luke tells of several direct encounters that the risen Jesus had with his followers in the days to come. The appearances culminate in the Book of Acts, when Jesus commissions his followers to witness to his message to the ends of the earth. He then ascends to be with God (Acts 1:3–11). Matthew and John also contain a number of stories of Jesus's post-resurrection appearances.

All these stories present Jesus's resurrection as his physical return. He lives with his followers for forty days before departing again. On the one hand, as mentioned above, no one expected Jesus as an individual to be raised from the dead. This was not an anticipated characteristic of the Messiah, but came as a surprise to everyone. Yet, on the other hand, such an event would not have been unimaginable for those who, as was common, believed in the eventual bodily resurrection of people of the covenant. "The evidence suggests that by the time of Jesus, most Jews either believed in some form of resurrection or at least knew it was standard teaching."[3] What surprised believers was that Jesus would have been resurrected immediately following his death, not that resurrection could happen.[4]

3. Wright, *Resurrection*, 129–30.

4. I will focus on the story of Jesus's resurrection and its meaning as part of the biblical portrayal of salvation. I will not focus on the difficulties within our modern worldview of accepting the historicity of Jesus returning to physical existence following his death. I believe that the issue of the historicity of Jesus's resurrection is beyond our ability definitively to resolve. Significantly, the evidence of the past 2,000 years seems to indicate that belief that Jesus's resurrection happened in history has not hindered Christians from virtually ignoring the main thrust of Jesus's own teaching about salvation, not to mention ignoring the anti-retributive justice message of the story of

What does this all mean?

Jesus's Resurrection Vindicates His Life

First of all, and perhaps most fundamentally, when God raised Jesus from the tomb, against all expectations, God vindicated Jesus's life as fully reflective of God's will for humankind. "By raising Jesus Christ from the dead, God revealed, confirmed, verified, and enacted the mission of the life and death of Jesus. The resurrection is God's concrete and unconditional 'yes' to Jesus' life and death."[5] When God raised Jesus, God vindicated his faithful life, including his faithfulness unto death. The story of this life does not end with his death. Contrary to how some might have seen it, Jesus's death was not an expression of God's judgment about Jesus. By raising Jesus, God reversed any negative implications people might be tempted to draw from Jesus's life.[6]

God shows God's approval of Jesus's way of life by raising him. The message of healing justice that Jesus embodied is revealed to be a message from the heart of God through this vindication and affirmation. Jesus proclaimed God's immediate presence in his ministry when he challenged the Powers and served the vulnerable. Thereby, he asserted that God's Spirit filled him and empowered him. The resurrection confirms that message as God's message.[7]

Jesus's basic strategy to bring salvation to the world included: (1) He welcomed all people even across the boundary lines of the cultural exclusivists. (2) He reiterated the core message of Torah concerning God's mercy and human responsibility. (3) He directly challenged the Powers of cultural exclusivism, religious institutionalism, and political authoritarianism and sought to loosen their holds on people's loyalties. (4) He simply proclaimed and demonstrated God's love. This strategy led to his execution in a terribly public, physically torturous, and humiliating way.

Jesus's death. That this would be so supports the conclusion that to focus on the historicity issue provides little assistance for understanding the role of Jesus's resurrection in the biblical portrayal of salvation. The relevance of the story of Jesus's resurrection for this book lay elsewhere than the affirmation (or non-affirmation) of its historicity. The meaning of Jesus's resurrection must be linked inextricably both with his life and teaching and with the events that surrounded his death. The point is the meaning of the story, not provable "scientifically" historical "facts."

5. Lorenzen, *Resurrection*, 242.
6. Goergen, *Death*, 161.
7. Herzog, *Jesus*, 250.

PART TWO: Jesus' Death and Salvation

The basic story of Jesus's life and death, should it have ended with his followers scattered and the Powers that corroborated to kill him triumphant, would not have provided much hope. In fact, the basic lesson of that story would have been that the Powers of violence, oppression, and death are more than likely to use whatever means necessary to eliminate those who challenge their hegemony. Jesus's life, morally exemplary as it may have been, would not likely have been seen to reflect God's will for human beings by many people. His life would more likely have been seen as tragic, an approach that was admirable to the few who might remember it but also a warning to all who might be tempted to follow his example. Walk this path and you too will end up abandoned.

However, the events recounted in the Gospels and the early chapters of Acts tell of a very different kind of conclusion to the story. They speak of the regathering of Jesus's followers and their transformation into people who came to believe (and live in light of the belief) that Jesus's life indeed expressed God's will—and that God did not abandon the one who lived that way.

Jesus took sides in his ministry. Had he simply withdrawn into neutrality or affirmation of the present status quo, he would never have faced crucifixion. He stood against the Powers by showing partiality toward the vulnerable, the poor, and the outcasts—to the point of putting his life in jeopardy. "By raising this Jesus from the dead, God affirmed and effectively enacted the partiality of Jesus."[8]

When Jesus died, God did not abandon him. The cross, with its extreme violence and public humiliation, called into question all the ways Jesus had stood for life in the face of death. "The resurrection counteracted the catastrophe of the cross. Jesus had been vindicated. His death did not mean rejection by God."[9]

Due to God's unprecedented act of raising Jesus, the message that emerges from the story of his life is one of hope and empowerment, not defeat and despair. The very way of God is more clearly than before revealed to be the way of welcome. God's way seeks to heal the vulnerable people of the world and stands against all types of violence and oppression. The basic thrust of Torah found concrete expression in this life—and was vindicated in Jesus's resurrection.

Jesus's resurrection brought clarity about his identity for his followers. When they realized he still lived they concluded that he was indeed

---

8. Lorenzen, *Resurrection*, 103.
9. Goergen, *Death*, 161.

Israel's Messiah. They did so not because they had a pre-existent belief that the Messiah would be resurrected. Rather, they concluded that Jesus was the Messiah because of the way the resurrection validated his life. They had hoped he was the Messiah. They had their hopes shattered, momentarily, but with the joy of Easter they realized that the Jesus they had followed, though condemned and executed, indeed truly was God's Messiah, contrary to the conclusions of the religious and political leaders.[10]

Jesus's life gave hope that healing for the world may be found through love that perseveres even in the face of profound resistance to that love. This hope found vindication in an act of God that actually went beyond the dreams of Jesus's followers.

God ratified Jesus's life and teaching by raising him. The message Jesus brought turned out indeed to be true—and would now be remembered as such. Jesus could wholeheartedly be affirmed as a true prophet who genuinely spoke for God. "It is through the raising of Jesus that God once and for all identified the whole earthly ministry of Jesus as the work of him who inaugurates the kingdom of God by his preaching and actions."[11]

Jesus's Resurrection Rebukes the Powers

When God raises Jesus from the dead, God not only endorses Jesus's way as God's way, but also rebukes the Powers that put Jesus to death. The law as interpreted and applied by those committed to cultural exclusivism, the temple as understood and defended by those committed to religious institutionalism, the state as operated by those committed to political authoritarianism all act against God's will for those structures. The law, the temple, and the state need not be forces for violence. However, in how they responded to Jesus they were.

Jesus's resurrection makes the point that his critique of those Powers for usurping God came not from some disaffected prophet railing against the status quo. Rather, Jesus's resurrection proves that Jesus's critique reflected the will of the God of the universe. Each of these Powers, in their own way, claimed to represent God and thereby justified their demand for loyalty. The law as represented by the keepers of cultural exclusivism was said to be direct communication from God. When they established and defended (with violence if necessary) strict boundary markers for the people of the covenant, the keepers of the law understood themselves to

---

10. Wright, *Resurrection*, 576.
11. Goergen, *Death*, 162.

be God's agents. They worked to sustain the people God had called in their identity as God's people—and to protect this identity fully in accordance with God's will.

These keepers critiqued Jesus's violation of the legal restrictions of work on the Sabbath and Jesus's sloppiness about who he fellowshipped with in the name of God. They believed they spoke for God when they opposed him on these fronts. Jesus, of course, strongly disagreed. Jesus claimed that, instead, he embodied God's true will.

In this conflict over who indeed did represent what God wanted, Jesus initially seemed to be the loser because of his execution. However, God acted decisively to vindicate Jesus and thereby sharply to rebuke those who understood the law to justify the violence and hostility visited on Jesus. Along with rebuking the Powers for their violence against him, Jesus's resurrection also rebukes the Powers for presenting the law in such a way that fostered violence and oppression toward all the people who allegedly did not measure up.

Jesus does seem explicitly to align himself with the law-as-it-should-be-understood. He challenges the keepers of the oral tradition because he believed they misunderstood and misapplied Torah. In this sense, then, Jesus rebukes the misuse of the law; he clearly teaches that the actual law-as-it-should-be-understood remains valid. Its application needed to be taken away from those who used is as a tool to oppress rather than liberate.

The other two structures, the temple and the state, do not command the same level of respect from Jesus. He does accept that the temple has a legitimate vocation—to be "a house of prayer for all the nations." And he is portrayed, in Luke at least, as coming from a family that respected the temple traditions. However, he seems ultimately to view the temple as extraneous to God's saving work.

So, the rebuke to the temple would seem to be more generally that such a structure typically distorts God's will. The temple could have served a legitimate role if it actually had been a welcome beacon to the nations. Since it was not, to its shame, other beacons to the nations (specifically, Jesus and his community) would arise. The temple, insofar as its leaders resisted God's work to bring light to the nations, became not the center of God's presence in the world but the center of rebellion against God.

When God raised Jesus from the dead, to borrow from Jesus's own enigmatic words as reported in John's Gospel (2:19), in a genuine sense God raised up God's authentic "temple," God's authentic beacon to the nations. Such a raising up rebukes the failed institution that had not fulfilled its vocation to be such a light.

Jesus Brings Salvation

Jesus seems to have had a somewhat parallel view of the state. On the one hand, as with his call to render unto Caesar what is Caesar's and unto God what is God's, he seems to allow for a legitimate role for human government. There are things we do rightly give to Caesar, though our ultimate loyalty belongs to God. And Jesus did have some positive encounters with members of Rome's occupying military forces.

On the other hand, the Gospels generally speak negatively about human government. They link Satan with political power in the story of Jesus's temptations in the wilderness and label the state's typical style of leadership as a type of "lording it over" that is forbidden to Jesus's own followers. Most seriously, government leadership as characterized by Pontius Pilate treated Jesus with disdain and issued the orders to put Jesus to death.

So, for Jesus not to stay dead serves to rebuke those forces that killed him. They were not all-powerful; more importantly, they actively rejected God's Son. The alternative type of politics Jesus embodied, to practice servanthood rather than to lord it over and to treat each person with respect rather than disdain, highlights the flaws in authoritarian politics. "That God had vindicated Jesus by resurrection . . . was empowering evidence that God was indeed engaged in the broader agenda of judging the empire."[12]

The ultimate rebuke toward the empire, the state turned authoritarian, came with the endorsement of Jesus as true king (Messiah) and true lord (Caesar) at the end of his life. God's raising Jesus from the dead definitively challenges those who trust in God to turn from giving higher loyalty to human kingdoms. The nations lord it over others and kill prophets. They tend to be Powers run amok that go far, far beyond their legitimate role of providing for the order and justice necessary for all human societies to function.

Rome exercised its "almighty" power in ending Jesus's life, just as it did with countless others crucified as political offenders. However, in this case the power turned out to be limited. Rome cannot keep Jesus dead. The most extreme act of violence the empire could take was unable to defeat God's purposes. "Even soldiers and stones (Matt 27:62–66), lies, imperial propaganda, and bribe money—a veritable catalog of elite manipulative strategies—can not do it (Matt 28:11–15)." The empire's governor, Pontius Pilate had the power to bring about death. In this case, though, that power was not allowed the final word.[13]

---

12. Horsley, *Jesus*, 132.
13. Carter, *Matthew*, 167.

PART TWO: Jesus' Death and Salvation

When it rebukes the Powers, Jesus's resurrection unmasks their use of the logic of retribution as antithetical to salvation. God does not operate in accord with the logic of retribution when God brings salvation to the world. Rather, the Powers operate according to this logic in trying to destroy the saving efforts of God.

When Jesus sought faithfully to live out the Torah approach that embodies salvation through care for the vulnerable ones in the community that places the mercy of God at the heart of human life, he ended up in conflict with the rules and expectations of the main cultural, religious, and political structures of his world. Because he "broke the rules," these structures responded with deadly retribution. The upholders of the law and sustainers of the temple would certainly have understood their retribution to reflect God's will.

Hence, in accord with the standards of the keepers of public order, Jesus did deserve punishment. Because of the high stakes in the Pharisaic quest to renew Israel in this time of great threat, this punishment would need to be severe. And because of the high stakes in volatile Jerusalem, seething with barely contained conflicts between the Roman occupation forces and various insurgents, Jesus's punishment when he exacerbated the tensions with his acts and words needed to be deadly. These responses followed the logic of retribution that required violators to be repaid with pain.

When God raised Jesus from the dead, God made it clear that this logic of retribution was not God's will. "God, in raising Jesus, was not merely showing that death has no power over him, but also revealing that the putting to death of Jesus showed humans as actively involved in death."[14] Jesus' resurrection makes clear that salvation is rooted in God's deep, persevering love, not God's inviolable holiness and anger that must be appeased when holiness is violated. The punishment that followed Jesus's actions, though meted out in the name of God and in the name of peace and order, ends up exposed as an act of hostility toward God.

Even with their trauma and despair, those who followed Jesus and affirmed his message came to realize that he indeed embodied God's healing justice and transformative power—precisely in his path that led to the cross. God emerged victorious against the onslaught of the violence of the Powers. "Belief in Jesus' resurrection implied that Jesus *was* God's last word."[15]

---

14. Alison, *Joy*, 117.
15. Placher, *Jesus*, 164–65 (Placher's italics).

Jesus's Resurrection Points to His Followers' Vocation

From the beginning of his public ministry, Jesus explicitly linked God's merciful gift of salvation with recipients' vocation actively to live merciful lives themselves. In so doing, he merely reinforced the message of Torah—as we have seen.

The purpose of God's gift of healing has from the time of Abraham and Sarah been to "bless all the families of the earth" (Gen 12:3). The purpose of the exodus from Egypt was for the Hebrew people to mediate God's mercy to the world (Exod 19:6). The giving of the Commandments followed directly from God's mercy (Exod 20:2), for the purpose of guiding the people in merciful living. The very heart of the Levitical holiness code emphasizes the Hebrews' responsibility to care for each other, especially the vulnerable ones in their community, but also to love the outsiders in their midst (Lev 19).

Jesus simply reemphasized this basic portrayal of God's purpose in intervening in human history: to bless all the families of the earth through a community of faith that embodies God's mercy and overtly expresses love for God and neighbor. One does not gain salvation without embodying its presence in merciful living. That is to say, the purpose of salvation is not simply to bless the recipient; the purpose is to move the blessing out into the world.

Let's look at Jesus's resurrection with the question of what the implications from it are for how we might understand the relationship between salvation and the effect of salvation on its recipients. When we do so, we should not be surprised to see that the accounts of Jesus's post-resurrection teaching emphasize that the main implication of Jesus's resurrection for his followers is not that they therefore will also be resurrected and go to heaven. Rather, the main implication is that because Jesus was raised, his followers are commissioned to go out into the world and share the good news of the presence of God's healing mercy. The Gospels say nothing along the lines of Jesus is risen, therefore you will be too. "Instead, we find a sense of open-ended commission within the present world: 'Jesus is risen, therefore you have work ahead of you.'"[16]

Jesus's resurrection provides his followers with a vocation. This vocation links with the content of Jesus's life and teaching; the resurrection does not redirect the content of the message. The resurrection itself does

---

16. Wright, *Resurrection*, 603. See also Wright, *Surprised* and *Simply*.

PART TWO: Jesus' Death and Salvation

not provide the content. The content remains what had been revealed in Torah and reemphasized by Jesus: God is merciful, join with others who have experienced God's mercy in a community of faith that will seek to bless all the families of the earth.[17]

The Gospel of Matthew emphasizes this point with Jesus's words that complete that Gospel. Matthew tells briefly of Jesus's return to his followers after his death. He met with them in Galilee, and before he left them again he gave them one last exhortation that may be understood as a kind of summary of what it now means for them that he had returned from death. "All authority in heaven and on earth has been given to me. Go therefore and make disciples of all nations, baptizing them in the name of the Father and of the Son and of the Holy Spirit, and teaching them to obey everything that I have commanded you. And remember, I am with you always, to the end of the age" (Matt 28:18–20).

This statement carries many implications for what Jesus's resurrection means for his followers. It speaks of his vindication and the final expression of his power. The Powers did not defeat him. It speaks of the main ramifications for his followers without any allusion to their own promised resurrection and eternal life (quite likely because this was already assumed by many Jews, especially those in the Pharisaic tradition; Jesus's own resurrection did not challenge that assumption). The main point, we could say, is this: now, get to work.

The primary meaning of Jesus's resurrection does not lie in the personal future of individuals after we die. The message is not, "you too can have life after death." Rather, what the story tells the believer is that God has a plan to transform the entire creation through the vocation of God's people—and you are to be part of this task. Jesus is raised, so now get involved in blessing all the families of the earth![18]

Because Jesus has been raised, he says to his followers, you may go out boldly and spread the message of the gospel to "all nations," "teaching them to obey everything that I have commanded you." Jesus will remain present with his followers as they carry out their vocation. "Witnesses are authentic and credible when their existence matches that to which they are witnessing, namely the story of Jesus as it is present in the power of the Spirit."[19]

---

17. Wright, *Resurrection*, 24–25.
18. Ibid., 649.
19. Lorenzen, *Resurrection*, 212.

Jesus Brings Salvation

So, the story links the resurrection inextricably with Jesus's life and teaching. Its meaning lies primarily in its reiteration that the content of Jesus's life does indeed reflect God's will for human beings and that the calling of Jesus's followers is to do as he did—with the great likelihood of facing the same consequences. Jesus's resurrection, according to his words in Matthew, promises that those who do take up their crosses and confront the Powers in the same way he did, will enjoy his presence with them. Because of God's faithfulness to Jesus even in death, they can count on God's faithfulness to them as well.

Luke's account in the beginning of the Book of Acts echoes many of the same points. Jesus rejoins his disciples and gathers them together for forty days of instruction (Acts 1:1–3). He promises the presence of his Spirit with them and enjoins them to "be my witnesses in Jerusalem, in all Judea and Samaria, and to the ends of the earth" (1:8). These were his last words. Here, too, then, the main significance of Jesus's resurrection for his followers is presented not in terms of their own blessing but of their vocation to share their blessing "to the ends of the earth."

We could add one other piece of evidence to link Jesus's resurrection with his followers' vocation to spread the blessing to others, the account in the Book of Acts of Paul's encounter with the risen Jesus. Acts 7–9 tell of an early Christian leader named Stephen who did take up his cross in imitation of Jesus, who echoed Jesus's direct confrontation with the Powers of cultural exclusivism and religious institutionalism, and faced deadly consequences as a result. At Stephen's execution, "a young man named Saul" was present, and "approved of their killing" Stephen (Acts 7:58; 8:1). This Saul then became a leader in the active and violent hostility expressed toward this emergent group of Jewish followers of Jesus. Then Saul met Jesus himself and had his life turned around.

With Saul's encounter with Jesus, we have a reiteration of the basic message about the ramifications of Jesus's resurrection that we saw above. Saul meets the risen Jesus and has his life turned around. (In Acts, Luke changes the name from "Saul" to "Paul," likely due to Paul's Gentile mission.) But the point is not that Paul now knows he will get to go to heaven after he dies (as a Pharisee, he already believed that); the point is that now Saul/Paul himself has a new vocation—one that he follows with unmatchable commitment for the rest of his days. This new vocation was to be part of the spreading of the message of God's healing love to the ends of the earth (significantly, the Book of Acts ends with an account of Paul spreading this message to Rome—likely with the implication that the gospel now had reached "the ends of the earth").

Jesus's Resurrection Reveals the Nature of Reality

The resurrection of Jesus indeed has cosmological ramifications. Most basically, it reveals the true nature of reality. The creator and sustainer of the universe is the one who brought Jesus back from the dead. In so doing, God underscores that as the recipient of such an unprecedented act, Jesus inextricably connects with God. When the early Christians confess Jesus as Messiah, Lord, and Son of God—titles that seem to have been fully only understood as a consequence of the resurrection—they affirm that Jesus's way is God's way, the way of the cosmos.

Jesus's resurrection verifies that love that suffers and perseveres constitutes the heart of the universe. This verification is of apocalyptic proportions. However, the nature of this apocalypse (= "revelation") is not that suddenly the world has changed. To the contrary, when linked with Jesus's life that is inextricably linked with Torah and the prophets, the revelation the resurrection gives makes clear that the universe (and God) have always been this way—Jesus's resurrection simply makes this more clear.

Jesus's resurrection, then, serves as a strong statement that the logic of retribution, based as it is on an understanding of God's holiness as inflexible, does not cohere with the nature of the cosmos. The God of Jesus, the God who revealed the divinity of Jesus through raising him from the dead, responds to violence with mercy. The God of Jesus breaks the cycle of violence that leads in turn to more (punitive) violence that thereby encourages an ever-repeating spiral of violence. As reflected in the vocation of the servant of the Lord in Isaiah's prophecy, and as reflected in the vocation of Jesus, the God of the Bible breaks this downward spiral by offering healing to sinners, not retributive violence.

God's response to the powers of death and their human agents, even after the enormity of their rebellion against God seen when they murdered God's son, is confirmed in the resurrection to be a response of reconciling love. God's nonviolence in the face of the worst of human violence underscores that God's intent in vindicating Jesus is healing not vengeance. As James Alison writes, "Jesus' resurrection is not revealed as an eschatological revenge, but as an eschatological pardon. In happens not to confound the persecutors, but to bring about a reconciliation."[20]

20. Alison, *Joy*, 98.

Jesus Brings Salvation

The resurrection of Jesus confirms the argument in this book that the biblical portrayal of salvation provides a strong basis to reject the logic of retribution. Jesus lived and taught mercy, not retribution. When he did so, he alienated the Powers of his time to the point that they joined together in deadly retributive violence. In his life and teaching, Jesus merely reiterated the basic salvation message we see in Torah and the Prophets. For God to vindicate Jesus so decisively underscores that the Powers are the enemies of salvation, not its agents. God's vindication also underscores that the universe itself rests on mercy, not retribution.

The holiness of God that transforms the world from brokenness to wholeness does so in that it heals, not that it punishes. This is the basis for our hope for wholeness.

TEN

God's Saving Justice
Paul on Salvation

THE INTERPRETER OF THE story of Jesus's life, death, and resurrection who has shaped the generations since most powerfully has been the Apostle Paul. Christian salvation theology has, for better and for worse, tended to be Pauline salvation theology. When we focus on Paul's thought in relation to the biblical salvation story, I will argue that Paul understands salvation in ways fully compatible with the Old Testament and the story of Jesus.[1]

Like his predecessors, Paul understands salvation in terms of God's merciful intention to bring healing to a broken world. Paul does not present salvation in terms of retributive justice or a mechanistic view of God's holiness and honor. Salvation, for Paul, is a gift of a relational God who seeks to free humanity from its self-destructive bondage to the powers of sin and death.

Paul's most extended argument related to salvation comes in the first three chapters of his letter to the Romans. So I will focus my attention on that argument. I do not assume that Paul has a perfectly coherent view of these matters in his various writings. But this Romans text is indeed an extended argument that does seem compatible with what he writes elsewhere. So I will treat it not as a full statement of Paul's views but as instead a reliable statement about the core of his thought.

---

1. Brondos, *Paul*, 67.

Paul's Main Concern in Romans

After various introductory comments, Paul begins his longest and most theologically complex letter with an extended discussion of salvation and justice (complementary motifs for him). This discussion runs from 1:16 through 3:31 and begins and ends with affirmations that justice and salvation go together, and their meaning has been revealed to humanity through the life, death, and resurrection of Jesus Christ.

In 1:16–17, Paul offers a thesis statement, both for the argument that concludes in 3:31 and for his letter as a whole:

> For I am not ashamed of the gospel; it is the power of God for salvation to everyone who has faith [i.e., to everyone who is faithful],[2] to the Jew first and also to the Greek. For in it the righteousness [or justice][3] of God is revealed through faith for faith [i.e., from God's faithfulness to human faithfulness]; as it is

---

2. The word translated "faith" (*pistis*) is a key term for Paul. It may be translated "faith" or "faithfulness." The meaning of this term continues to be a point of intense debate. In my view, with this term Paul has in mind a way of life that encompasses trust in God, belief in the content of Torah and the gospel of Jesus Christ, and faithful living. With this holistic meaning in mind, I prefer the term "faithfulness"—not in the sense of a legalistic and externally-oriented adherence to a certain set of rules but in the sense of an entire way of life (that imitates the way of Jesus in his ministry).

3. Here we have a second crucial term with a contested translation. Following writers such as N. T. Wright, Michael Gorman, and Neil Elliott, I prefer "justice" to "righteousness." Neither term precisely captures what Paul has in mind with *dikaiosune* and its various derivatives. However, I believe that our term "justice" more closely captures Paul's meaning than "righteousness." Regardless, part of my reason for preferring justice (and "injustice," "just," and "justification") is that consistency in translating these terms helps us discern the development of Paul's argument better than if we use the terms more common in recent translations ("righteousness," "wickedness," and "justification") that obscure the direct connection among these various concepts.

Gorman writes: "Paul says that his gospel reveals the justice of God (Rom 1:17; 3:21), God's *dikaiosyne*—a phrase often translated 'the righteousness of God.' We can certainly retain the noun 'righteousness,' but if we do, we should probably exchange the related verb 'to justify' for something like 'to rightwise,' 'to set right,' or even 'to make righteous.' However, these are all a little awkward, and they are subject to quite individualistic interpretation. So we probably do better to keep the verb 'justify' and use the noun phrase 'justice of God'—understood as God's *saving* and *restorative* justice—to remind us of the close connection between justification and justice. Moreover, 'the (saving) justice of God' reminds us also that Paul is saying that the gospel is about a special kind of divine character trait and activity—*God's* justice—that is in some sense parallel to but radically different from other kinds of justice, such as Roman justice or American justice. It is also important to note that 'the justice of God' does *not* mean God's punitive justice" (Gorman, *Reading*, 119).

PART TWO: Jesus' Death and Salvation

> written, "the one who is righteous [just] will live by faith [faithfulness]." (Rom 1:16–17)

After setting out the problems to which the gospel speaks, the nature of salvation God provides, and the universality of the human need for salvation, Paul concludes his argument in this section (Rom 3:21–31) with a sense of resolution—he emphasizes the role Jesus plays in bringing salvation:

> But now, apart from [works of the] law,[4] the righteousness [justice] of God has been disclosed and is attested by the law and the prophets, the righteousness [justice] through faith in Jesus Christ [i.e., the faithfulness of Jesus Christ[5]] for all who believe [i.e., are faithful]. For there is no distinction, since all have sinned and fall short of the glory of God; they are now justified [i.e., made whole[6]] by his grace as a gift, through the redemption that is in Christ Jesus, whom God put forward as a sacrifice of atonement [i.e., a self-sacrifice enabling reconciliation[7]] by his blood, effective through faith [faithfulness]. He did this to show his righteousness [justice], because in his divine forbearance he had passed over the sins previously committed; it was to prove at the present time that he himself is righteous [just] and that he justifies [i.e., makes whole] the one who has faith in Jesus [i.e., shares in the faithfulness of Jesus]. (Rom 3:21–31)

---

4. Paul reference to the "law" here in 3:21 echoes what he has just written in 3:20 that human beings will not be justified "by deeds prescribed by the law"—which is most likely a reference to the exclusivist, legalistic, and self-righteous approach to core commands by the "law-abiders" Paul has thoroughly critiqued beginning in Romans 2:1. So he's saying, "apart from the legalistic approach to the law."

5. Much of the debate about faith/faithfulness centers on this verse. As indicated by the intensity of the argument, it seems clear that the appropriate translation here cannot be determined strictly on grammatical and philological grounds. We need to look mostly at bigger theological concerns and the general development of Paul's argument in this section. I choose the "faithfulness of Jesus Christ" option because it makes better sense in the context of Paul's logic here to understand that what is crucial is how Jesus himself embodied the life of faithfulness—and is our model for what the life of God's justice looks like. Jesus's faithfulness makes it possible for his followers to be faithful. See Hays, *Faith*.

6. This is a paraphrase emphasizing that "justice," "just," and "justify" are relational and restorative terms more than legalistic, forensic, and impersonal terms. The justified person in Paul's account is a person who has been made whole through trust in and following after Jesus and finds healing from brokenness, alienation, and injustice (as Paul himself had)—more than a person "declared" innocent or worthy of God's love as a legal fiction.

7. See the discussion below.

IDOLATRY: THE PROBLEM PAUL ANALYZES

So, precisely what problem does Paul believe humanity needs to be saved from? The term he uses most often in our passage is "sin." From a careful reading of Romans 1:18—3:20, we may find at the heart of the sin problem for Paul the dynamic of idolatry, people giving ultimate loyalty to entities other than God. Paul describes two distinct kinds of idolatry here.

These may be characterized as the idolatry of the nations and the idolatry of the covenant people—or, we could say using Paul's language here, the idolatry of the Greeks and the idolatry of the Jews (recognizing that by "Jews" here Paul most likely has in mind Jewish members of the Roman assembly of followers of Jesus). Both types of idolatry put something in the place of the merciful God Paul has learned to serve through linking his life with the faithfulness of Jesus. The idolatry, in both cases, produces injustice and violence.

Idolatry I: The Nations (Rome)

After the introduction to his argument in 1:16-17, Paul turns to the big problem. He analyzes how people move from the rejection of truth to lack of gratitude to trust in created things to out of control lust to injustice and violence. This dynamic itself manifests "wrath"—not direct intervention by God but God "giving them up" to a self-selected spiral of death.

As Paul will make clear in Romans 5:1-11 and 11:32, God's intentions toward humanity are salvific. Hence, we make a mistake if we interpret "wrath" as God's punitive anger directly aimed at people God has rejected. We should understand "wrath" in relation to the gospel. "Wrath" refers to how God works in indirect ways to hold human beings accountable, "giving them up" to the consequences of their giving their loyalty to realities other than life and the giver of life.[8]

In 1:17 we have the salvific "revelation" of God's justice. In the next verse, we have the suppression of truth that leads to the "revelation" of

---

8. Dunn, *Theology*, 42: "For Paul 'the wrath of God' denotes the inescapable, divinely ordered moral constitution of human society, God's reaction to evil and sin. God's righteousness as creator, the obligation appropriate to him as creator, has determined that human actions have moral consequences. Thus the consequence of disowning the dependence of the creature on the creator has been a futility of thought and a darkening of experience (1:21). Focusing reverence on the creature rather than the creator has resulted in idolatry, debased sexuality, and the daily nastiness of disordered society (1:22-31). God's wrath, we might say, is his handing over of his human creation to themselves."

PART TWO: Jesus' Death and Salvation

wrath. With "justice," people see created things for what they are (pointers to the creator), not as false gods worthy of ultimate loyalty. Such sight leads to life. With "wrath," the act of giving loyalty to created things results in truth being suppressed and a spiral of lifelessness.

God has built within creation itself directives that should lead to "justice" (linking "justice" here with a basic stance of gratitude towards life that encourages kindness, generosity, and wholeness in relationships). Many people have not lived in gratitude (1:22) and as a consequence brokenness characterizes much of human life.

The "revelation" of wrath (1:18) concerns God giving those who trust in idols up to descent into self-destructive behavior (1:24). People make an "exchange." They trade their humanity as God's children for "images" that resemble created things. This trade leads to an exchange of justice for wrath, an exchange of life for death, a spiral of injustice. This need not happen. God has shown the world what is needed. "What can be known about God is plain to them, because God has shown it to them . . . , seen through the things God has made" (1:19–20). However, when human beings exchange trust in "the glory of God" for trust in images that resemble created things they lose their ability to discern God's revelation. Paul echoes Psalm 115, where people become like the lifeless images they worship.

When created things are worshiped they no longer reveal the God who stands behind them and gives them their meaning. The paradigmatic expression of this dynamic for Paul is how inter-human love—which indeed reveals God in profound ways—comes to be reduced to lust, and relationships become unjust, broken, contexts for alienation.

Paul writes that "for this reason" (1:26) God gave those consumed by lust (the "lusters") "up to degrading passions." When they exchange trust in God for worship of created things, the lusters are led into "unnatural" behavior. What is unnatural is when intimate human relationships become occasions for death and alienation instead of life and wholeness.

As Neil Elliott has suggested, Paul may have in mind the recent history of the Roman emperor's court and its prolifigate sexual behavior that had scandalized many. When the emperor Caligula went down, many understood this to be an act of cosmic vindication.[9] Paul sees lust as the problem (not homosexuality per se) because of how it diminishes humanness, reflects worship of "degrading passions" rather than God, distorts the revelation of God in the human, and fosters injustice.

---

9. Elliott, *Liberating*, 194–95; and Elliott, *Arrogance*, 78.

In 1:28, Paul once more refers to the dynamic where "God gives them up," in this case to a "debased mind." They cannot see reality as it is. The revelation of God's love becomes "wrath" for them rather than whole-making justice. When people trust in things other than God, their ability to think and perceive and see and discern is profoundly clouded.

Paul refers to "things that should not be done" that result from "the debased mind" that follows from "God giving them up" (1:28) that happens when people "exchange the glory of the immortal God for images resembling a mortal human being or birds or four-footed animals or reptiles" (1:23). The reference to "things that should not be done" points ahead to the vice list in 1:29-31, with a wide-ranging description of the injustice and violence of those who trust in creation rather than the creator—paradigmatically, the Roman Empire's leaders.

In this discussion of idolatry in 1:18-32, Paul wants his readers to see their would-be Benefactors (the rulers of the empire) as God's rivals. The Benefactors claim to act on behalf of the gods and for the sake of "peace" (they use terms such as "Good News," "Savior," and "Peace of Rome"). They desire people's trust and loyalty. These Benefactors are actually unjust and violent. Rome's "peace" is actually based on the sword—it is a counterfeit peace.[10]

When people worship "created things," the progression moves inexorably toward injustice—suppression of truth (1:18), refusal to give thanks to God (1:21), darkened minds (1:21), the exchange of God's glory for images (1:23), being "given up" to degrading lusts (1:24), the worship of the creature rather than creator (1:25), degrading passions (1:26), shameless acts (1:27), debased minds (1:28), and profound injustice and violence (1:29-31).

The Powers that exploit this progression into idolatry replace God as the center of people's lives and as the objects of worship. In doing so, they distort people's minds so that instead of recognizing that those who practice such injustice deserve judgment people instead "applaud" their unjust Benefactors (1:32).

Idolatry II: Works of the Law

Paul now adds a critique of the way people in the covenant community embrace idolatry in relation to the law. Following James Dunn, I will use

---

10. Elliott, *Arrogance*, 78-83

the term "works of the law" for what Paul criticizes here—in distinction from Torah in and of itself, which Paul (like Jesus) embraces.

Dunn sees Paul's use of the term "works of the law" in Galatians 2:16 ("We know that a person is justified, not by the works of the law but through faith in Jesus Christ") as helping us distinguish between Paul's critique of how his opponents understood the law and his own affirmation of the continuing validity of the law (Romans 13:9: "The commandments, 'You shall not commit adultery; You shall not murder; You shall not steal; You shall not covet'; and any other commandment, are summed up in this word: 'Love your neighbor as yourself' ").[11]

Behind Paul's critique here is his own earlier commitment to works of the law as boundary markers. He protected the "true faith" with extreme violence. Paul as Saul the Pharisee, before he met Jesus, had made an idol of works of the law in a way that made him just as guilty of injustice as the leaders of the Roman Empire in his harsh persecution of Jesus's followers.[12]

Paul's concern in 1:18-32 centers on idolatry and the need to be free from the bondage idolatry fosters. If one points fingers at other idolaters while denying one's own tendency to worship idols, one will never find such freedom. Hence, "the very same things" (2:1) that those who point fingers (the "judgers") are guilty of are themselves forms of idolatry. Paul experienced his own exchange—God for the boundary markers that required a violent defense. Paul's "degrading passions" were not sexual but ideological—and led to the same result, violence.

The words Paul quotes in 2:2, "we know that God's judgment on those who do such things is in accord with truth," come from the judgers alluded to in 2:1. When they embrace God's judgment on others, the judgers actually condemn themselves because they too are unjust. They mistakenly believe that when they condemn the idolatry of 1:18-32 while they remain idolaters themselves they have God on their side. When they claim that their judging accords with "truth" (2:2), the judgers actually align themselves with the "debased minds" who worship the creation rather than the creator and in doing so actually suppress the truth (1:18).

---

11. Dunn, "New Perspective," 213 (Dunn's italics): "Paul's objection is not to *ritual* law, but to exclusivist or particularist attitudes which came to expression in and are reinforced by certain rituals. Not the rituals as such, but the attitude behind them, expressed typically as a 'boasting' in works of the law (Rom 2:17-23; 3:27ff.)."

12. For a discussion of Paul's conversion from violence to nonviolence, see Gorman, "While."

God's Saving Justice

Paul had committed his own acts of violence in the name of the "truth."[13] However, after he met Jesus he learned that violence is always a sign of falsehood. The truth he thought he served was actually a lie. The works of the law that he defended turned out to be idolatrous. So, as a judger he was just as much of an idolater as the lusters who ran the Roman Empire.

Paul makes affirmations about God in 2:4 that oppose all forms of idolatry. The antidote to idolatry is recognition of God's unconditional and abundant mercy. God's kindness comes first, then comes repentance.

The revelation of "the day of wrath" (2:5) may be understood in terms of the revelation of the true path to God through the witness of Jesus. This revelation illumines how the various idolatries bring death. When Paul writes of "God's just judgment" in 2:5 he uses the same terms translated as "God's decree" in 1:32. The "decree" is what the lusters know but ignore in their injustice. The "judgment" is what will be revealed to the judgers "on the day of wrath." This parallel usage implies that the injustices of 1:29–31 and the judging of 2:1–2 are the same kind of phenomena; both blind people to God's authentic justice. By denying the life-giving justice of God, both types of idolaters condemn themselves to experience this justice as wrath.

Condemnation comes to everyone who does evil—Jew first and also Greek (2:9). The description of the two types of idolatry encompasses all kinds of people. Crucially, though, Paul immediately follows this terrifying word with a word of hope. Salvation also comes to all kinds of people, Jew first and also Greek (2:11). Salvation enters through God's chosen people and spreads to all the families of the earth. The judgers (such as Saul the Pharisee) forgot that salvation for them was intended to lead to salvation for all, that God chose them in order to bless all the families of the earth (Gen 12:1–3).

Paul associates "sin," a term he introduces in 2:12, with the idolatry he describes. He sets out the basic dynamic in 1:21: sin and idolatry arise when people live without trust and gratitude, become futile in their thinking and darkened in their minds, and practice injustice and move toward lifelessness. "Sinning under the law" (2:12) seems basically to mean to make an idol of some rule or other and using it to underwrite injustice (as with Saul the Pharisee).

---

13. Gorman, *Inhabiting*, 94.

PART TWO: Jesus' Death and Salvation

Paul argues that the law itself is not the problem.[14] He affirms in 2:14 that some Gentiles "do the law" even while ignorant of the written Torah. They do it "naturally," the idea linking back to Paul's allusion in 1:18–32 that it is *unnatural* to worship the creature, to be ungrateful, to practice injustice, and to exchange the creature for the creator.

The faithfulness or justness or authentic obedience of Gentiles who do not know the written Torah shows that "what the law requires is written on their hearts" (2:15: to trust God, to live in gratitude, to do justice). This comment echoes Paul's earlier affirmation that "ever since the creation of the world God's eternal power and divine nature, invisible though they are, have been understood and seen through the things God has made" (1:20).

In 2:23–24, Paul asserts that "boasters in the law" dishonor God. For the judgers, the law had become a boundary marker. As such, the law (reduced to works of the law) had become a tool for violence. It had become a basis to assert a cosmic division between circumcised and uncircumcised, rather than part of an affirmation of "the fundamental solidarity-in-difference of Jews and Gentiles as together creatures of the one God."[15] When those charged with witnessing to God's justice for the benefit of all instead witness to injustice, it is as if they are not part of God's covenant people at all; their "circumcision has become uncircumcision."

Paul asserts that some who are physically "uncircumcised" do indeed "keep the requirement of the law" (2:26), implying that "the requirements of the law" boil down to living with gratitude, generosity, and justice—or, as Paul writes later in Romans, the law boils down to loving one's neighbor (13:8–10). "Real circumcision is a matter of the heart," Paul writes, in the sense that one's actual circumcision is not about a physical ritual but about one's genuine commitment to God's love and justice, a commitment that finds expression in one's actions.

Paul does insist that we are "all" under the power of sin (3:9), but in saying this he is not so much asserting that each individual is (he has clearly stated that some do keep the law) as arguing that the Jews and Gentiles are equally liable to be under the power of sin (equally likely to be either lusters or judgers).

Later in Romans, Paul illumines further the problems with the idolatry of works of the law in his agonizing reflections in chapter seven. As Robert Jewett suggests, we best read Paul here to reflect his own experience

---

14. Brondos, *Paul*, 81.
15. Harink, "Paul," 376.

as one who committed terrible acts of violence in the name of what turned out to be an idolatrous view of the law.[16]

The very act of striving to follow the letter of Torah leads to living in the "flesh," unleashing one's "sinful passions" (7:5). These sinful passions led to Paul's "zeal" when he practiced violence against followers of Jesus (Gal 1:14; Phil 3:5-6). When Paul writes, "the very commandment that promised life proved to be the death of me" (7:10), he has in mind how he applied the law in ways that deeply hurt others and that way experienced death himself. No wonder he was so profoundly shattered when he met Jesus and realized that the one he had persecuted was truly the Messiah of the God he had sought so zealously to serve.

Paul had staked his life on his responsibility zealously to enforce the "truths" of Torah—and ended up becoming a murderer who violated the truth of Torah as profoundly as anyone possibly could. Paul states flatly, "sin, seizing an opportunity in the commandment, deceived me and through it killed me" (7:11). This truly happened in Paul's own life. His embrace of the legalistic approach to Torah coupled with an embrace of the need to enforce works of the law with violence, and opened him to be dominated by the very power of sin he thought he was opposing.

The law itself is "spiritual." It is of the Holy Spirit. However, when Paul's zealotry sought to use it as a basis for injustice, he showed himself to have been "sold into slavery under sin." As a consequence, Paul was utterly bamboozled concerning the true message of Torah. "I do not understand my own actions. For I do not do what I want, but I do the very thing I hate." What he wanted to do was serve the God of Israel, faithfully practice Torah, and live a holy life. However, he actually worshiped idols instead of God. His mind was darkened. He ended up not serving God but doing the opposite ("the very thing I hate"); he served an idol.

The more "successful" Saul the Pharisee was in persecuting and "faithfully" following his rigorous path, the more he sinned. This turned out to be the wrong path. It set him actively opposing God. He indeed sought to follow the true and good law of God—and was shockingly deceived. When his eyes were opened (Jesus's revelation to him of Jesus's true identity), Paul realized that the "true Torah" (as love of neighbor, 13:8-10) condemned what he was doing.

16. Jewett, *Romans*, 436: "The 'sinful passions that came through the law' are to be differentiated from sensual passions or human weaknesses because the allusions to Paul's own previous experiences as a competitively zealous Pharisee and an opponent of the church seems so clear. How else is one to explain the extraordinary role of law in promoting sinful passions rather than, as traditionally believed, holding them in check?"

Paul dwelt in a "body of death" (7:24), both in the sense of being the cause of death to others and of being spiritually dead himself. He needed to be "rescued." He needed outside intervention to save him when he did not even realize he needed to be saved. He was subsumed in a "body of death." However, the rescue came, which is the story of Paul's gospel.

"Thanks be to God through Jesus Christ our lord," he concludes chapter seven (7:25). Jesus intervened and shook Paul's world to the foundations. Through this rescue, Jesus made his own identity clear: God's Messiah, the one worthy of trust who reveals the meaning of Torah. When Paul trusted in Jesus and realized that Jesus's God was his God, Paul did find liberation from the bondage that had turned him into a murderer. As a consequence, he was transformed from an exclusivist persecutor to a person "enriched by otherness."[17]

The Universality of the Dominance of Sin

In his critique of the idolatry of the judgers, Paul does not reject Judaism. He alludes to Abraham and Sarah's calling when he answers his rhetorical question, "then what advantage has the Jew?" (3:1), with an emphatic "much, in every way" (3:2). They were "entrusted with the oracles of God" (3:2)—that is, they were given Torah and the calling to bless all the families of the earth (Genesis 12:3). That some of Abraham and Sarah's descendants have been unfaithful does not annul the faithfulness of God. God's promise to bless all the families of the earth through the people of the covenant remains in effect (Paul makes this point in Romans 9–11).[18]

As bad as the idolatry of those who use Torah to justify sacred violence was, Paul makes clear here that this expression of sin is matched by the sin of the idolaters who give their loyalty to the Roman Empire. People in both categories, Jew and Greek, are all under the power of sin.[19] Paul underscores this point in 3:10-18 with a series of scriptural proof texts that lay out the universality of bondage to the power of sin. This bondage creates the basic problem that humanity—Jew and Greek—needs salvation from.

Paul concludes his critique in 3:20: "For no human being will be justified in his sight [a quote from Psalm 143:2] by deeds prescribed by the law, for through the law comes knowledge of sin." That is, no one will be

---

17. Volf, *Exclusion*, 51.
18. Jewett, *Romans*, 243.
19. Wright, *Justification*, 175.

made whole and gain salvation by using the letter of the law as the basis for condemning others in order to strengthen their own standing before God. Paul here in a nutshell captures the folly of the path he himself had taken with his sacred violence against the followers of Jesus. He thought he served God; in fact he assured his alienation from God.

The true law exposes the sins of us all. It helps us see when we exchange love for neighbors with trust in idols. At such times, instead of practicing justice we instead practice injustice and violate God's will for our lives. This problem characterizes Jews and Greeks alike. This is the problem: the universality of the domination of the "power of sin" (3:9) over all groups of people. Being a member of the empire does not save one—nor does being a member of the religious institutions that had emerged around Torah. In fact, when such membership fosters injustice it has become a curse, a ticket to alienation and idolatry.

Paul's logic here follows this path: humanity is trapped in bondage to systems of injustice that claim to be our Benefactors and agents of God's will. This claim is false; such systems (be they Roman or Jewish) enslave rather than liberate. We choose this bondage when we ignore God's kindness and respond to what God does for us with ingratitude rather than gratitude. This ingratitude toward God is manifested in human beings worshiping created things rather than the Creator. This worship of created things may involve empire idolatry or it may involve Torah legalism and violent protection of the boundary lines of the religious institution.

In making this choice to worship created things we evoke "wrath" (Rom 1:18). Paul links "wrath" directly with God's justice, in some sense portraying them as two sides of one coin—God reveals justice to faithful people; God reveals "wrath" to idolaters. Paul portrays this "wrath" as neither personal and punitive anger on God's part nor as impersonal principles of holiness and retribution—both in tension with God's mercy. Rather, "wrath" refers to the process of God "turning us over" that allows us to worship as we please with self-inflicted consequences.

Paul illustrates this problem as he himself experienced it in Romans seven.[20] He cries out in frustration, the good that I would do (to enforce the law, keep the faith community pure, and thereby honor God) turns out to lead to evil. The trust in the law was trust in it as a basis for hating the neighbor instead of trust in the merciful God behind the law who commands love of neighbor (including enemies). God's wrath was seen in how this process of idolizing works of the law led to alienation and

---

20. Jewett, *Romans*, 266–67.

PART TWO: Jesus' Death and Salvation

death instead of life. As Paul reports his experience in chapter seven, he concludes with the core question relating to salvation: Who will deliver us (7:24)? How might we find liberation, redemption, transformation, salvation? What is the good news in our present darkness?

THE RESOLUTION: JUSTICE APART FROM WORKS OF THE LAW

Paul answers the question about deliverance in 3:21–31. These verses provide a remarkable (and dense) summary of how he understands salvation—that parallels what we have seen in the Old Testament and in the Gospels. In brief, like the Old Testament and Gospels, Paul also emphasizes that salvation has simply to do with turning to God and trusting in God's mercy.

The resolution to the problem of bondage to the power of sin comes "apart from law," i.e., the law idolatry Paul has just critiqued. He ended his critique by stating that justification will not happen based on "works of the law" (3:20). It will not be circumcision or zealotry in defense of the standards of the covenant community nor the proclamation of one's identity as an Israelite nor ritual purity and over-againstness vis-à-vis Greeks that will resolve the problem.

The resolution has to do with the justice of God, going back to the beginning of Paul's argument where he proclaims that the justice of God is revealed in the gospel of salvation (1:16–17). God's justice is not something to fear or to counter-pose to God's mercy. It makes whole and brings salvation as a gift. In relation to the problem Paul has described, we could see God's justice as God's initiative to liberate human beings from bondage to the powers of sin.

This justice has been disclosed. The Greek word, *pephanerotai*, echoes the term used in 1:17, *apokalypsis*. God has disclosed or revealed the truth—the very thing idolaters suppress (1:18). God will not be deterred by human obstinacy. Humanity needs a breakthrough that will empower us to see the truth of God. In seeing this truth, humanity will be able to understand God truly, the human situation truly, and creation truly—all bound together by God's love.

This disclosure that Paul will describe "is attested by the law and prophets." This helps us understand Paul's intentions. He puts his understanding of the gospel in continuity with the biblical story—"the law and prophets" literally means the entire Bible. We must remember this continuity as we go in to interpret Paul's words here. Whatever he goes on to say, he insists that his gospel directly links with the Bible's message.

Paul affirms Torah (when properly understood as a gift from God calling for love of neighbor and not as a basis for sacred violence). The contrast that he has in mind, then, does not center on a contrast between "Judaism" and "Christianity" or a contrast between Torah and mercy. Rather, Paul means to contrast gratitude and wrath, to contrast justice and injustice. Torah as properly understood sides with gratitude and justice over against wrath and injustice. "Torah witnesses to the purpose of human life for both the circumcised and the uncircumcised, which is to do the good that Torah itself commands (Romans 2) and the gospel enables."[21]

The "disclosure" that Paul will now turn to, then, does not disclose a new economy of salvation over against the old economy of the Old Testament. Rather, the disclosure reiterates what has been disclosed from the start (this point will be made clear in chapter four when Paul presents pre-circumcision Abraham as the model of saving faithfulness).

The justice of God is seen in Jesus's faithfulness (3:22).[22] Jesus discloses the true nature of God, the path to life, and the agenda of the Powers that seek to separate humanity from God's love (Romans 8:38-39). Jesus's faithfulness breaks the illusions that make idolatry possible (both in relation to empire and in relation to Torah-legalism). The contrast could not be greater for those with eyes to see. Jesus's path led to his being accused, condemned, and executed by the leaders of the Empire in Jerusalem and the leaders of the religious institutions—all of whom claimed to be Benefactors but turned out to be tyrants (see Mark 10:42-45).

God's justice disclosed through Jesus brings salvation "for all who believe." What Paul refers to here is not so much doctrinal assent as the connection of heart and soul with Jesus and his way.[23] Those "who believe" are those who see Jesus and God for who they are, who see the Powers for what they are, and who commit their lives to the path of justice set out in Jesus's life and enabled now by the presence of Jesus's Spirit (see Rom 8:9-11). This path involves trust in God alone as the true God. Jesus models this trust when he rejects both empire and religious institutionalism in the wilderness shortly after his baptism (Luke 4:1-13).

---

21. Harink, "Paul," 377.

22. Wright, "Romans," 470.

23. This motif of participation in Jesus is central in Michael Gorman's account of Paul's view of salvation in Gorman, *Inhabiting*.

PART TWO: Jesus' Death and Salvation

This healing justice is made available to everyone "without distinction" since everyone needs it ("all have sinned and fall short of the glory of God," 3:23). The point here, again, is not about every single individual. Rather, Paul emphasizes that neither "citizenship" in the empire nor in ethnic Israel saves anyone—both communities are in bondage to the power of sin, as seen in their dependence upon injustice and violence to sustain their boundary lines and identity.[24]

The key point in this passage, though, is what follows: "all . . . are now justified by God's grace as a gift, through the redemption that is in Christ Jesus" (3:24). Paul earlier asserted the universality of bondage to sin in order now to assert the universality of liberation from this bondage. Just as God called Abraham and Sarah as a gift, just as God liberated the Hebrews from slavery in Egypt as a gift, just as God gave Torah as a gift, just as God sustained the promise through exile as a gift, so too now Paul reminds his readers of God's mercy through the ministry of Jesus Christ as a gift—a gift that brings redemption from bondage to the power of sin.

Jesus himself lived free from this bondage. He did not serve idols but lived in grateful service to the true God, worshiping the Creator rather than created things. In doing so, he exposed the Powers for the false gods they are. His self-sacrificial love even in the face of the deadly violence of the Powers stood at the center of this exposure. And, crucially, God vindicates Jesus's faithfulness by raising him from the dead, making the nature of true faithfulness clear for all with eyes to see. In this clarity lies the hope for liberation from bondage to the power of sin.

Paul emphasizes that God initiates the needed liberation—strictly out of God's mercy.[25] Just as God "put forward" Moses and freed the Hebrews from slavery in Egypt, Paul asserts that God "put forward" Jesus to free Jew and Greek alike from enslavement to the power of sin. God is not the recipient of this act but the doer of it. In no sense, according to Paul's argument, does the liberation come from God's own retributive justice. Rather, the liberation comes as a gift that a merciful God gives as an expression of God's restorative justice.

God puts Jesus forward as a "sacrifice of atonement" (3:25). What does Paul mean by "sacrifice of atonement" (Greek: *hilasterion*)? The meaning of this term continues to be highly contested.[26] Let's note here some points about the broader context of Paul's thought (with the assumption that his

---

24. Jewett, *Romans*, 279.
25. Wright, "Romans," 471.
26. Ibid., 474.

meaning here is not to be determined by focusing on this one isolated term). God is responsible for this saving action, the one who offers the sacrifice (not the one who receives it).

How is Jesus a "sacrifice"? Not as a blood offering to appease God's anger or honor or holiness but as one who freely devoted his own life to persevering in love all the way to the end. Thus, the "sacrifice" should be understood as Jesus's self-sacrifice expressed in faithful living, his way of being in the world. How does Jesus's self-sacrifice act as an "atonement"? Jesus's self-sacrifice reveals God's saving justice (that is, God's mercy) that is available to everyone (Jew first and also Gentile) with eyes to see and responsive hearts.

The "atonement" (at-one-ment, reconciliation) is not a sacrifice to God that satisfies God's neediness (that God is not needy for sacrifices has been established back with Ps 50). The "atonement" illumines the truth that humanity has suppressed (Rom 1:18), truth that helps (or allows) sinners to see God's welcoming mercy clearly. This illumination makes "one-ment" with God possible—not from God's side (God has always welcomed sinners) but from the human side (when we see accurately we will be freed from our fearfulness toward God that leads to ingratitude and trusting in idols instead of God).[27]

The "sacrifice of atonement" is given "by Jesus' blood" (3:25). What does "blood" signify here? Does God after all need a blood-sacrifice to satisfy God's anger or honor or retributive justice or sense of "evenness"? Hardly. Since God never did need or even desire such a sacrifice, it is impossible to imagine that Paul has such a sacrifice in mind here.

We have seen in our earlier chapters that the Old Testament makes it clear that God does not need offerings—God is not "hungry" (see Ps 50:1–15 and various anti-sacrificial references in the prophets). Rather, the need for offerings rests on the human side. Offerings are necessary to concretize for the human imagination the reality of God's mercy and the expectations God has for life lived in light of that mercy. Jesus himself made it clear that God desires works of mercy rather than ritual sacrifices that take the place of such works (see his quotes of Hosea in Matt 9:13 and 12:7, "I desire mercy not sacrifice," and his actions of bypassing the sacrificial temple system with his direct offer of forgiveness).

Paul has also made it clear in Romans 1–3 that God's justice expresses God's merciful will for salvation, not God's retributive inclination to punish. Paul does mention "wrath," but as I suggest above, we best see this

---

27. Jewett, *Romans*, 285–86.

PART TWO: Jesus' Death and Salvation

"wrath" as itself an expression of God's forbearing love that allows human beings to choose to worship created things and become like them.

So, then, what does Paul mean by "blood" here? It seems to symbolize Jesus's life of self-giving, giving to the point of being killed by the Powers. This "self-sacrifice" by "blood" is "effective through faithfulness" Paul states (3:25). That is, Jesus's faithfulness makes the sacrifice as he faithfully devotes his life to love of God and neighbor; our faithfulness in "taking up our cross" links us with Jesus's self-sacrificial way of life and, hence, with his path of freedom from bondage to the powers of sin.

God "did this" (i.e., "put forward Jesus") to show God's justice. Our sense of what Paul means here, of how "putting forward Jesus" expresses God's justice, will be determined by how we define "justice" in this broader Romans passage. Note, in 1:16–17 Paul links the revelation of God's justice directly with the bringing of salvation. Here in 3:21–24, Paul links the disclosure of God's justice directly with sinners being justified (made whole, saved) by God's grace.

Clearly, the revelation of God's justice in Jesus has to do with God's healing and restorative work. So, God "put forward Jesus" out of love in order to heal—not out of mechanistic holiness that requires a violent sacrifice in order to satisfy God's honor or turn away God's anger. Jesus's work expresses restorative justice, not retributive justice. This "showing of God's justice" leads to the direct consequence of reconciliation between former human enemies (Jew and Greek) and between God and God's human enemies (see Rom 5:1–10).

Paul now adds that in God's "divine forbearance" God had "passed over the sins previously committed" (3:25). God cares about healing more than punishment or more than having God's honor satisfied. Jesus's own faithfulness had at its heart the welcome of sinners and the forgiveness of sins apart from temple sacrifice or rigorous adherence to Pharisaic oral laws. In this welcome, Jesus embodied God's "divine forbearance."

By "putting forward Jesus," God proves that God is "just" (3:26). "Justice" here is to make things right, to restore relationships, to create wholeness—not to punish, as in retributive justice. Jesus's own faithfulness in his life models what God's justice is like. As a "just" God, God heals and makes whole ("justifies") those people who share in Jesus's faithfulness (3:26)—that is, those who trust in and identify with Jesus's own faithfulness, making his way their way.

Because God's mercy serves as the basis for salvation, we have no reason to "boast" (3:27). By "boasting," Paul has in mind the kinds of attitudes and behaviors that characterized his own life as a judger (or, we could say, a law-idolater). These included exclusivist attitudes, practicing sacred violence, and self-righteousness about his ethnic and religious identity.[28] These were possible because of a sense of superiority that is contrary to the appropriate response to God's mercy shown to sinners (which include Jews first but also Greeks).

The "boasting" that is excluded here followed directly from trusting in works of the law. These works are the opposite of faithful works—boundary maintenance with "necessary" violence as opposed to love of neighbor (friend and enemy). The law that excludes boasting is the "law of faith" (or, we could say, the law of faithful acts of love and generosity). The contrast Paul makes here has to do not with a distinction between ethics and belief ("works" versus "faith") but between exclusivism versus inclusive, healing, restorative justice.

Paul offers an important summary statement that requires careful unpacking in light of what we have seen as his message in Romans 1–3: "A person is justified by faith apart from works prescribed by the law" (3:28). By "justified by faith" Paul means how we are made whole through faithfulness. This faithfulness involves trusting in Jesus in such a way that one commits oneself to following Jesus's way of life. The desire and ability to follow this way of life come from having hearts transformed by God's love. By "apart from works prescribed by the law" Paul means apart from the boundary marking idolatrous legalism that appropriates Torah for nationalistic and exclusivistic purposes that, in turn, lead to injustice and "sacred" violence.[29]

Paul's notion of justification includes at its heart reconciliation among human beings.[30] Paradigmatically for Paul, justification leads to Jews reconciled with Gentiles, joined together in one community of followers of Jesus's way. Paul's rhetorical question in 3:29 confirms this interpretation ("Is God the God of Jews only?"). God is not simply the God of Jews. The election of Abraham and Sarah happened in order that their descendants bless all the families of the earth, not only the "chosen people." God is God of Gentiles also. This assertion of Paul's was not an innovation; he insists that this universality of God's healing love is the true message of Torah and the prophets.

---

28. Wright, "Romans," 480.
29. Ibid., 481.
30. Gorman, *Inhabiting*, 80.

Paul concludes that God justifies (makes whole) in only one way (3:30). God justifies on the ground of faithfulness. This is true for circumcised and uncircumcised alike (a point emphasized in Paul's discussion of Abraham's justification in chapter four). The emphasis on one method for justification reiterates what Paul wrote earlier: Justification is offered by God's justice apart from [works of] the law but attested to by the law and prophets (3:21). Justification has to do with faithfulness (Jesus's and his followers'), not with ethnic identity, relation to the empire, a punitive sacrifice, or doctrinal belief.

Justification and salvation are about a living relationship with God that is manifested in love of neighbor. Paul makes this affirmation clear in 13:8–10 where he again summarizes Torah. Jesus famously, of course, already made this understanding clear when he responded to the question about how we attain eternal life with the reiteration of Torah and the prophets: love God with your entire being and love your neighbor as yourself (Matt 22:34–40). For Paul in Romans, the embodiment of this saving commitment to love finds its paradigmatic expression in the social wholeness of reconciled Jew and Gentile in the community of faith.[31]

Paul's final comment in our passage is to once more emphasize that the saving faithfulness he understands the gospel to be centered on does not stand over against Torah. It is not even in tension with Torah. This saving faithfulness is precisely what Torah itself calls for. With this faithfulness, "*we uphold Torah*" (3:31).[32]

God's Saving Justice

According to Paul in Romans 1–3, the fundamental need humanity has is liberation or salvation from the power of sin. He defines "sin" as most basically expressed in the dynamics of idolatry, where human beings do not give God gratitude for what is but rather put their trust in created things and set off a dynamic where they exchange wholeness for brokenness.

Paul describes this bondage to the sin/idolatry plague as universal—characteristic of those whose idols lead to ultimate trust in the Roman Empire and a spiral down into self-destructive lust and injustice and violence toward others and of those whose idols lead to ultimate trust in the Law as a boundary marker that requires violence and injustice to defend.

---

31. Yoder, *Politics*, 212–27.
32. Jewett, *Romans*, 303.

God's Saving Justice

These various expressions of idolatry leave human beings in bondage to whatever Power they give ultimate loyalty to—with the consequence of living lives characterized by "wrath" rather than genuine justice. So, what is needed is something to break this spiral toward death. That "something" is the core element of Paul's theology of salvation.

The resolution to this crisis of humanity may be found in God's revelation of the true nature of humanity's problem and God's solution. The resolution is a process of illumination. God provides sight and breaks the hold of blindness that idolatry has on humanity with its misplaced loyalties. God does this when God shows the world through the life, death, resurrection, and exaltation of Jesus the true nature of reality and God's relationship to it. To embrace this revelation from God leads to freedom from bondage, salvation from the spiral of death, and an exchange of "wrath" for healing justice.

God's present disclosure in Jesus of the truth of creation and present and future reality is at the same time both the summation of the law and prophets and separate from law-as-idol. This particular ideal had demanded ultimate loyalty from Paul himself and resulted in his own acts of blasphemous violence when he persecuted Jesus's followers. Paul understands Torah to be good and life-giving so long as it is understood to point without compromise toward love of neighbor (Romans 13:8–10). However, when the law provides justification for violence in the name of purity and exclusivity it becomes an idol.

Those who do recognize the revelation of God's saving justice in Jesus for what it is need only trust that that revelation is true. Such trust leads to salvation. If it is authentic, it also leads to the believer participating in Jesus's way. Later in Romans Paul will describe this participation in terms of life in the Spirit and in terms of shared communal life characterized by mutual appreciation of various spiritual gifts, the rejection of vengeance, and the embrace of love of neighbor as the summation of life lived under Torah.

Paul makes clear, in full continuity with the Bible's salvation story, that the salvation he describes comes to humanity due to God's initiative. As Paul presents God here, God has no need for appeasement or satisfaction prior to revealing God's healing mercy. The mercy exists without limit and is given unconditionally. God is the initiator in the process of salvation, not the recipient. We see no hint here of anything needed on God's side of the human/divine relationship as a precondition for God's saving work.

PART TWO: Jesus' Death and Salvation

So, the "justice of God" that stands at the center of Paul's theology of salvation from start to finish is restorative justice, not retributive justice. God seeks to help humanity see God's true nature, creation's true nature, as merciful. God breaks through idolatry's blinding dynamics in the witness of Jesus. God in this way seeks to convey to any with eyes to see and ears to hear that God's welcome remains unconditional for all who turn toward it.

Paul adds no new spin to the Bible's salvation story. He reiterates what the call of Abraham, the exodus, the gift of Torah, the sustenance of the community in exile, and the message of Jesus have all (in harmony with one another) expressed: God is merciful and offers empowerment for just living for all who embrace that mercy and let it transform their lives.

God's mercy frees people from bondage to the Powers. Such freedom empowers people of faith to experience themselves and to be agents for others transformed living. Believers may move from injustice and violence toward genuine wholeness and shalom. And, Paul confirms God's healing strategy as seen in Genesis 12 and witnessed to throughout the story. Those human beings who trust in God's way of wholeness are called to embrace the vocation to be witnesses of this wholeness and thereby bless all the families of the earth.

Paul's distinctive contribution in Romans 1–3 to the biblical salvation story lies in his powerful portrayal of the problem of idolatry both in the empire and in the faith community. He witnesses, based on his own life, to the transforming power of God's mercy embodied in the ministry of Jesus. This power is sustained in the presence of the Spirit of the risen Jesus Christ among the community of his people. As Michael Gorman concludes: "The notion of making peace between humans and God and between formerly alienated humans is so central to the core of Pauline doctrinal and ethical thought that it is impossible to develop a faithful construal of Pauline thought without peacemaking and/or reconciliation at the core."[33]

Just as Paul, walking in the Spirit of the risen Christ, now powerfully practices shalom-making despite his earlier career of extreme and blasphemous violence, so too may all others who accept the disclosure of God's justice in Jesus.[34] Paul reiterates that God's justice is disclosed in Jesus, not in Caesar and not in works of the law.

---

33. Gorman, *Inhabiting*, 143.
34. Brondos, *Paul*, 134.

ELEVEN

Salvation through Revelation

THE BOOK OF REVELATION provides a closing summary of the Bible's salvation story in the form of an extended vision that interprets Jesus's message of salvation. One way to read Revelation is as an attempt to apply the salvation story the Gospels tell (in the context of the overall biblical salvation story) to life in the Roman Empire near the close of the first century. John presents two salvation stories locked in mortal conflict—the story of the Lamb and the story of the Beast.[1]

At the heart of each story is an account of power. What does it take to conquer? What does it take to achieve victory? Revelation challenges the empire's notions of salvation, power, and victory and presents the Bible's notions as a viable alternative. At it sees the Dragon as the power behind the empire, Revelation teaches that "what most distinguishes the rule of God from that of the [Dragon] is that the latter uses coercive force."[2]

John compares and contrasts these two salvation stories in order to inspire peaceable living. He challenges his readers, who identify themselves as believers in Jesus, to follow the same path that Jesus took. Jesus confronted the Powers with his practice of embodied restorative justice and his faithful witness. The Powers responded with extreme violence and executed him on the cross. Then God vindicated Jesus's witness by raising him from the dead and unveiling him as the true ruler of the earth. John presents this "pattern of Jesus" as the norm for those who would take his name: faithful witness, resurrection, and ruling through self-giving love.

In face of the relentless assault of the Powers—spiritually, ideologically, and physically—on people throughout the empire, John presents

1. Howard-Brook and Gwyther, *Unveiling*, 157–94.
2. Barr, "Doing," 98.

this revelation of the actual nature of the human environment. He draws directly on and reiterates the biblical story of salvation we have examined in this book.

The basic content of Revelation's revelation concerning salvation is the same as we have seen to be characteristic of the rest of the Bible: God creates and sustains the universe in love; due to choices to turn from God and trust in idols, human hearts have been damaged; the message of salvation proclaims simply turn back from the idols and trust in God's love. In my summary of how Revelation presents salvation, I will touch on six texts.

Revelation One

The first words of the book tell us this is a "revelation of Jesus Christ." That is, this book is a revelation about Jesus that gives a vision of how his salvation transforms the world. Chapter one asserts that Jesus is very, very powerful. He is powerful in relation to the nations ("the ruler of the kings of the earth," "on his account all the tribes of the earth will wail") and in relation to the churches ("he holds the keys to death and Hades").

What is the nature of Jesus' power? The book challenges us to accept Jesus' Lamb-power[3] as the fundamental power of history. Lambs don't kill and dominate and instill fear and justify violence in the name of a "realistic" need for peace and order, nor do they violently punish their enemies. "Lamb theology is the whole message of Revelation. Evil is defeated not by overwhelming force or violence but by the Lamb's suffering love on the cross. The victim becomes the victor."[4]

This is how John describes Jesus: "the faithful witness, the firstborn of the dead, and the ruler of the kings of the earth" (1:5). These three descriptors present in a nutshell what we could call the pattern of Jesus: Faithful living, to the point of suffering due to his resistance to the domination system, even to the point of death. Vindication by God, the witness sustained even through death, resurrection, sustained hope, true power. And ruler of the kings of the earth. What does "rulers of the kings of the earth" mean? The book will explain—and the outcome of this rule will be salvation even for these enemies of God ("The kings of the earth will bring their glory into [the New Jerusalem] . . . [and] people will bring into it the glory and the honor of the nations," 21:24–26).

---

3. On the "Lamb" metaphor, see Johns, *Lamb*.
4. Rossing, *Rapture*, 111.

In Revelation, the visions John sees reveal Lamb-power as the true power of the universe. Even in the face of a sword wielding empire. The exalted Lamb is exalted as Lamb, not as warrior. The exalted Lamb is exalted because of his faithful witness to persevering compassion and love. "Fundamental to Revelation's whole understanding of the way in which Christ establishes God's kingdom on earth is the conviction that in his death and resurrection Christ has already won his decisive victory over evil."[5]

The threefold pattern of Jesus sets the stage for the revelation of Jesus Christ that makes up Revelation. This Jesus loves us and has freed us from our sins by his blood (1:5b). All three components of this sentence must be held together: Jesus's love, Jesus's acts of providing for freedom, and the role of Jesus's "blood" in this freeing.

The love stems from the love of the Creator for the creation, even in its brokenness and alienation. The underlying motivation for God that fuels "what must soon take place" (1:1) is God's love. We have only a few markers in the course of Revelation to remind us of this fundamental reality, so it is important to take note of John's beginning emphasis here.

The work of love that Jesus embodies has as its goal the setting free of enslaved creation, especially enslaved humanity. The visions that follow will drive home in powerful ways the identity of the agents and the consequences of this enslavement. John emphasizes at the start that everything Jesus does as God's agent in our world stems from love and has as its purpose the freeing of humanity from all that enslaves. The "sins" John alludes to here are likely a general reality more than any particular acts. The fundamental sin in the Bible is idolatry, trusting in things rather than in God. The consequence of idolatry is enslavement, wherein the idol seduces and controls the idolater.

Freedom from the control of sin, from enslavement to the Powers that seduce humanity into idolatry, comes through Jesus "blood." As with elsewhere in the Bible, the term "blood" is used here without explanation of what precisely is meant by the term. In the context of the rest of the Bible and of what is to come in Revelation, we may hypothesize for now that by "blood" John has in mind the overall life, death, and resurrection of Jesus. That is, it is not Jesus's literal blood that frees but what the blood symbolizes—Jesus's life of freedom from the Powers and idolatry and sin, lived to the end in faithfulness even in face of violence and the most devastating kind of execution. God's vindication in making Jesus "first born of

---

5. Bauckham, *Theology*, 73.

PART TWO: Jesus' Death and Salvation

the dead" reveals to the cosmos that God's love survives the worst bloodletting of which the Powers are capable.

Jesus provides a "freedom from": freedom from the Powers and from idolatry and from sin, all the aspects of life that lead to enslavement. However, Jesus also provides "freedom for." Jesus frees those who follow him so that they might be "a kingdom, priests serving his God and Father" (1:6). We must remember that "kingdom" is a political term, spoken of here in the present tense. The freedom-for is a freedom here and now to live as communities that embody the way of the Lamb and display to the cosmos that Jesus indeed is the ruler of the kings of the earth.

What follow in Revelation will be visions directly concerned with a struggle between two present and demanding kingdoms. The Roman Empire is a "kingdom," too. When John speaks of Jesus "making us a kingdom" he means to say that followers of Jesus have chosen to enter his kingdom and, in a genuine sense, to exit Rome's kingdom. The book will conclude with a clear juxtaposition of this choice, one of the fundamental choices that energizes John's visions. Babylon or New Jerusalem? These are the two rival kingdoms. John's burden is to present those in the churches with the realities and demands of God's kingdom. Those who are the "priests" who serve Jesus's God do so through their embodied love and their resistance to the loyalty demanded by the kingdom that directly competes with God's.[6]

REVELATION FIVE

The initial vision in Revelation (1:10—3:22) focuses on Jesus's presence among and messages to "the seven churches that are in Asia" (1:4). These messages challenge the churches to commitment to Jesus's way of "conquering" in face of the empire's threats.[7] Then, John sees an "open door in heaven" followed by a theophany (chapter four) that portrays the "one on the throne" as the recipient of widespread worship.

At the beginning of chapter five, John sees a "scroll" in the right hand of the one on the throne. That this scroll is in God's "right hand" emphasizes its weightiness as does the fact that it is so securely bound with seven seals. Though we are not told directly, we surely are to understand the contents of this scroll to be the fulfillment of God's work with creation, a

---

6. Gorman, *Reading Revelation*, 76.
7. Ibid., 96–97.

message of salvation.⁸ But the message cannot simply be given. Someone must be found to open the scroll and bring the message to its fruition. To John's bitter frustration, given that he longed for salvation, "no one in heaven or on earth or under the earth was able to open the scroll or look into it" (5:3). We can only speculate as to why this is the case. One idea, though, is that everyone misunderstands the way the scroll is to be opened. Everyone looked for the power of domination as the power to bring history to its conclusion.

No one is found and John weeps bitterly (5:4). Then he is told to weep no more because one has indeed been found. He hears that a king, great and powerful enough to break open the scroll has made an appearance—at least this is the sense one gets from what John hears. It is "the Lion of the tribe of Judah, the Root of David," a great conqueror who can open the scroll.⁹

This is all for dramatic effect. John of course already knows the identity of this victor. However, the drama is important. Many did expect that the deliverer would indeed be an all-powerful king of the type of King David of old. This would be the hoped for Messiah longed after for many generations, the one who would "redeem Israel" (Luke 24:21) with great force. This expectation is what John hears.

What John actually sees makes for a dramatic re-emphasis on the claim from chapter one that Jesus, the faithful witness, actually has become ruler of the kings of the earth (1:5): "Then I saw between the throne and the living creatures and among the elders a Lamb standing as if it had been slaughtered … [who] went and took the scroll from the right hand of the one … on the throne" (5:6–7). What John sees, though, is not actually different from what he hears. It is just that the mighty king who has the power to open the scroll and bring the story of humanity to its healing end is the gentle, compassionate, consistently loving, self-sacrificial Jesus who conquers by persevering on the path of love, all the way to the cross and beyond.¹⁰

We must notice, though, just how profound the exaltation of this slain and raised Lamb is here. This vision may present the highest christology in the entire New Testament.¹¹ The Lamb stands right next to the throne. He is not part of worshiping creation but actually himself becomes

---

8. Kraybill, *Apocalypse*, 98.
9. Bauckham, *Climax*, 180–81.
10. Swartley, *Covenant*, 340–41.
11. Maier, *Apocalypse*, 185–86.

PART TWO: Jesus' Death and Salvation

the object of worship. What follows in chapter five in relation to the Lamb almost exactly echoes what John reports in chapter four in relation to the one on the throne.

So, we have a profound affirmation of the godness of the Lamb. This affirmation precisely follows from the self-emptying of the Lamb (see Philippians 2). It is as the one whose persevering love leads to a cross that the Lamb embodies God as nothing else does. Hence, the most important revelation here is not that Jesus is divine. The most important revelation is what this affirmation tells us about God.

The one on the throne is seen most clearly and best understood in terms of the persevering love of the Lamb. This vision thus becomes a radical and transformative theophany. We see God here, indeed, God on the cross, God as bringing victory and transformation and healing to creation through self-giving love. "Christ's sacrificial death belongs to the way God rules the world. The symbol of the Lamb is no less a divine symbol that the symbol of 'the One who sits on the throne.'"[12]

The worship service then culminates in an ever-widening set of affirmations: "Worthy is the Lamb that was slaughtered to receive power and wealth and wisdom and might and honor and glory and blessing!" (5:12). The worship ripples wider and wider, including praise from every tribe and nation, then from angels beyond count, and then—amazingly—from "every creature in heaven and on earth and under the earth and in the sea" (5:13).

John drives home with every bit of rhetorical force he can muster that Jesus shows us the character of God and the means of victory. And this revelation of what God is like and how God works gains the strongest imaginable endorsement from creation itself. So, the slain and raised Lamb not only reveals God's character, he reveals the character of God's created universe by the response he generates from "every creature" when he takes the scroll.

The Lamb's victory is praised as having already been won. As will be reemphasized in creative ways in the visions to follow, in the life, death, and resurrection of Jesus salvation has come. There will be no other battle. No other victory—other than actions and commitments that reinforce the victory already won, and that conquer in precisely the same way (faithful witness to the very end confirmed by God's nonviolent vindication through resurrection).

---

12. Bauckham, *Theology*, 64.

Salvation through Revelation

The most fundamental expression of God's power is the self-giving love of the Lamb. This love cannot be conquered even by the empire's crucifixion. Whatever we can imagine as the empire's greatest expression of might cannot defeat this vulnerable Lamb. To realize that this is God's power transforms how we understand the One on the throne and the "Revelation of Jesus Christ" that is the focus of the book of Revelation.

John portrays God's power in chapter five. The power of the Lamb, the power of God, is not to be understood as the power of unlimited coercion, as brute strength, as the power to impose God's will no matter what. That is not how the scroll is opened. That is not how salvation is won. God's power is not unlimited coercion but the power of self-giving, persevering love. The gospel tells us that the way of victory for the messiah came through the Jesus's self-sacrifice, not through matching sword for sword.

The Lamb is worthy to take the scroll, the Lamb has true power, because it was willing to be slain for the sake of God's truth. This act was not an isolated happening, something the Lamb did so that none of his followers would have to. Rather, this act of the Lamb was something his followers are to imitate. In chapters two and three, Jesus called upon the people in the seven churches to be conquerors. Jesus called upon the people in the seven churches to follow his way even if that led to their death. God vindicated Jesus's faithfulness through resurrection. So too will God vindicate the faithfulness of all who follow Jesus's way.

Immediately after the vision of the Lamb as triumphant, John sees a series of great plagues that are triggered by the breaking of the seals to the giant scroll. The source and meaning of these plagues are complicated. In chapter twelve's vision, John seems to indicate that the Dragon (Satan) making war on the earth and the followers of the Lamb (12:17) stands behind the plagues—though they also in some sense serve God's purposes. With chapter thirteen, though, the role of the Dragon and his Beast becomes clear.

Revelation Thirteen and Fourteen

The vision begins with a Beast rising out of the sea, the sea being the domain of the Dragon who is named as Satan (12:9) and is the power behind the Beast. The actions of the Beast are an expression of the war the Dragon wages against followers of the Lamb (12:17). The Beast, with its "diadems" and "throne" (13:1–2) and worldwide authority (13:7), symbolizes

PART TWO: Jesus' Death and Salvation

empire.[13] This vision presents the salvation story John opposes in its most vivid and harsh light. That the Beast gains his power from the Dragon echoes Jesus's temptation narrative where Satan offers Jesus leadership of the empire.

John has more in mind than simply the Roman Empire, though. Verse three refers to the Beast suffering what seems to be a mortal wound and then being healed. When any particular empire receives a mortal would (that is, is defeated), that is not the end of the Beast. It simply continues on in a succeeding empire or kingdom or other political power structure. The wound that killed one empire heals, and the Beast continues in power in another empire. The Bible shows Babylon as succeeded by Assyria, followed in turn by Persia, then Greece, and then Rome—all manifestations of the Beast. The Beast is an image for all authoritarian human political institutions that separate people from God.[14]

Rome's demand that people render to Caesar that which belongs to God compelled many people of faith to resist Rome to the death. John believed that when it made this demand the empire became demonic. He vigorously represented this in 13:4: "They worshiped the Dragon, for he had given his authority to the Beast, saying, 'Who is like the Beast, and who can fight against it?'"

"Let anyone who has an ear listen," verse nine asserts. In the messages to the churches, these words accompanied the promise to "conquerors," those who follow what Jesus says to them. By putting these words here, John underscores that what follows has crucial importance for his audience. In the face of the awful power of the Beast what must they do? How might they contribute to the fulfillment of God's promises of salvation for the world? "If you are to be taken captive, into captivity you go; if you kill with the sword, with the sword you must be killed. Here is a call for the endurance and faith of the saints" (13:10). Just as Jesus stuck to the path of love even in the face of violence, so too must his followers. Like their savior, they are called to win a victory not based on brute, coercive power. The revolutionary's sword is still a sword.

With this challenge for patient endurance, John calls his readers to refuse to fight back with violence against the attacks of the Beast, since only in this way can the Beast be halted in its tracks. Evil is self-propagating. To repay violence with violence only perpetuates violence and makes no contribution to peace and healing. Genuine salvation is linked with

---

13. Ibid., 37.
14. Howard-Brook and Gwyther, *Unveiling*, 157–58.

consistency with the pattern of Jesus: faithful witness, resurrection, and vindication.

A second beast (13:11), called the False Prophet, portrays the ideological dimension of the Beast's kingdom. The Dragon and the Beast deceive. Their power comes from what people give them with trust in them. The False Prophet "deceives the inhabitants of the earth, telling them to make an image for the Beast that had been wounded by the sword and yet lived; and it was allowed to give breath to the image of the Beast so that the image of the Beast could even speak and cause those who would not worship the image of the Beast to be killed" (13:14–15).

The "image of the Beast" likely refers to emperor worship in that specific context. More generally, it refers to whatever concrete thing facilitates idolatry of human kingdoms. John's vision demands that followers of Jesus refuse to offer the Beast the worship it demands and refuse to resist the Beast with violence as those who fought the Romans during the Jewish War in Jerusalem in 66–70 CE had done. This creates a challenging picture, then. Salvation is linked with likely martyrdom and being crushed by the might of the empire.[15]

The vision does not end here, though. The first five verses of chapter fourteen stand in important contrast to chapter thirteen and make a powerful contribution to Revelation's version of the Bible's salvation story. Chapter thirteen shows the true nature of emperor worship and all other similar demands for ultimate loyalty made by imperial states and the need for people of faith to say no even if it means suffering and tribulation. Then 14:1–5 shows the Lamb's victory and it shows that those who follow him share that victory. The conquering the Beast does (13:7) was, in a sense, illusory. The faithful ones' actual fate will be to join the crucified and vindicated Lamb that sings on Mt. Zion.

Revelation, at its heart, teaches that the Lamb of God has defeated the Powers of evil. This act leads to the eventual healing of creation, healing that includes the transformation of the nations and their kings. This affirmation arose in the midst of a practical awareness of the power of evil in the world. This vision of transformation tells John's readers that they fight against the Beast when they, as 14:4 says, "follow the Lamb wherever he goes." Chapter five tells us that the Lamb who was slain stands as the master of history. The Lamb who defeated evil through the way of love reveals the path to salvation.

---

15. Gorman, *Reading Revelation*, 135–36.

PART TWO: Jesus' Death and Salvation

According to these visions for the followers of the Lamb there are two parts to reality, both true at the same time. One, the Beast makes war upon them. For John himself, being warred upon meant exile to the island of Patmos (1:9), for Jesus it meant crucifixion. For others too, it meant martyrdom. But the other part of reality, the deeper one, is that of redemption, of oneness with God, of hope and empowerment in the midst of tribulations and persecutions and evil.

Rome's call for emperor worship lies behind these visions. Shortly before Jesus was born, a movement toward emperor worship arose within the Roman Empire. It began more as worship of the empire than of the specific emperor due to the gratitude that people felt for the social order and stability afforded by the *Pax Romana* ("peace of Rome"). But because the emperor symbolized the empire and was more tangible, this worship soon focused on him.[16]

The emperors at first only tolerated this religious devotion as they resisted being treated as divine. But soon the social value of emperor religion became obvious. With the empire's many nationalities, its elite soon realized a common religion of emperor worship could be a helpful way to ensure unity within the empire. People could practice their own faith as well as long as they would confess the emperor's lordship. Believers such as John assumed they could not go along with this. Jesus was lord, not Caesar. For followers of Jesus to refuse to render worship to Caesar led the empire to see them as threats to the stability of the social order.[17] The empire did not see them as heretics who did not believe the correct doctrine. Rather, the empire saw them as rebels who refused loyalty due to the emperor. Revelation thirteen portrays the empire's response.

John's vision could not end with chapter thirteen's seemingly hopeless picture. Despite the overwhelming power and authority that the Beast possesses, John sees in chapter fourteen the holder of the ultimate power of the universe and the guarantor of authentic salvation. He sees the Lamb surrounded by his people. The 144,000, chapter seven shows us, is not a small, limited number but symbolizes the entire people of God, "a great multitude that no one could count" (7:9).[18] The Lamb's salvation story, John insists, stands; it repudiates the Beast's salvation story.

---

16. Howard-Brook and Gwyther, *Unveiling*, 113.
17. Ibid., 117.
18. Bauckham, *Theology*, 76–77.

REVELATION NINETEEN

Revelation contains several visions that portray terrible plagues befalling the earth. They culminate in the total destruction shown in chapter sixteen. However, the world does not actually end. More visions follow that focus on the destruction of the powers behind the evil that plagues the earth in chapters seventeen and eighteen. With the Powers of evil crushed, the scene is set for a great celebration in the beginning of chapter nineteen, the "marriage supper of the Lamb."

John, though, has yet another major judgment scene to portray, one that is a kind of sequel to the plague visions. After the sixth bowl plague, demonic spirits from the mouth of the Dragon, the Beast, and the False Prophet "go abroad to the kings of the whole world, to assemble them for battle on the great day of God the Almighty" (16:14). Before John sees this "battle," though, we get the judgments of chapters seventeen and eighteen that focus on the destruction of the "Great Whore," Babylon—the empire that embodies the ways of the Dragon (its spills "the blood of prophets and of saints, and of all who have been slaughtered on earth," 18:24). This judgment vision, though, reveals a difference between the Powers of evil and the humans they deceived ("all nations were deceived by your sorcery," 18:23).

With the Powers judged in chapters seventeen and eighteen, the multitude can gather for celebration—19:1–2: "Salvation and glory and power to our God; for his judgments are true and just; he has judged the Great Whore who corrupted the earth with her fornication, and he has avenged on her the blood of her servants."

The character of this "avenging" work of God becomes the focus starting in 19:11. We should link the vision presented here both with the earlier vision from chapter five of the Lamb who carries the meaning of history and with the outcome of the book, the vision of the New Jerusalem. Remarkably, the "kings of the earth" present to God the "glory of the nations."

After the celebration in 19:1–10, "heaven is opened" for a new vision. Jesus returns to the scene. It appears he will act as God's warrior-judge, upon first glance the expected actions of the "Lion of the Tribe of Judah" of 5:5; the conquering judge at long last. However, as we read on we realize that the war is over before it even starts, due to Jesus's faithful witness that led to his crucifixion. What we see in 19:11–21 is not a battle but simply the carrying out of God's final victory.[19] The Beast and False Prophet are

---

19. Gorman, *Reading Revelation*, 154–55.

PART TWO: Jesus' Death and Salvation

thrown into the lake of fire. "All the rest" (those who were deceived) are judged by the word of Christ (the sword that comes out of his mouth, 19:21).

The white horse that Jesus rides (19:11) symbolizes victory. He has conquered through his death and resurrection. He comes already the victor to this apparent battle with the forces of the evil. This "battle" was foreseen in 16:14. The outcome of the "battle" in no way is in question.

The rider is called "faithful and true"; that is, "the faithful and true witness" of 1:5. He remained faithful and true to God even when it meant a martyr's death and thereby gained the white horse. He wins the "war" because he remains faithful to the way of the cross in the face of temptations to take up the sword to further his ends. The rider approaches the scene "clothed in a robe dipped in blood" (19:13) already shed before the battle begins. Jesus can already ride the white horse because the battle is over due to his faithful witness.[20] The "armies of heaven" (19:14), likely the "saints" wearing their bridal linen (19:7–8), carry no weapons. They too are already victorious. The only weapon mentioned is the sword that comes out of Jesus' mouth—his word, the gospel (cf. Heb 4:12; Eph 6:17) that brings the enemies of God to their knees.[21]

The Beast and the kings and armies are all ready for battle (19:19). They are deceived to think one will occur. However, the battle is long past. We see that when Jesus simply captures the Beast and False Prophet and throws them into the fiery lake (19:20) without a battle. Jesus, in his death and resurrection, won the only battle necessary to defeat evil.

John presents a "rebirth of images." He uses battle imagery to present a picture of Jesus winning the ultimate battle with the Powers of evil, not through a bloodbath in the future but in the past historical event of his witness and its vindication in resurrection.[22] This "battle" scene from chapter nineteen underscores how the Lamb conquers. He contrasts with the Beast who seeks to conquer through force.

The vision of 19:11–21 stands in between John's contrasting portrayals of the fate of the two great cities of Revelation. At the beginning of chapter seventeen, we read, "then one of the seven angels who had the seven bowls came and said to me, 'Come, I will show you the judgment of the great whore who is seated on many waters, with whom the kings of the earth have committed fornication, and with the wine of whose fornication

20. Maier, *Apocalypse*, 188.
21. Blount, *Can I Get*, 82.
22. Bauckham, *Theology*, 106.

the inhabitants of the earth have become drunk.' So he carried me away in the spirit into the wilderness" (17:1–3). Then, in chapter twenty-one we read, "then one of the seven angels who had the seven bowls full of the last seven plagues came and said to me, 'Come, I will show you the bride, the wife of the Lamb.' And in the spirit he carried me away to a great, high mountain" (21:9–10).

In between these twin visions, chapter nineteen provides the denouement to the scene set up at the end of chapter sixteen. The allies of the Dragon gather "for battle on the great day of God the Almighty" (16:16). However, in chapter nineteen, when this "battle" is described, it turns out not to be a battle at all.

The two kinds of power for conquering in Revelation correspond with the two cities, the two objects of loyalty vying for adherents.[23] The Beast's power for conquering, characteristic of Babylon, rests on violence and domination, top-down power that enforces its will by crushing its enemies. The Lamb's power for conquering, characteristic of New Jerusalem, rests on resistance through love and adherence to peace that seeks to convert its human enemies. According to Revelation twenty-one, the very "kings of the earth" who join the Beast in facing the white rider at the great "battle" end up bringing their glory into New Jerusalem as transformed people.

Revelation Twenty-one and Twenty-two

The Bible's vision of wholeness is presented the most clearly at the very end, the last two chapters of Revelation. The angel tells John that God "will wipe every tear from [our] eyes. Death will be no more; mourning and crying and pain will be no more" (21:4). Then John sees a vision of the city of healing and wholeness, the New Jerusalem.

> The angel showed me the river of the water of life, bright as crystal, flowing from the throne of God and of the Lamb through the middle of the street of the city. On either side of the river is the tree of life with its twelve kinds of fruit, producing its fruit each month; and the leaves of the tree are for the healing of the nations. Nothing accursed will be found there. But the throne of God and of the Lamb will be in it, and his servants will worship him; they will see his face, and his name will be on their

---

23. Maier, *Apocalyse*, 37. See also Rossing, *Choice*.

PART TWO: Jesus' Death and Salvation

foreheads. And there will be no more night; they need no light of lamp or sun, for the Lord God will be their light. (22:1–5)

God had promised to Abraham and Sarah that their descendants would be a light to the nations and bring healing and salvation. This promise finds fulfillment in the New Jerusalem. The nations are healed. People see God face to face. The Lord God becomes their light. The two foundation stones of hope—God's past acts of salvation and God's promise—merge. The true victory of God, the actual battle with and defeat of the Powers of evil, are past events in Revelation. Jesus has conquered death. Revelation's hope is based on what Jesus already did.

The new heaven and earth are cleansed of evil. They are heaven and earth as good, the way they were created to be. The holy city (21:2), the beautiful bride, stands in stark contrast to Babylon. A vision of this city empowers John's readers to perceive the allurements of Babylon for what they are and resist. At 21:5–8, for the first time since chapter four, John hears the voice of God: "I am making everything new!" God's work is not reserved for a new creation, after the old has been discarded. Rather it is the process of recreating by which the old becomes new.

In one sense, the holy city in 21:9–14 is future, but in another sense it exists in the present and, like Babylon does, invites people to enter it. This contrast highlights the present choice of cities. "The New Jerusalem vision is meant to be God's vision by which we live our lives right now, as followers of the Lamb and of Lamb power in our world."[24]

The New Jerusalem is actually constructed of people. The people of God are the bride. They are the walls and foundations of the city and they inhabit the city. The twelve tribes of Israel make up the walls (21:12) and the twelve apostles make up the foundation (21:14). Together they symbolize the entire people of God. The city represents a people. The earthly temple and the earthly Jerusalem have been replaced by people living in the direct presence of God. Everything that the temple of old represented at its best is now transferred to the life of the city.[25] God's glory fills everything. Merely to be in the city is to be with God. God Almighty is seen in the Lamb (21:23). Jesus defines who God is. The light of the world becomes also the light by which the nations walk (21:24). They will no longer be deceived.

In John's earlier visions, the nations are deceived by Satan and are subservient to the Beast and "the kings of the earth." But the deceiver is

---

24. Rossing, *Rapture*, 142.
25. Howard-Brook and Gwyther, *Unveiling*, 185–90.

defeated and removed. Now the song of 15:4 is fulfilled: "All nations shall come and worship you." The nations that once offered their riches to the city of the Beast will yield them instead to the city of God and the Lamb (21:24, 26).[26] This implies a sanctification of the entire order of the created world and its products. Nothing from the old order that has value in the sight of God is kept from the new. Verse twenty-seven reminds us that the city is truly holy and pure. Those who enter it do not do so because God compromises, but because they themselves have been transformed and made whole.

In 22:2, the fruit of the tree of life symbolizes abundant life. The river of living water also powerfully expresses the idea of bountiful life. The "healing of the nations" from the "leaves of the tree of life" likely refers to the hurts caused by the plagues. The nations are healed from the awful effects of the dragon and his cohorts. If Babylon is characterized by terror and deception and injustice, the New Jerusalem is the exact opposite. It is the place where the nations walk in harmony and justice and peace, where the light of the glory of God guides everyone's path.

A key element in John's vision is that the New Jerusalem, in all its brilliance and beauty, is not something people visit or take residence in. Rather, it is something people become. The New Testament often speaks of "the people of God" as the bride of Christ. Here, in 21:9–11, we are told that John "saw the bride, the wife of the Lamb," which was the holy city, Jerusalem, coming down out of heaven from God, possessing the glory of God.

New Jerusalem is people, the countless multitudes that John sees singing praises to the Lamb throughout the book. But along with these renewed people will be all of creation, purified and set free from the bondage of decay and death; not worshiped instead of God, but cared for and enjoyed as part of God's creation.[27]

Salvation According to Revelation

The book of Revelation presents, we could say, two contrasting and competing salvation stories. The one, which John caricatures with polemical force, proclaimed Caesar as "savior," "lord," and the master of history. The second, which John embraces, proclaimed Jesus as savior, lord, and master of history. Through his plague visions, judgment visions, and worship

26. Bauckham, *Climax*, 315–16.
27. Bredin, *Ecology*, 165–80.

visions, John conveys the two directions these respective stories take their adherents.

Culminating the Bible's emphasis from the story of creation on, John juxtaposes the kingdom of God with the empires and nations of the world. These stand as the two basic social options in history. When the book concludes with heaven and earth joining together in the New Jerusalem, John emphasizes (as has the biblical salvation story from the start) that choices of loyalty between God's kingdom and the nations were always both religious and political choices.

Revelation appropriately concludes the biblical account because John has brought to the surface and sharply portrayed the basic issues that have concerned about all of the biblical writers. Central to God's response to the brokenness that severed the original harmony that characterized the good creation has been to create communities that would know God's peace and bless all the families of the earth (Gen 12:1–3). These communities received liberating empowerment and guidance from God—exodus and Torah—as merciful expressions of God's will for wholeness.

From the very start, though, the ways of the nations with their idolatry, injustice, and power politics have troubled the covenant people and disrupted their attempts to embody God's shalom. The great empires always stand as threats, both in how they often seek to crush the possibility of the independent, shalom-oriented social witness God seeks from God's people and in how they provide a competing account of the core values that shape human communities. For Torah, the core values center on mutuality, respect, care for the vulnerable, and inclusion of all stakeholders into processes of governance and discernment. For the empires, the core values center on the aggrandizement of power and wealth in the hands of the elite, exploitation of the vulnerable, and disempowerment of the many.

In John's presentation, the veneer of respectability and claim for divine support for the way of empire is torn away.[28] John reveals with his visions the "beastly" nature of his particular empire (Rome) that, as so many others had before, sought to shape the covenant people in ways contrary to the heart of Torah. Rome offered many rewards for those who would willingly accept its demands and many severe punishments for those who did not. John's intent is to lay bare the actual source of Rome's power—not God at all but the Dragon (Satan) himself.

John's agenda, though, is not to cultivate resentment and rebellion. Rome is but a passing phenomenon that does not actually have the power

---

28. Howard-Brook and Gwyther, *Unveiling*, 227–28.

to determine people's ultimate fate. Rather, John has a positive agenda that in many ways echoes the positive agenda of the original revelation of Torah, an agenda reiterated by the Old Testament prophets, Jesus, and Paul.

The embodiment of this positive agenda, of course, is Jesus. When John labels his book a "revelation of Jesus Christ," he has in mind the Jesus who healed. Revelation, like the Gospels and epistles (and the law and prophets), is about embodiment of God's healing strategy. What does John want to inspire his readers to do? "Follow the Lamb wherever he goes." Like the Lamb, the followers play a key role in revealing the true character of the Master of the Universe. The God of Revelation is the God of Jesus and the God of Abraham and Moses. That is, the God of Revelation is a God who seeks to heal and effects healing through persevering love.

The message of salvation John offers is simple, in line with the simple message I have traced from throughout the Bible: Turn from the idols and trust in God's love. John presents the Beast in unflattering terms in order to facilitate such a turn in his readers. Though they may profess faith in Jesus, many in John's audience (as reflected in the critique of several of the churches in the messages from Jesus in chapters two and three) found mixing profession of faith in Jesus with accommodation to the empire to be acceptable. For John, such a mix actually ends up being a repudiation of trust in Jesus and his way.

Though John portrays the consequences of accommodation with the Beast to have potentially terrible consequences (though note that even the kings of the earth—the Beast's strongest human allies—are welcomed into the New Jerusalem in the end), the path toward healing was not complicated. Simply turn, follow the Lamb, and trust in his revelation of the character of the true God.

Revelation does have language of judgment, of vengeance, of death and blood. Jesus's crucifixion is presented as the fulcrum point of human history. However, the book does not point toward this death as a sacrifice to God that makes salvation possible. To the contrary, as implied in the title of the book itself, Jesus's crucifixion gains its significance as a "revelation" that shows all with eyes to see that God's love stands above the Beast's domination practices.

The initial statement about Jesus at the book's beginning makes clear how he shows the world God's character. This book is a "revelation of Jesus Christ" (1:1), who is worthy of praise and discipleship because of his "faithful witness" (i.e., his life of persevering love that led the empire to execute him) that results in his resurrection ("the firstborn of the dead"),

PART TWO: Jesus' Death and Salvation

and status as "ruler of the kings of the earth" (1:5). He "freed us from our sins by his blood" (i.e., his faithful witness to the death empowers us to turn away from the sin of idolatry) and "made us a kingdom" (a community that stands over against the "kingdoms" of the nations and empires) to serve God (1:6). As a consequence of Jesus' witness "every eye will see him" and "all the tribes of the earth will wail" (1:7). The salvation comes as a gift of God. Ultimately this "wailing" from "all the tribes of the earth" is best understood as a wail of recognition that leads to salvation.

"You [the Lamb] ransomed for God saints from every tribe and language and people and nation; you have made them to be a kingdom and priests serving our God" (5:10). "A great multitude that no one could count, from every nation, from all tribes . . . cried out . . . 'Salvation belongs to our God who is seated on the throne, and to the Lamb" (7:9). "Lord, who will not fear and glorify your name? For you alone are holy. All nations will come and worship before you" (15:4). "The city has no need of sun or moon to shine on it, for the glory of God is its light, and its lamp is the Lamb. The nations will walk by its light and the kings of the earth will bring their glory into it" (21:23–24).

The second half of Revelation gives us two different visions contrasting the two salvation stories. In 13:1—14:5, the Beast and Lamb provide the counter stories. In 17:1—22:5, it is two cities who provide the contrast—Babylon and the New Jerusalem. Both visions emphasize the centrality of Jesus' faithful witness, the call for people of faith to follow his way, and the ultimate impotence of the Beast/Babylon/Dragon story to provide life. This latter story evokes terrible fear, brings death to prophets, and makes human beings into commodities. But it does not bring life and it is bound to self-destruct.

John means his account of the Beast in chapter thirteen to be read in relation to the empire's best attributes. He says, in effect, that the Pax Romana, attractive as it may be as a source of peace and comfort for those who embrace its story, actually is empowered by the Dragon and in claiming its divine status is uttering the worst blasphemies. Its peace rests on systemic violence. It seems irresistible, in part because of the effective ideological work of its propagandists (the "False Prophet").

For those who recognize the empire for what it is (perhaps we could infer here respect from John for the Jewish revolutionaries of the 66–70 CE resistance in Judea), saying no is crucial. However, in contrast to the revolutionaries, it must not be centered on the sword. Violence does not offer salvation; it only adds to the Beast's dynamic of destructiveness.

The other story stands in the midst of the peace-but-really-systemic-violent chaos of the empire story. The empire story is not the true story. The Lamb stands with the multitudes who "follow the Lamb wherever he goes" (14:4). These 144,000, we learn from chapter seven, are the countless multitudes from all nations who worship the true God and not the Beast. They are freed for this worship when they see God for who God truly is due to the witness of the Lamb.

The visions of Babylon in chapters seventeen and eighteen show that it goes down in a conflagration triggered by the great harlot, who symbolizes the empire and becomes "drunk with the blood of the saints and the blood of the witnesses to Jesus" (17:6). We notice, in relation to the judgment, that the destruction visited upon the spiritual Powers of evil (Beast, Dragon, and False Prophet) results in the nations and the kings of the earth being healed.

The victory that sends the Powers down, we see reiterated in chapter nineteen, is the victory of Jesus' faithful witness and God's vindication.[29] The judgment of the Powers itself serves the healing that Jesus devoted his life to: as a result of his embodied testimony that conquers the Powers, healing comes to all creation, including God's worst human enemies.

Chapter nineteen echoes chapter five. Jesus wins by creative love. As a consequence, those with faith worship him (chapter five) and the Powers are crushed (chapter nineteen). Those who are in between—the human allies of the Powers who have been deceived by the Beast and False Prophet—meet with a complicated fate. They are "killed" by the "sword" that comes from the rider's mouth (19:21), but in such a way that leads to their presence in the New Jerusalem. "Jesus makes war not with a sword of battle but 'by the sword of his mouth.' The word is Jesus' only weapon—this is a reversal as unexpected as the substitution of a lamb for a lion. These reversals undercut violence by emphasizing Jesus' testimony and the word of God."[30]

The New Jerusalem welcomes all who want to be there. The door is never closed, and it is a place of healing. "Nothing unclean" will be found there, implying that the presence of the kings of the earth links with their transformation. They do not enter as allies of the Beast but as people who have found healing and see now that life is to found in the Lamb.

---

29. Maier, *Apocalypse*, 96.
30. Rossing, *Rapture*, 121.

TWELVE

Conclusion: Is There an Atonement Model in this Story?

FOR MANY CHRISTIANS, THE "biblical view" of salvation centers on Jesus's death. The doctrine of salvation ("soteriology") is defined in terms of how Jesus's death makes salvation possible. It is linked closely with the atonement, which is commonly defined as "how Christ accomplished our justification (i.e., being found just or righteous before God) through his sacrifice on the cross."[1]

I have attempted in this book to show that the Bible's portrayal of salvation actually does not focus on Jesus's death as the basis for reconciliation of humanity with God. Not all accounts of salvation that place Jesus's death as central explicitly argue in favor of retributive justice as part the divine economy that must be satisfied by a sacrifice such as Jesus's death. However, I suspect that any view of Jesus's death as a sacrifice necessary for salvation at least implicitly accepts retributive justice as an element of the process of providing for salvation.

I will leave it for a sequel to this book, though, to take up issues of historical theology and the development and logic of atonement theologies that developed much later than the biblical era. What I have done here is focus on the biblical story itself without explicitly interpreting it as compatible or incompatible with particular atonement models.

I have made a case: (1) to see that salvation in the Bible is not centered on Jesus's death as a necessary prerequisite for salvation to be made available, and (2) to see that the dynamics of justice that undergird salvation in the Bible are best understood as restorative and not retributive. In a nutshell, I argue that the biblical story of salvation portrays God as

1. Long, "Justification," 79.

Conclusion: Is There an Atonement Model in this Story?

reaching out to human beings with mercy. The God of the Bible responds to human brokenness, violence, and sinfulness with healing love. In telling the salvation story in this way, the Bible refutes the logic of retribution.

We see in the present-day United States the consequences of when human beings order important elements of social life more by the logic of retribution than the logic of mercy—an ever-expanding spiral of violence. Ironically, some of the strongest advocates in our culture for the appropriateness of, for example, shaping our criminal justice system according to the logic of retribution, are professing Christians—those who should be most responsive to the biblical story of salvation.

To conclude my treatment of salvation, justice, and the logic of retribution, I will first go back to review the basic argument I have presented, then reflect briefly on a hermeneutical strategy for thinking about the pro-violence elements of the Bible, and then discuss how the logic of mercy might be applied to present-day concerns regarding criminal justice.

THE BASIC ARGUMENT

One crucial element of the popularity of the logic of retribution in the United States is a common belief that God wills that violations of the public peace be punished. If God requires retaliation, repaying violence with violence, then official violent sanctions are appropriate, even a positive good. This logic provides a basis to justify warfare, certainly—along with, for many people, a basis to justify the use of corporal punishment on children. In chapter one I looked in more detail at how the logic of retribution justifies punishing criminal offenders—and the problematic consequences of the uses of such punishment.

However, no matter how widespread the use of punitive responses to wrongdoing and the basis for such responses in beliefs about God, we cannot avoid the reality that all such beliefs are human beliefs. Hence, all such beliefs are, by definition, finite and relative—and subject to challenge and revision. This book challenges the logic of retribution on the basis of theological beliefs. I have maintained a fairly narrow focus on a core element of our beliefs about God—our understanding of the Bible's portrayal of God in relation to effecting salvation for human beings.

If salvation stems from a holy and pure God being governed by the need to destroy sin and impurity unless God's righteous anger is dealt with, then the logic of retribution may be validated. However, if salvation according to the Bible instead may be most accurately understood

PART TWO: Jesus' Death and Salvation

as contrary to the logic of retribution, governed by God's simple healing mercy—unearned by human repayment, unconditional except for human acceptance of it—one of the main bases for affirming the logic of retribution will be refuted.

Chapters two through four summarized the core or "primal" biblical story of salvation. The Old Testament emphasizes a few key moments at the heart of salvation: (1) the calling of Abraham and Sarah to parent descendants (miraculously, given Sarah's barrenness) who would form a people who will bless all the families of the earth; (2) the liberation of these descendants from slavery in Egypt and the threat of annihilation they faced there at the hands of Egypt's god-king Pharaoh; (3) the coalescing of these liberated slaves into a coherent peoplehood shaped by Torah, given by God to the people through their leader, Moses; (4) the establishment of this community in the promised land to enable them to sustain their peoplehood in a real-world environment; and (5) the sustenance of this community even in the face of the destruction of their main political and religious institutions by the Babylonians through the promises voiced by the prophets and the perseverance of Torah as their organizing blueprint.

The story portrays each of these five "moments" as expressions of God's unilateral mercy. Each is a gift of a loving God, not the fruit of human action, rituals, or payments to God. In none of these cases are we led to believe that God was constrained by holiness or the need to balance the scales of justice before the gift is given. Certainly, at least in some cases, violence, even punishment, may be seen as an element of the story. Human beings do reap consequences for their injustice and resistance to God. However, in terms of the basic gift, the violence is peripheral. The gift does not require that there be pre-payment of appeasement or punishment. The gift is unearned; the violence is not inherent in its bestowal.

The centrality of the gift may be seen in the role the law and sacrifices play in salvation. Both are second steps, responses to the gift. God acts directly to give life to Abraham and Sarah; then they offer sacrifices. God acts directly to liberate the Hebrew slaves from Egypt; then God gives the law to shape the people's responsive living. Salvation is not the consequence of obedience to the law or the offering of sacrifices. To the contrary, obedience to the law and the offering of sacrifices are consequences of salvation.

Because of God's gift, the Hebrews express their gratitude by giving offerings to God—the offerings of their goods and of their actions. To be sure, with regard to sacrifices, provision is also made for sin offerings beyond gratitude offerings. However, these are not ways to appease

Conclusion: Is There an Atonement Model in this Story?

God's righteous anger so much as concrete expressions of remorse that are offered as responses to forgiveness. The entire system as portrayed in Leviticus presupposes God's mercy and is not based on the logic of retribution. God provides for the Hebrews' communal health through ritual as an expression of love, not of detached balance-the-scales-of-justice holiness.

The perseverance of God's love and the basic mercy-oriented commitment of God to sustain the Hebrew people as a channel for blessing all the families of the earth are borne out through the story of God's response to the Hebrews' own sinfulness. Prophets emerged in the generations after the Hebrews, contrary to God's will, installed a human king so as to be "like the nations." These prophets testified to God's ongoing commitment to the people and to the covenant God had made with them. Prophets such as Amos, Hosea, and Micah spoke sharp words of critique in response to Israel's injustice, violence, and idolatry. They asserted that Israel would face dire consequences should the people not turn back.

However, even though some of these warnings are expressed in punitive language, they sought to effect healing changes. They are framed by promises of such healing. The prophets presented the path back to God as simple and straightforward: all listeners must do is turn back. God, the gracious God who brought them out of slavery, waits with open arms should they do so. God requires no appeasement—"I desire mercy, not sacrifice."

So, these prophets, even amidst their sharp critiques, reinforce the basic message of the salvation story. Salvation is a gift; it simply requires trust, while its fruit is faithful living. Reject the gift and you will face consequences—but even then, God awaits your return should you choose to do so. The point of the consequences is not punishment, nor is it that God is unable to forgive without the scales of justice being balanced. Rather, the consequences remind people that wholeness requires harmony with the God of the universe. The consequences themselves point toward God's healing love that must be trusted in for it to heal.

The events ultimately vindicate the prophets. First of all, the Hebrews' unwillingness to trust God and instead trust in the ways of the nations and their power politics and injustices leads to the failure of the Hebrew kingdoms, first the northern kingdom of Israel and then the southern kingdom of Judah. Secondly, though, and more profoundly, the underlying message of God's persevering love remains when the Hebrew people's tradition and community survives the fall of Jerusalem. According to the prophecies in

PART TWO: Jesus' Death and Salvation

Second Isaiah, this survival itself is a gift. God's will for healing emerges as more fundamental than God's anger at the people's unfaithfulness.

It is not as a nation-state successful in power politics that Israel is sustained. Abraham's descendants do keep their identity. They are scattered widely, but also retain a presence back in Judea. They remain at the mercy of the empires and always long for something more secure. Still, the promise to Abraham remains in effect and the tradition survives.

The next stage in the biblical story of salvation emerges when a prophet arises in Galilee, a kind of Jewish in-between area, nearer than the diaspora, but outside of Judea. This prophet shares a name with one of the Old Testament's main heroes: Joshua/Jesus. This name also expresses an aspiration. Jesus means "savior" or "liberator." As presented in the four Gospels, Jesus overtly linked himself with his forebears—not only Joshua, but Moses, Elijah, and a few other key prophets.

Remarkably, given how Christian theology has evolved in the centuries since Jesus's lifetime to assert a disjunction between "Christian salvation" and "Old Testament salvation," Jesus's message actually places him squarely within the mainstream of the Old Testament salvation story. For Jesus, salvation is a gift. Obedience follows as a response to the gift. Jesus affirms Torah as the source of guidance for this obedience-as-a-response-to-God's-mercy.

The God of the Exodus liberates captives from the Powers—and Jesus embraces this understanding of God. The God of Hosea responds to wandering Israel with mercy—and Jesus embraces this understanding of God. For example, Jesus tells how God responds to the wandering prodigal son with mercy. Jesus gives no hint of the need for some kind of sacrificial violence a la the logic of retribution as a prerequisite for salvation. Simply repent and trust in the good news of the presence of God's kingdom and respond with lives shaped by love—just as in the time of Abraham, of Moses, of Joshua, of Second Isaiah.

So, the story of Jesus stands in continuity with the Old Testament salvation story. It embraces the logic of mercy, not the logic of retribution. In Jesus, as in the Old Testament, God responds to brokenness not with punitive violence but with unconditional mercy. The spiral of violence that leads to vengeance that leads to brokenness and more violence must be resisted. Forgiveness trumps retribution.

The story of Jesus goes further, though. Amos, Hosea, and Micah underscored the truthfulness of that original story and also deepened it. So also Jesus affirmed what was already known about God and salvation and

Conclusion: Is There an Atonement Model in this Story?

yet added clarity and depth to the "old, old story." What came clearer with Jesus's story was the nature of the human predicament and the relevance of the biblical salvation story for this predicament. Rather than, as later theology often assumed, operating according to the logic of retribution, Jesus exposed retributivism as prevalent in the Powers of cultural exclusivism, religious institutionalism, and political authoritarianism, and as contrary to the will of God.

The story of Jesus's death does add something essential to the biblical portrayal of salvation that precedes it, as traditional Christian theology affirms. But this essential element is nearly the opposite of what the traditional theology says it is. Jesus's death reveals the logic of retribution to be the tool of evil, not the God-ordained rule of the universe. If Jesus's basic salvation message proclaims liberation from the Powers, the story of his death reveals the true character of some of the main Powers that bind people.

Jesus proclaimed and embodied emphases from Old Testament prophets: Torah as a gift from God meant to enhance human well-being and the sustenance of liberated existence ("the Sabbath is for human beings, not human beings for the Sabbath"), worship as an expression of all in the community's access to God and as an invitation to all the families of the earth ("the temple is meant to be a house of prayer for the nations"), and political life characterized by service and mutuality ("the Gentiles' leaders lord it over them; it must not be so with you").

With such a message, Jesus ended up in conflict with the Powers who found themselves threatened by his alternative consciousness. Pharisees, Sadducees, Herodians, and Romans alike asserted that Jesus violated their standards for behavior. By doing good in the way he did, by faithfully expressing God's will for human life, Jesus found himself in conflict with the principles of the guardians of society's alleged peace and order.

This conflict makes clear the problematic nature of these principles for peace and order. The Powers of cultural exclusivism, religious institutionalism, and political authoritarianism claim to serve God and society's welfare. However, their standards place them at odds with the one who actually embodies the will of the true God and, hence, the authentic peace that does serve society's welfare.

Jesus, remarkably, as he becomes aware of the tensions between his vision of authentic peace and the Powers, pushes the tensions further. When confronted by Pharisees, Sadducees, and Pilate, Jesus does not defer to their power but instead acts even more vigorously to express God's

PART TWO: Jesus' Death and Salvation

will for healing (even on the Sabbath), for the temple being a light for the nations, and for God's truth being affirmed. Jesus brings to the surface the brutality of his opponents.

Jesus's conflict with the Powers leads to their acts that silence him with extreme violence, in the name of their service to the gods of peace and order. When he remains firmly committed to the path of liberation, Jesus exposes the Powers as unworthy of the kind of trust they demand that, when given, leads to bondage.

The story of Jesus's death contributes to the larger biblical story of salvation insofar as it: (1) reinforces the truthfulness of the prophetic message of God's mercy as a critique of and alternative to the peace and order of power politics, (2) highlights the tension between Torah as revealed through Moses and the distortion of the law as an instrument of cultural exclusivism, (3) reveals the underlying violence of religious institutionalism and political authoritarianism, and (4) decisively refutes the belief that the logic of retribution reflects God's will.

Understanding the story of Jesus's death, for those who believe Jesus embodies human life as God intends it to be lived, will undermine uncritical acceptance of the demands for loyalty made by culture, religion, and state. Those who heed this story will find that they operate with a strong hermeneutic of suspicion toward any attempts by the Powers to follow the logic of retribution as a means to reinforce their domination.

The final element of the story points both backward (and underscores the truthfulness of Jesus's way that underscored the truthfulness of the Old Testament's prophetic message) and forward (and offered hope that the way of Jesus indeed does express life that cannot be conquered by the Powers of death). God raises Jesus from the dead. Jesus's resurrection vindicates his message. Rather than being ill-fated and naïve, a kind of quixotic idealism in the face of the "real world's" overwhelming force, Jesus's way links inextricably with the creative powers that form the universe. God blessed the way Jesus lived and taught, and God verified the message given at the time of Jesus' baptism: "This is my son, the beloved, with whom I am well pleased" (Matt 3:17).

Jesus' resurrection confirms that Jesus's own resistance to the Powers deserves to be followed. He challenged their hegemony; he proclaimed alternative ways to their exclusivism, institutionalism, and authoritarianism; he remained utterly committed to nonviolence even in the face of their brutality.[2]

---

2. Wink's *Engaging* remains our best treatment of this combination of critique,

Conclusion: Is There an Atonement Model in this Story?

The differences between the Bible's salvation story and atonement theology are significant enough to conclude that we do *not* find an atonement model in this story. The Bible's salvation story does not base salvation on Jesus's death. As David Brondos concludes, "Jesus' death may have been seen as the center and starting point" of traditional atonement theology. However, for the Bible "what was redemptive was the whole story, that is, all the events making up that story; the cross was redemptive only to the extent that it formed a part of that story."[3]

My reasons for concluding that we do not have an atonement model in this story include: (1) The story places the emphasis on God's mercy as the basis for salvation, not on Jesus's death. Atonement theology, when it defines salvation in terms of the cross, cannot help but add complicating layers to the dynamics of salvation, whereas the Bible's story itself from start to finish remains simple. God makes salvation available due to God's mercy—period.

(2) The story presents justice as restorative much more than as retributive. Salvation is "just" because it restores relationships and heals brokenness due to God's merciful initiative. This is contrary to the retributive notion that God's justice requires punishment and sacrifice to be satisfied as a prerequisite for making salvation possible.

(3) For atonement theology, Jesus's death is the core content. It provides a heretofore missing and necessary basis for salvation being made available. For the Bible's salvation story, the basis for salvation is given at the very beginning and never changes: it is God's mercy. Jesus's death provides no new content in relation to the essence of salvation. Jesus's death does confirm the origin basis for salvation and, crucially, reveals how powerfully the Powers resist his embodiment of God's mercy. Likewise, Jesus's resurrection does not change the basis for salvation but rather confirms it when it vindicates Jesus's way of life that reiterates the original basis for salvation, which is God's mercy.

Reflecting on the Bible's "Dark Side"

As I near the end of this book, I want to acknowledge that my focus has been limited in my treatment of biblical themes. I have traced what I understand to be the basic salvation story and sought to find there our best approximation of the Bible's portrayal of God's will for human beings. I

---

alternative consciousness, and unwavering adherence to creative nonviolence.

3. Brondos, *Paul*, 194–95.

believe that if we understand the Bible's salvation story as being a refutation of the logic of retribution rather than an expression of such logic, we will conclude that God Godself does not respond to wrongdoing with violence, but rather with mercy—and, hence, that we also should refuse to follow the logic of retribution in how we respond to wrongdoing.

However, the biblical materials are indeed diverse and, we could even say, messy. It is not without reason that many peace-minded people have turned from the Bible (especially the Old Testament) as a hopelessly "bloody book"—nor, that many who support the use of appropriate violence find in the Bible strong support for their position.

I decided for this book not directly to take on this perception of the Bible as being pro-violence. I chose rather to construct a positive case for the core message of mercy rather than to try to refute the counter-veiling evidence piece by piece. I took this path largely due to my belief that to focus on the problems would detract from the need simply to lay out the positive case. However, I recognize value in at least a brief hermeneutical reflection on how I might deal with this countervailing evidence.

I grant that the Bible, especially the Old Testament, does contain stories and direct teaching that speak of vengeance, retribution, and punishment. How should one who reads the Bible in light of the way of Jesus best understand these materials?

(1) We should probably recognize that the Bible contains within itself a variety of perspectives, some even mutually exclusive of others. So we should not be surprised, or even necessarily troubled to find pro-violence sentiment in the broader context of an ultimately anti-violence perspective. If we read the Bible in light of its overall message, we can accept that some elements are in tension with that message without actually threatening its viability.

We see a fairly clear example of this dynamic in the contrast between how the story of Jehu's vengeance upon King Ahab's descendants is recounted in 1 Kings and then the use of it later on in the prophet Hosea. The initial account seems to portray Jehu's violence in positive terms; Hosea, on the other hand, condemns it. The tension seems to be resolved when we recognize how Hosea's critique fits much better with broader biblical themes of the Hebrew people's calling to be a light of peace to the nations and God's own forbearance toward the rebellious Hebrew people as captured so poignantly in Hosea 11.[4]

---

4. Brenneman, "Prophets."

Conclusion: Is There an Atonement Model in this Story?

(2) The perspective of biblical writers differs from our modern sense of a materialistic universe that operates according to impersonal laws of cause and effect. In the Bible, everything comes from God. God is involved in all actions and reactions. So for biblical people to speak of God's connections with events in the world has somewhat different connotations that it would for modern people. For Jesus to say, for example, that God causes the rain to fall on the just and the unjust alike is basically saying, in modern terms, that God has created the world in such a way that when rain falls, it does not discriminate upon whom it falls but simply wets all in its path. But, for the biblical way of speaking of reality, it is God that does it, even if it is actually a natural and impersonal process.

Hence, at least some of the biblical language about God's involvement in judgment and "punishment" may actually simply be a way of speaking of the natural and impersonal processes of the world. That is, the world is set up so that when people violate the basic harmony of healthy human inter-relating, they will face negative consequences. We could call this "providential punishment," a sense that God has providentially established the world in such a way that human beings reap the natural negative consequences of sinful acts.

When the people of Israel follow the paths of disorder and disrespect for the dictates of Torah (that are dictates for harmony with the created order), they will be "judged" and "punished" by reaping the natural consequences of such departures from God's will. To say that God is part of this process is not to say that God acts in direct, unusual ways to punish particular people for particular acts so much as to say that God is part of the way the universe works. The imprecision of the "judgment" that characterizes many stories bears this suggestion out. For example, the Hebrew people suffered significant trauma as a consequence of the terrible sins their king David committed with Bathsheba and Uriah. David himself did not bear the brunt of those consequences; they were visited more upon his descendants. God was behind this providentially; however, God cannot be said directly and with precision to have punished David in a way that was commensurate with David's sins.

(3) The story makes clear throughout that the threats, and even carried-out incidents, of judgment and retribution served the broader purposes of God's work for salvation. Even the "providential punishing" is not an end in itself but ultimately serves redemptive ends.

Each of the three eighth-century prophets that we considered in chapter three (Amos, Micah, and Hosea) spoke sharp words of critique

PART TWO: Jesus' Death and Salvation

and uttered dire threats of judgment. In each case, though, the books end not with visions of ongoing punishment but with visions of healing and restoration. The threats were not meant to express God's will to punish; rather, the threats must be linked with the visions of healing and thus seen as having a redemptive, not punitive, intent.

(4) Mercy in the Bible means God heals that which is broken and does not simply accept brokenness and sinfulness. The vision that concludes the Bible illustrates this. Revelation portrays the New Jerusalem as welcoming those heretofore seen to be God's enemies, the "kings of the earth" and "the nations." However, this city is also portrayed as a place into which nothing unclean will enter. The leaves of the tree of life in the New Jerusalem are for the healing of the nations. Hence, the vision refers to transformation, not simply acceptance. This transformation is a gift, of course, an expression of God's mercy.

The healing requires resistance to the brokenness. The consequences of sinfulness, when seen as part of God's providential work to effect healing ("providential punishment") may therefore be seen as for human beings' welfare, even as they are "imprecise" and not always directly life-giving.

(5) So, if we look at the whole, we will see that retribution is secondary in the overall biblical perspective; mercy is central. The underlying logic is one wherein retribution, to the extent it is part of the picture at all, serves God's merciful, healing intentions. The biblical salvation story rests upon the logic of mercy, not the logic of retribution.

HEALING JUSTICE

To conclude, I would like to return briefly to the issue I used in chapter one to illustrate the costliness of the logic of retribution when it governs how we respond to wrongdoing—criminal justice.[5] What would a concept of justice look like if it were based, instead, on the logic of mercy—that is, on respect and concern for the people involved, on a commitment to respond constructively? Could such a relational or restorative approach to justice not only be articulated but actually implemented? Is it imaginable that the actual underpinning of salvation in the Bible (mercy) could shape a different kind of public policy that would avoid the kinds of human suffering exacerbated by the traditional retribution-oriented salvation theology I outline in chapter one?

---

5. Some of what follows is drawn from Grimsrud and Zehr, "Rethinking."

Conclusion: Is There an Atonement Model in this Story?

In fact, in recent decades a movement has emerged that has made significant progress in implementing such an approach—known as "restorative justice."[6] One of the earliest efforts that led to the current restorative justice movement came in the 1970s when two Canadian Mennonite peace workers, frustrated with existing criminal justice practices, conducted a series of "victim-offender reconciliation" encounters between two juvenile offenders and the numerous people these young men had victimized in a drunken spree. This led to the implementation of various forms of victim-offender mediation or reconciliation throughout North America, Europe, and elsewhere and to the development of restorative justice theory.

Restorative justice has drawn on various sources including non-retributive Christian and Jewish readings of the Bible as well as other religious traditions, and the conflict resolution movement as well as the seemingly contradictory movements for victim rights and alternatives to prison. Feminist theory has provided an important awareness of the patriarchal nature of our structures, including the justice system, but has also enriched the stream with its emphasis on an ethic of relationship. The stream is fed in important ways from a variety of traditional values, practices, and customs. Indeed, two of the most promising forms of restorative justice, Family Group Conferences and Circle Sentencing, come directly from aboriginal or indigenous values adapted to modern legal systems.

In contrast to the "retributive" paradigm of justice, the concept of restorative justice that underlies these approaches might be summarized like this: (1) Crime is primarily a violation of, or harm to, people and relationships. (2) Violations create obligations. The aim of justice is to identify needs and obligations so that things can be "made right" to the extent possible. (3) The process of justice should, to the extent possible, involve victims, offenders and community members in an effort mutually to identify needs, obligations, and solutions.

The restorative justice concept can be framed in a variety of ways, but two ideas are fundamental: restorative justice is harm (rather than rule) focused and it promotes the engagement of an enlarged set of stakeholders. Most restorative justice efforts can be seen as following from these two concepts.

---

6. One prominent account of the origins, philosophy, and practical approach of restorative justice is Zehr, *Changing*. Zehr demonstrates that important elements of this movement draw on similar theological perspectives to those articulated in this book. See also Sawatsky, *Justpeace*, and Redekop, *Changing*.

Restorative justice views crime first of all as harm done to people and communities. Our legal system, with its focus on rules and laws, often loses sight of this reality, that crime is essentially harm; consequently, it makes victims at best a secondary concern of justice. A harm focus, however, implies a central concern for victims' needs and roles. Restorative justice, then, begins with a concern for victims and how to meet their needs, for repairing the harm as much as possible. A focus on harm also implies an emphasis on offender accountability and responsibility—in concrete, not abstract, terms. Too often we have thought of accountability as punishment, that is, pain administered to offenders for the pain they have caused. In reality, this has very little to do with actual accountability.

Mainstream justice processes rarely encourage offenders to understand the consequences of their actions or to empathize with victims. On the contrary, the adversarial game requires offenders to look out for themselves. Offenders are discouraged from acknowledging their responsibility and are given little opportunity to act on this responsibility in concrete ways. The "neutralizing strategies"—the stereotypes and rationalizations that offenders use to distance themselves from the people they hurt—are never challenged. However, if crime is essentially about harm, accountability means being encouraged to understand that harm and to begin to comprehend the consequences of one's behavior. Moreover, it means taking responsibility to make things right in so far as possible, both concretely and symbolically.

The principle of engagement suggests that the primary parties affected by crime—victims, offenders, members of the community—should be given significant roles in the justice process. Engagement implies involvement of an enlarged circle of stakeholders as compared to the traditional justice process.

The three central questions of the retributive justice paradigm might be characterized like this: What laws have been broken? Who "done" it? What do they deserve? The comparable questions for a restorative approach then might be these: Who has been hurt? What are their needs? Whose obligations are they? "What does the Lord require?" asks the prophet Micah, and begins the answer like this: "To do justice. . . ." But what does justice require? The latter question is central to restorative justice. What does justice require for victims? For offenders? For communities?

Out of the traumas of victims' experiences come many needs.[7] They badly need what might be called somewhat ambiguously "an experience

---

7. Zehr, *Transcending*, 185–98.

Conclusion: Is There an Atonement Model in this Story?

of justice." This has many dimensions. Often it is assumed that vengeance is part of this need but various studies suggest that this is not necessarily so. The need for vengeance often may mostly be simply the result of justice denied.

The experience of justice seems to include public assurance that what happened to the victim was wrong, that it was unfair, that it was undeserved. Victims need to know that something is being done to make sure that the offense does not happen again. Often they feel the need for some repayment of losses, in part because of the statement of responsibility that is implied. So restitution and apologies from an offender can play an important role in the experience of justice.

Victims also need answers; in fact, crime victims often rate the need for answers above needs for compensation. Why me? What could I have done differently? What kind of person did this and why? These are just a few of the questions that haunt victims. Without answers, it can be very difficult to restore a sense of order and therefore to heal.

Another area is sometimes termed "truth-telling"—opportunities for victims to tell their stories and to vent their feelings, often repeatedly, to people that matter: to friends, to law enforcement people, perhaps even to those who caused this pain. Only by expressing their anger and by repeatedly telling their stories can many victims integrate this terrible experience into their own stories, their own identities.

Also important is the need for empowerment. In the crime, an offender has taken power over victims' lives—not only of their body and or property during the incident itself, but over their subsequent emotions, dreams and reality. Indeed, many victims find that, at least for awhile, the offense and the offender are in control of their psyche. That is profoundly unnerving. Without an experience of justice and healing, this too can last a lifetime.

Offenders need to be held accountable, but in ways that encourage them to grow in empathy and responsibility. However, they certainly have other needs as well. Instead of isolation, offenders need encouragement to be reintegrated—or integrated—into the community. They also need opportunities for personal transformation. This implies focus on developing competencies (instead of the usual focus on deficiencies). It requires that they have an opportunity to have their own needs—including the harms and sense of victimization that may have led to their actions—addressed.

Although retributive justice is done in the name of the "community" (which actually means the state), in reality the actual human community

PART TWO: Jesus' Death and Salvation

of those affected by the crime is left out of this process and its needs addressed only abstractly, if at all. Fears and stereotypes are heightened rather than addressed. People are encouraged to view things in simple dichotomies—them and us, guilty or innocent—rather than appreciate the rich nuances of real-life people and situations. Worst of all, perhaps, when the community is left out of the justice process, important opportunities for growth and community building are missed. When conflicts are processed appropriately, they provide the means to build relationships between people and within communities; take this away, and you take away a fundamental building block of community and of crime prevention.

Communities have needs well as responsibilities that must be addressed. To address these needs, a diverse set of practices has emerged in various communities. Most work in a cooperative relationship with the existing justice system, receiving referrals from it. Many are designed to provide alternative sentencing options or alternatives to arrest or prosecution. Others, such as those that work with severe violence, may be primarily designed to assist the healing of victims and offenders, with minimal impact on legal outcomes. Most, however, involve some form of victim-offender conferencing. They involve an opportunity for a facilitated dialogue between victim and offender, often with a written restitution agreement as part of the outcome.

Justice needs to be redefined in new terms, if not explicitly in the language of mercy, then in the language of peace and respect. Criminologists Richard Quinney and John Wildeman set the context like this: "From its earliest beginnings . . . the primary focus of criminology has been on retribution, punishment, and vengeance in the cause of an existing social order . . . rather than a criminology of peace, justice and liberation. . . . If crime is violent and wreaks violence on our fellows and our social relations, then the effort to understand and control crime must be violent and repressive."[8] However, such an approach only intensifies the spiral of violence leading to greater violence. What is needed is something that breaks the cycle of violence, a "peacemaking school of criminology."[9]

Such a peacemaking approach must take seriously (and vigorously critique) the philosophical and theological roots to retributive criminology. As this book has tried to show, the deepest roots of Western theology, found in the Bible, are indeed fully compatible with new, peacemaking approaches to criminal justice. The growing restorative justice movement

---

8. Quinney and Wildeman, *Problem*, 40–41.
9. Schwartz, *Dreams*.

Conclusion: Is There an Atonement Model in this Story?

shows that such a peacemaking school has great potential to impact our society's criminal justice practices in more humane ways. And in doing so, it will vindicate the Bible's salvation story.

Bibliography

Alexander, Michelle. *The New Jim Crow: Mass Incarceration in the Age of Colorblindness*. New York: The New Press, 2010.

Alison, James. *The Joy of Being Wrong: Original Sin Through Easter Eyes*. New York: Crossroad, 1998.

Anderson, Bernhard W. *The Eighth-Century Prophets: Amos, Hosea, Isaiah, Micah*. Minneapolis: Fortress, 1978.

Anselm. "Cur Deus Homo?" Translated by Janet Fairweather. In *Anselm of Canterbury: The Major Works*, edited by Brian Evans and G. R. Evans, 260–356. New York: Oxford University Press, 1998.

Avery-Peck, Alan J. "Oral Tradition (Early Judaism)." In *Anchor Bible Dictionary*, edited by D. N. Freedman, 5:34–37. New York: Doubleday, 1994.

Barr, David L. "Doing Violence: Moral Issues in Reading John's Apocalypse." In *Reading the Book of Revelation: A Resource for Students*, edited by David L. Barr, 97–108. Atlanta: Society of Biblical Literature, 2003.

Bauckham, Richard. *The Climax of Prophecy: Studies on the Book of Revelation*. Edinburgh, UK: T. & T. Clark, 1993.

———. *The Theology of the Book of Revelation*. New York: Cambridge University Press, 1993.

Beale, G. K. *We Become What We Worship: A Biblical Theology of Idolatry*. Downers Grove, IL: InterVarsity, 2008.

Beilby, James, and Paul R. Eddy, eds. *The Nature of the Atonement: Four Views*. Downers Grove, IL: InterVarsity, 2006.

Belousek, Darrin W. Snyder. *Atonement, Justice, and Peace: The Message of the Cross and the Mission of the Church*. Grand Rapids: Eerdmans, 2012.

Berman, Harold J. *Law and Revolution: The Formation of the Western Legal Tradition*. Cambridge, MA: Harvard University Press, 1993.

Berman, Joshua A. *Created Equal: How the Bible Broke with Ancient Political Thought*. New York: Oxford University Press, 2008.

Bianchi, Herman. *Justice as Sanctuary: Toward a New System of Crime Control*. Bloomington, IN: Indiana University Press, 1994.

Birch, Bruce C., et al. *A Theological Introduction to the Old Testament*. Nashville: Abingdon, 1999.

———. *Let Justice Roll Down: The Old Testament, Ethics, and Christian Life*. Louisville: Westminster John Knox, 1991.

Blount, Brian. *Can I Get a Witness? Reading Revelation through African-American Culture*. Louisville: Westminster John Knox, 2005.

Borg, Marcus J. *Conflict and Holiness in the Teachings of Jesus*, 2nd ed. Harrisburg, PA: Trinity Press International, 1998.

Bibliography

Bredin, Mark. *The Ecology of the New Testament: Creation, Re-Creation, and the Environment.* Colorado Springs, CO: Biblical Publishing, 2010.

Brenneman, James E. "Prophets in Conflict: Negotiating Truth in Scripture." In *Peace and Justice Shall Embrace: Power and Theopolitics in the Bible,* edited by Ted Grimsrud and Loren L. Johns, 49–63. Telford, PA: Pandora, 1999.

Brock, Rita Nakashima and Rebecca Parker. *Proverbs of Ashes: Violence, Redemptive Suffering, and the Search for What Saves Us.* Boston: Beacon, 2001.

Brondos, David A. *Paul on the Cross: Reconstructing the Apostle's Story of Redemption.* Minneapolis: Fortress, 2006.

Brooks, Roger. "Mishnah." In *Anchor Bible Dictionary,* edited by D. N. Freedman, 4:871–73. New York: Doubleday, 1994.

Brown, Raymond E. *The Death of the Messiah: From Gethsemane to the Grave.* New York: Doubleday, 1994.

Brueggemann, Walter. *1 & 2 Kings.* Macon, GA: Smyth and Helwys, 2000.

———. *An Introduction to the Old Testament: The Canon and Christian Imagination.* Louisville: Westminster John Knox, 2003.

———. *Genesis.* Louisville: John Knox, 1982.

———. *Isaiah 40–66.* Louisville: Westminster John Knox, 1998.

———. *Reverberations of Faith: A Theological Handbook of Old Testament Themes.* Louisville: Westminster John Knox, 2002.

———. *The Bible Makes Sense.* Winona, MN: St. Mary's, 1977.

———. *The Land: Place as Gift, Promise, and Challenge in Biblical Faith,* 2nd ed. Minneapolis: Fortress, 2002.

———. *The Prophetic Imagination,* 2nd ed. Minneapolis: Fortress, 2001.

———. *Theology of the Old Testament: Testimony, Dispute, Advocacy.* Minneapolis: Fortress, 1997.

———. *Tradition for Crisis: A Study in Hosea.* Atlanta: John Knox, 1968.

Capps, Donald. *The Child's Song: The Religious Abuse of Children.* Louisville: Westminster, 1995.

Carroll, John T. and Joel B. Green. *The Death of Jesus in Early Christianity.* Peabody, MA: Hendrickson, 1995.

Carter, Warren. *Matthew and Empire: Initial Explorations.* Harrisburg, PA: Trinity Press International, 2001.

Clements, Ronald E. Clements, *God and Temple.* Philadelphia: Fortress, 1965.

Cole, Graham A. *God the Peacemaker: How Atonement Brings Shalom.* Downers Grove, IL: InterVarsity, 2009.

Daly, Robert J. "Baal (Deity)." In *Anchor Bible Dictionary,* edited by D. N. Freedman, 1:545. New York: Doubleday, 1992.

———. *Christian Sacrifice: The Judaeo-Christian Background Before Origen.* Washington, DC: Catholic University Press, 1978.

———. *The Origins of the Christian Doctrine of Sacrifice.* Philadelphia: Fortress, 1978.

Donahue, John. *The Gospel in Parable.* Minneapolis: Fortress, 1987.

Douglass, James W. *The Nonviolent Coming of God.* Maryknoll, NY: Orbis, 1991.

Dunn, James D.G. *Jesus, Paul, and the Law.* Louisville: Westminster John Knox, 1990.

———. *Jesus Remembered: Christianity in the Making.* Grand Rapids: Eerdmans, 2003.

———. "The New Perspective in Paul." In *Jesus, Paul, and the Law: Studies in Mark and Galatians,* 183–214. Louisville: Westminster John Knox, 1990.

———. *The Partings of the Ways: Between Christianity and Judaism and Their Significance for the Character of Christianity*. Harrisburg, PA: Trinity Press International, 1991.

———. *The Theology of Paul the Apostle*. Grand Rapids: Eerdmans, 1998.

Elliott, Neil. *Liberating Paul: The Justice of God and the Politics of the Apostle*. Maryknoll, NY: Orbis, 1994.

———. *The Arrogance of the Nations: Reading Romans in the Shadow of Empire*. Minneapolis: Fortress, 2008.

Erickson, Millard. *Christian Theology*. Grand Rapids: Baker, 1984.

Evans, C.A. "Midrash." In *Dictionary of Jesus and the Gospels*, edited by Joel B. Green, et al., 544–48. Downers Grove, IL: InterVarsity, 1992.

Fretheim, Terence E. *The Message of the Book of Jonah*. Minneapolis: Augsburg, 1977.

Garland, David. *Peculiar Institution: America's Death Penalty in an Age of Abolition*. Cambridge, MA: Harvard University Press, 2010.

———. *The Culture of Control: Crime and Social Order in Contemporary Society*. Chicago: University of Chicago Press, 2001.

Gerbrandt, Gerald Eddie. *Kingship According to the Deuteronomic History*. Chico, CA: Scholars, 1986.

Gilligan, James. *Preventing Violence*. New York: Thames and Hudson, 2001.

———. *Violence: Our Deadly Epidemic and Its Causes*. New York: Putnam, 1996.

Gingerich, Ray and Ted Grimsrud, eds. *Transforming the Powers: Peace, Justice, and the Domination System*. Minneapolis: Fortress, 2006.

Goergen, Donald J. *The Death and Resurrection of Jesus*. Collegeville, MN: Michael Glazier, 1988.

Gorman, Michael. *Inhabiting the Cruciform God: Kenosis, Justification, and Theosis in Paul's Narrative Soteriology*. Grand Rapids: Eerdmans, 2009.

———. *Reading Paul*. Eugene, OR: Cascade, 2008.

———. *Reading Revelation Responsibly: Uncivil Worship and Witness: Following the Lamb Into the New Creation*. Eugene, OR: Cascade, 2011.

———. " 'While We Were Enemies': Paul, the Resurrection, and the End of Violence." In *Inhabiting the Cruciform God: Kenosis, Justification, and Theosis in Paul's Narrative Soteriology*, 129–60. Grand Rapids, MI: Eerdmans, 2009.

Gorringe, Timothy. *God's Just Vengeance: Crime, Violence, and the Rhetoric of Salvation*. New York: Cambridge University Press, 1996.

Gottwald, Norman K. *The Hebrew Bible in Its Social World and Ours*. Atlanta: Scholars, 1993.

Green, Joel B. and Mark D. Baker. *Recovering the Scandal of the Cross: Atonement in New Testament and Contemporary Contexts*. Downers Grove, IL: InterVarsity, 2000.

Greven, Philip. *Spare the Child: The Religious Roots of Punishment and the Psychological Impact of Physical Abuse*. New York: Knopf, 1991.

Grimsrud, Ted. *God's Healing Strategy: An Introduction to the Bible's Main Themes*, 2nd ed. Telford, PA: Cascadia, 2011.

———. "Healing Justice: The Prophet Amos and a 'New' Theology of Justice." In *Peace and Justice Shall Embrace: Power and Theopolitics in the Bible*, edited by Ted Grimsrud and Loren L. Johns, 64–85. Telford, PA: Pandora, 1999.

Grimsrud, Ted, and Howard Zehr. "Rethinking God, Justice, and Treatment of Offenders." In *Religion, the Community, and the Rehabilitation of Offenders*, edited by Thomas O'Connor, 259–85. New York: Haworth, 2002.

Bibliography

Hanson, Paul. *The People Called: The Growth of Community in the Bible*. San Francisco: Harper and Row, 1986.

Hardin, Michael, and Brad Jersek, eds. *Stricken By God? Nonviolent Identification and the Victory of Christ*. Grand Rapids: Eerdmans, 2007.

Harink, Douglas. "Paul and Israel: An Apocalyptic Reading." *Pro Ecclesia* 16.4 (2007), 359–80.

Hays, Richard. *The Faith of Jesus Christ: The Narrative Substructure of Galatians 3:1–4:11*, 2nd ed. Grand Rapids: Eerdmans, 2002.

Herzog, William R. *Jesus, Justice, and the Reign of God: A Ministry of Liberation*. Louisville: Westminster John Knox, 2000.

Heschel, Abraham Joshua. *The Prophets*, vol. 1. New York: Harper and Row, 1969.

———. *The Prophets*, vol. 2. New York: Harper and Row, 1971.

Hirst, John. "The Australian Experience: The Convict Colony." In *The Oxford History of the Prison*, edited by Norval Morris and David J. Rothman, 236–65. New York: Oxford University Press, 1998.

Hooker, Morna D. *The Gospel According to Mark*. Peabody, MA: Hendrickson, 1991.

Horsley, Richard A. *Jesus and Empire: The Kingdom of God and the New World Disorder*. Minneapolis: Fortress, 2003.

———. *Jesus and the Powers: Conflict, Covenant, and the Hope of the Poor*. Minneapolis: Fortress, 2011.

House, H. Wayne and John Howard Yoder. *The Death Penalty Debate*. Waco, TX: Word, 1991.

Howard-Brook, Wes. *"Come Out, My People!" God's Call Out of Empire in the Bible and Beyond*. Maryknoll, NY: Orbis, 2010.

Howard-Brook, Wes, and Anthony Gwyther. *Unveiling Empire: Reading Revelation Then and Now*. Maryknoll, NY: Orbis, 1999.

Hughes, Robert. *The Fatal Shore: The Epic of Australia's Founding*. New York: Knopf, 1987.

Hylton, Wil S. "Sick on the Inside: Correctional HMOs and the Coming Prison Plague." *Harper's Magazine* (August 2003) 43–54.

Jeffrey, Steve, et al. *Pierced For Our Transgressions: Rediscovering the Glory of Penal Substitution*. Wheaton, IL: Crossway, 2007.

Jewett, Robert. *Romans: A Commentary*. Hermeneia. Minneapolis: Fortress, 2006

Johns, Loren L. *The Lamb Christology of the Apocalypse of John: An Investigation into Its Origins and Rhetorical Force*. Tübingen: Mohr/Siebeck, 2003.

Josipovichi, Gabriel. *The Book of God: A Response to the Bible*. New Haven, CT: Yale University Press, 1988.

Kaufman, Gordon D. *In Face of Mystery: A Constructive Theology*. Cambridge, MA: Harvard University Press, 1993.

Kraybill, Donald B. *The Upside-Down Kingdom*, 2nd ed. Scottdale, PA: Herald, 1990.

Kraybill, J. Nelson. *Apocalypse and Allegiance: Worship, Politics, and Devotion in the Book of Revelation*. Grand Rapids: Brazos, 2010.

Levenson, Jon. *Sinai and Zion: An Entry into the Jewish Bible*. San Francisco: HarperCollins, 1985.

Limburg, James. *Hosea—Micah*. Atlanta: John Knox, 1988.

Lind, Millard C. "The Concept of Political Power in Ancient Israel." In *Monotheism, Power, Justice: Collected Old Testament Essays*, 135–52. Elkhart, IN: Institute of Mennonite Studies, 1990.

———. "Law in the Old Testament." In *Monotheism, Power, and Justice: Collected Old Testament Essays*, 61–81. Elkhart, IN: Institute of Mennonite Studies, 1990.

———. *Monotheism, Power, Justice: Collected Old Testament Essays*. Elkhart, IN: Institute of Mennonite Studies, 1990.

———. *Yahweh Is a Warrior: The Theology of Warfare in the Old Testament*. Scottdale, PA: Herald, 1980.

Logan, James Samuel. *Good Punishment? Christian Moral Practice and United States Imprisonment*. Grand Rapids: Eerdmans, 2008.

Long, D. Stephen, "Justification and Atonement." In Timothy Larson and Daniel J. Treier, eds., *The Cambridge Companion to Evangelical Theology*, 79–92. New York: Cambridge University Press, 2007.

Lorenzen, Thorwald. *Resurrection and Discipleship: Interpretive Models, Biblical Reflections, Theological Consequences*. Maryknoll, NY: Orbis, 1995.

Maier, Harry O. *Apocalypse Recalled: The Book of Revelation After Christendom*. Minneapolis: Fortress, 2002.

Mays, James Luther. "Hosea." In *The HarperCollins Study Bible*, edited by Wayne A. Meeks, 1340. New York: HarperCollins, 1993.

McHugh, Gerald Austin. *Christian Faith and Criminal Justice: Toward a Christian Response to Crime and Punishment*. Mahwah, NJ: Paulist, 1978.

Mendenhall, George. *The Tenth Generation: The Origins of the Biblical Tradition*. Baltimore: Johns Hopkins University Press, 1973.

Meyer, Ben F. "Jesus Christ." In *Anchor Bible Dictionary*, edited by D. N. Freedman, 3:773. New York: Doubleday, 1992.

Milgrom, Jacob. *Leviticus 1–16*. Anchor Bible. New York: Doubleday, 1991.

Miller, Alice. *For Your Own Good: Hidden Cruelty in Childrearing and the Roots of Violence*. New York: Farrar Straus and Giroux, 1983.

Miller, J. Maxwell, and John H. Hayes. *A History of Ancient Israel and Judah*. Philadelphia: Westminster, 1986.

Miller, Patrick D. *The Ten Commandments*. Louisville: Westminster John Knox, 2009.

———. *The Religion of Ancient Israel*. Louisville: Westminster John Knox, 2000.

Myers, Ched. *Binding the Strong Man: A Political Reading of Mark*. Maryknoll, NY: Orbis, 1988.

Paul, Shalom M. *Amos: A Commentary on the Book of Amos*. Hermeneia. Minneapolis: Fortress, 1991.

Placher, William. *Jesus the Savior: The Meaning of Jesus Christ for Christian Faith*. Louisville: Westminster John Knox, 2001.

Potter, Harry. *Hanging in Judgment: Religion and the Death Penalty in England*. New York: Continuum, 1993.

Quinney, Richard and John Wildeman. *The Problem of Crime: A Peace and Social Justice Perspective*. Mountain View, CA: Mayfield, 1991.

Redekop, Paul. *Changing Paradigms: Punishment and Restorative Discipline*. Scottdale, PA: Herald, 2008.

Rensberger, David. *Johannine Faith and Liberating Community*. Philadelphia: Westminster, 1988.

Rogerson, J. W. "Sacrifice in the Old Testament: Problems of Method and Approach." In *Sacrifice*, edited by M. F. C. Bourdillon and Meyer Fortes, 45–59. New York: Academic, 1980.

Bibliography

Rossing, Barbara. *The Choice Between Two Cities: Whore, Bride, and Empire in the Apocalypse*. Harrisburg, PA: Trinity Press International, 1999.

———. *The Rapture Exposed: The Message of Hope in the Book of Revelation*. Boulder, CO: Westview, 2004.

Salderini, Anthony T. "Scribes." In *Anchor Bible Dictionary*, edited by D. N. Freedman, 5:1015. New York: Doubleday, 1994.

Sanders, E. P. *The Historical Figure of Jesus*. New York: Penguin, 1993.

Santos, Michael G. *Inside: Life Behind Bars in America*. New York: St. Martin's, 2006.

Sawatsky, Jarem. *Justpeace Ethics: A Guide to Restorative Justice and Peacebuilding*. Eugene, OR: Cascade, 2008.

Scalia, Antonin. "God's Justice and Ours." *First Things* 123 (May 2002) 17–21.

Schlosser, Eric. "The Prison-Industrial Complex." *The Atlantic Monthly* 282.6 (December 1998) 51–77.

Schneidau, Herbert N. *Sacred Discontent: The Bible and the Western Tradition*. Berkeley, CA: University of California Press, 1976.

Schwager, Raymund. "Christ's Death and the Prophetic Critique of Sacrifice." *Semeia* 33 (1985) 109–23.

Schwartz, Regina. *The Curse of Cain: The Violent Legacy of Monotheism*. Chicago: University of Chicago Press, 1997.

Schwartz, Sunny. *Dreams from the Monster Factory: A Tale of Prison, Redemption, and One Woman's Fight to Restore Justice to All*. New York: Scribner, 2009.

Seow, Choou-Leong. "The First and Second Books of Kings." In *The New Interpreter's Bible*, volume 3, edited by Leander Keck, 1–296. Nashville: Abingdon, 1999.

Shuntz, William J. *The Collapse of American Criminal Justice*. Cambridge, MA: Harvard University Press, 2011.

Stott, John R. W. *The Cross of Christ*. Downers Grove, IL: InterVarsity, 1988.

Swartley, Willard M. *Covenant of Peace: The Missing Peace in New Testament Theology and Ethics*. Grand Rapids: Eerdmans, 2006.

———. *Israel's Scripture Traditions and the Synoptic Gospels: Story Shaping Story*. Peabody, MA: Hendrickson, 1994.

Trible, Phyllis. "Jonah." In *The New Interpreter's Bible*, edited by Leander E. Keck, 7:461–530. Nashville: Abingdon, 1996.

Van Buren, Paul. *A Theology of the Jewish-Christian Reality, Part 2: Christ in Context*. New York: Harper and Row, 1988.

Van Wijk-Bos, Johanna W. H. *Making Wise the Simple: The Torah in Christian Faith and Practice*. Grand Rapids: Eerdmans, 2005.

Volf, Miroslav. *Exclusion and Embrace: A Theological Exploration of Identity, Otherness, and Reconciliation*. Nashville: Abingdon, 1996.

Weaver, J. Denny. *The Nonviolent Atonement*, 2nd ed. Grand Rapids: Eerdmans, 2011.

Wengst, Klaus. *Pax Romana and the Peace of Jesus Christ*. Minneapolis: Fortress, 1987.

Willoughby, Bruce E. "Amos." In *Anchor Bible Dictionary*, edited by D. N. Freedman, 1:211. New York: Doubleday, 1992.

Wink, Walter. *Engaging the Powers: Discernment and Resistance in a World of Domination*. Minneapolis: Fortress, 1992.

———. *Naming the Powers: The Language of Power in the New Testament*. Minneapolis: Fortress, 1984.

———. *The Human Being: Jesus and the Enigma of the Son of Man*. Minneapolis: Fortress, 2002.

———. *Unmasking the Powers: The Invisible Forces That Determine Human Existence.* Minneapolis: Fortress, 1986.
Wright, N. T. *How God Became King: The Forgotten Story of the Gospels.* New York: HarperOne, 2012.
———. *Jesus and the Victory of God.* Minneapolis: Fortress, 1996.
———. *Justification: God's Plan and Paul's Vision.* London: SPCK, 2009.
———. *The Resurrection of the Son of God.* Minneapolis: Fortress, 2003.
———. "Romans." In *The New Interpreter's Bible*, edited by Leander E. Keck, 10:393–770. Nashville: Abingdon, 2002.
———. *Simply Jesus: A New Vision of Who He Was, What He Did, and Why He Matters.* New York: HarperOne, 2011.
———. *Surprised By Hope: Rethinking Heaven, the Resurrection, and the Mission of the Church.* New York: HarperOne, 2008.
Yoder Neufeld, Thomas R. *Killing Enmity: Violence in the New Testament.* Grand Rapids: Baker Academic, 2011.
Yoder, John Howard. *The Jewish-Christian Schism Revisited.* Grand Rapids: Eerdmans, 2003.
———. *The Politics of Jesus*, 2nd ed. Grand Rapids: Eerdmans, 1994.
Young, Frances M. *Sacrifice and the Death of Christ.* London: SPCK, 1975.
Zehr, Howard. *Changing Lenses: A New Focus for Crime and Justice,* 3rd ed. Scottdale, PA: Herald, 2005.
———. *Transcending: Reflections of Crime Victims.* Intercourse, PA: Good Books, 2001.

Author Index

Alexander, Michelle, 12
Alison, James, 180, 184
Anderson, Bernhard, 62, 67
Anselm, 3, 5, 6, 9
Augustine, 6, 9
Avery-Peck, Alan J., 118

Baker, Mark, 89, 109, 167
Barr, David L., 207
Bauckham, Richard, 209, 211, 212, 214, 216, 218, 221
Beale, G. K., 59
Beilby, James, 5
Belousak, Darrin W. Snyder, 2
Berman, Harold J., 9
Berman, Joshua A., 41
Bianchi, Herman, 9, 17, 19, 23
Birch, Bruce C., 29, 30, 38, 40, 42, 44, 47, 113, 115, 131, 133, 136, 150, 153
Blount, Brian, 218
Borg, Marcus J., 85, 119, 122, 123, 125, 127
Bredin, Mark, 221
Brenneman, James E., 57, 234
Brock, Rita Nakashima, 90
Brondos, David A., 85, 186, 194, 206, 233
Brooks, Roger, 118
Brown, Raymond E., 103, 107
Brueggemann, Walter, 28, 29, 34, 36, 41, 43, 45, 49-54, 58, 60, 64, 121, 132, 136, 137, 149, 151, 153, 155, 157-59

Calvin, John, 6
Capps, Donald, 3
Carroll, John T., 96, 97, 98, 109, 147
Carter, Warren, 163, 166, 168, 179
Clements, Ronald E., 132, 135, 136
Cole, Graham A., 5

Daly, Robert J., 43, 46, 59, 86
Donahue, John, 84
Douglass, James W., 109
Dunn, James D. G., 119, 123, 125, 126, 141, 144, 147, 189, 191, 192

Eddy, Paul R., 5
Edwards, Jonathan, 7
Elliott, Neil, 187, 190, 191
Erickson, Millard, 6
Evans, Brian, 9
Evans, C. A., 117
Evans, G. R., 9

Fretheim, Terence E., 116

Garland, David, 8, 10, 12, 13, 16
Gerbrandt, Gerald Eddie, 156
Gilligan, James, 4, 12, 13, 16-18
Gingerich, Ray, 92
Goergen, Donald J., 109, 175-77
Gorman, Michael, 187, 192, 199, 203, 206, 210, 215, 217
Gorringe, Timothy, 2, 3, 8, 9, 11, 19
Gottwald, Norman K., 34, 40

Author Index

Green, Joel B., 89, 96–98, 109, 147, 167
Greven, Philip, 7
Grimsrud, Ted, 7, 29, 63, 92, 236
Gwyther, Anthony, 207, 214, 216, 220, 222

Hanson, Paul, 40
Hardin, Michael, 2
Harink, Douglas, 194, 199
Hayes, John H., 133, 137
Hays, Richard, 188
Herzog, William R., 69, 74, 95, 100, 101, 102, 119, 125, 127, 138, 139, 140, 141, 143, 145, 175
Heschel, Abraham Joshua, 58, 60, 64, 65, 67, 68
Hirst, John, 13
Hooker, Morna D., 146
Horsley, Richard A., 55, 161, 162, 165, 179
House, H. Wayne, 3, 11
Howard-Brook, Wes, 149, 158, 207, 214, 216, 220, 222
Hughes, Robert, 13–15
Hylton, Wil S., 17

Jeffrey, Steve, 6
Jersek, Brad, 2
Jewett, Robert, 194–97, 200, 201, 204
Johns, Loren L., 208
Josipovici, Gabriel, 24

Kaufman, Gordon D., 8
Kraybill, Donald B., 118, 120, 121, 140, 149
Kraybill, J. Nelson, 211

Levenson, Jon, 42, 47, 132
Limburg, James, 57, 62, 66
Lind, Millard C., 33, 40–42, 155
Logan, James Samuel, 12, 17
Long, D. Stephen, 3, 4, 226

Lorenzen, Thorwald, 172, 173, 175, 176, 182
Luther, Martin, 6

Maier, Harry O., 211, 218, 219, 225
Mays, James Luther, 59
McHugh, Gerald Austin, 17
Mendenhall, George, 151
Meyer, Ben F., 70
Milgrom, Jacob, 45, 46
Miller, Alice, 3
Miller, J. Maxwell, 133, 137
Miller, Patrick D., 42, 46
Myers, Ched, 160

Parker, Rebecca, 90
Paul, Shalom M., 53, 60, 62, 63
Placher, William, 180
Potter, Harry, 3

Quinney, Richard, 240

Ramsey, Paul, ix
Redekop, Paul, 237
Rensberger, David, 107, 108, 164, 165, 166
Rogerson, John W., 44–46, 86
Rossing, Barbara, 208, 219, 220, 225
Russell, John, 14

Salderini, Anthony T., 122
Sanders, E. P., 118
Santos, Michael G., 17
Sawatsky, Jarem, 237
Scalia, Antonin, 8, 23
Schlosser, Eric, 17
Schneidau, Herbert N., 24
Schreiner, Thomas, 5
Schwager, Raymund, 146
Schwartz, Regina, 36
Schwartz, Sunny, 240
Seow, Choou-Leong, 51
Shunz, William J., 10

Stott, John R. W., 6
Swartley, Willard M., ix, 145–47, 211

Van Buren, Paul, 119
Van-Wijk-Bos, Johanna, 40
Volf, Miroslav, 196

Weaver, J. Denny, 9
Wengst, Klaus, 160, 162, 163, 165
Wildeman, John, 240
Willoughby, Bruce E., 65
Wink, Walter, 76, 86, 92, 97, 111, 159, 232
Wright, N. T., 21, 73, 76, 80, 100, 104, 106, 109, 139, 142, 145, 164, 174, 177, 181, 182, 187, 196, 199, 200, 203

Yoder, John Howard, ix, 3, 11, 40, 74, 86, 126, 163, 204
Yoder Neufeld, Thomas R., 144, 168
Young, Frances M., 45

Zehr, Howard, 7, 9, 11, 236, 237, 238

Scripture Index

OLD TESTAMENT

Genesis

	27, 32, 149
1	29
1–12	77–78
4	43
8:21	37
12	31, 37, 206
12:1–3	31, 43, 58, 193, 222
12:3	31, 104, 128, 181, 196
17	121
19	35
37–50	150

Exodus

	40, 150
1–15	37, 154
1:8	32, 150
1:10–11	150
1:13–15	150
2:23	152
2:23–25	32
6:6	70
6:12	121
6:30	121
15:1	33
19:6	40, 181
20:1–17	82
20:2	42, 81, 181
20:3	81
21:8	85
21:30	85
32	44

Leviticus

	40, 60, 74, 141, 229
1–7	44
4–6	45
14	122
17:11	45, 86
19	43, 49, 98, 100, 181
19:2	125
19:18	80, 82
19:33–34	33, 41
24:5–9	123
25:8–12	74
25:42	42
25:47–52	85
26:41	121

Numbers

	40
28:9–10	124

Deuteronomy

	40, 41, 153
6:5	80, 82
7:8	38
10:16	121
13:5	42
15:15	42
17	152, 154, 155
17:14–17	153
17:14–20	41

Scripture Index

Deuteronomy (cont.)
17:17	154
17:18–20	153
17:20	41
20:1	42
21:23	173
24:18	42
24:22	42
28:68	155
30:6	121

Judges
19–21	57
21:25	151

1 Samuel
2:1–10	70
4	130
8:1–3	151
8:5	152
8:10–18	56, 152
8:18	152
8:19–20	152
8:22	152
21:1–6	123

1 Kings
	153, 156, 234
1–11	153
3:1	155
6–7	131
7:8	155
8:12–13	132
9:6–8	154
9:24	155
11	154
11:1	155
11:4	154
12:14	154
17:1–16	74
18:17	51
21	50, 56, 65
21:16	51
21:20	51
21:29	51

2 Kings
	153, 156
5:14	74
9:13	103
9–10	56
17:5–23	156
18–20	156
23:28–29	156
25:1–22	136

Ezra
	116
1–2	136
7:11–26	137

Nehemiah
	116
2:1–8	137

Psalms
22	33
27:1	29
50:1–15	201
72	153
77	33
78	33
78:22	29
87	156
89:10	70
89:13	70
101	153
105	33
106	33
110:1	105
114	33
115	190
118:22–23	146
135:18	59
136	33
143:2	196

Scripture Index

Isaiah

	184
2:2–4	32
5:1–7	146
14:4–21	155
19	156
36–39	156
37:23–29	155
40	36
40–55	30, 37, 38
40:3–5	71
43	36
43:1	36
43:1–7	85
43:4	37
44:21–23	85
44:28	158
45:1	158
47	157
47:5–7	158
47:10–11	158
49:6	71
51:1–3	37
52:7	29
52:10	29
54:9–10	37
56	145
56:7	104, 145

Jeremiah

	35
6:10	121
7	135, 145
7:1–11	104
7:9–11	135
7:11	145
9:25–26	121
31:31–34	36
43–44	156
46	156
52:28–30	136

Ezekiel

8–11	136
28:1–19	155
29–32	156
40–48	137

Daniel

1:20	163
2–4	158
2:37–45	163
4:31	162
4:34–37	158
4:36	163
7:13–14	105

Hosea

	20, 35, 46, 47, 52–57, 59, 61–63, 65, 114, 201, 229, 230, 234
1:2	59
1:4	56
1:10–11	65
2:14–20	65
3:1	59
4:1–2	57
4:6	61
5:1	59
5:6	61
6:6	21, 64, 66, 124, 142
6:9	57
8:11–13	61
9:1	59
9:1–9	59
10:9	57
10:11–12	63
10:12	64
10:13	56
10:13–14	57
11	4, 34, 35, 39, 43, 53, 234, 235
11:1	34, 54
11:2	35, 52
11:8	35
11:8–9	58
11:9	35
12:6	62, 64
14:1–3	62

Scripture Index

Amos
20, 46, 47, 52–56, 58, 60–64, 114, 229, 230, 235
1:11	56
1:13	56
2:6–7	55
2:9–10	53
3:1–2	53, 60
3:9–10	56
4:4	60
5:6	62
5:14–15	63
5:21–23	61
6:12	55
9:7–8	53
9:11–15	65
9:14–15	65

Jonah
116, 117, 156, 157
4:2	117

Micah
20, 47, 52–55, 57, 59, 61, 63, 66, 114, 229, 230, 235
2:1–2	55
2:8	57
3:1–3	55
3:9–11	56
4:1–3	32
4:1–5	57
5:1–10	58
5:13	59
6:4–5	61
6:6–8	61, 63
6:8	64, 66
6:12	58
7:14–15	66
7:18–20	66

Nahum
156
3:18–19	156

Haggai
137

Zechariah
137
1:17	138

Malachi
4:5–6	70

Sirach
12:4	83
12:6	83
33:20	83

1 Maccabees
13:51	103

2 Maccabees
10:7	103

~

New Testament

Matthew
21, 73, 84, 85, 96, 114, 122, 142, 143, 161, 174, 182
1:21	73
2:3	143
2:4	143
3:17	232
4:23	78
4:23—9:35	79
5–7	79
5:17	114
5:17–18	73
8:1–4	79, 122
8:5–13	79
8:10	79
8:14–15	79
8:16–18	79
8:19	122
8:28–34	79, 122

Scripture Index

Matthew (cont.)

8–9	79
9:2–8	79
9:3	122
9:6	122
9:9	79
9:10–11	122
9:13	21, 142, 201
9:18–25	79
9:27–31	79
9:32–33	79
9:33	79, 80
9:35	78
11:3	78
11:4–5	78
11:19	78
11:13	70
12:1–14	123, 124, 129
12:2	123
12:3	123
12:5	123
12:6	124
12:7	21, 124, 142, 201
12:10	124
12:11	124
12:12	124
12:14	125, 128
12:15	125
17:9–13	70
19:16–26	80
22:34–40	204
22:35–40	73
22:37–40	114
23:23	101
25:31	84
25:40	84
25:45	84
27:17	165
27:22	165
27:62–66	179
28:11–15	179
28:18–20	182

Mark

21, 75, 85, 98, 103, 105, 109, 122, 144, 147, 148

1:14	75
1:15	1, 75
1:40–45	144
2:6–7	98
2:16	98, 144
2:18	98
2:23–28	123
2:24	98
2:27	124
3:1–5	161
3:1–6	123
3:2	98
3:6	98
3:30	144
5:1–17	144
5:9	162
5:24–34	144
6:14–15	70
7:5	118
8:31	85
9:31	85
9:36	83
10:17–22	80
10:42	162
10:42–43	85, 113
10:42–45	199
10:45	85
11:1	144
11:7	147
11:8	103
11:11	144
11:12–14	144
11:15	144
11:15–16	103
11:17	143
11:18	104, 145, 146
11:20–21	144
11:27	146
11:28	104
12:1–12	105, 145
12:12	146
12:41–44	147

Scripture Index

Mark (*cont.*)

13	146
13:1–2	105
13:2	146
14:1	146
14:1–2	105
14:32–50	105
14:53	105
14:58	146
14:61	148
14:61–62	105
14:63–64	106, 147
15:25–34	109
15:29	146
15:38	146
15:39	147, 148
15:46–47	109
16:8	174

Luke

21, 69, 70, 71, 72, 80, 81, 96, 97, 98, 99, 103, 107, 114, 122, 142, 143, 171, 174

1:5	69
1:16–17	70
1:31–33	70
1:46–55	70
1:49–53	96
1:54–55	70, 72
1:68	70
1:69	71
1:71	71
1:72–73	71
1:78–79	71
2:4	71
2:11	71
2:21	71
2:21–40	142
2:22	142
2:22–24	71
2:24	142
2:25–26	71
2:28–32	71
2:32	74, 142
2:36	71
2:38	72
2:46	143
2:49	143
4:1–13	72, 199
4:5	97
4:9	97
4:13	97
4:22	97
4:28	97
4:16–30	73, 97
4:19	74
4:21	72
4:24	74
4:25–27	74
5:17	97
5:21	97
6:1–11	123
6:22–23	82
6:35–36	83
6:36	125
7:36–50	98
7:39	98
7:47	98
8:30	162
9:7–9	99
9:9	99, 107
9:22	99
9:23–25	99
9:51	99, 102, 170
10:16	99
10:25	80
10:25–37	80
10:28	80
11:33–34	102
11:39–44	100
11:42	100
11:45	101
11:45–52	101
11:49	101
11:53–54	101
13:1	96, 160
13:31–33	102
15:11–32	83

Luke (*cont.*)

15:12	83
15:15	83
15:18–19	83
15:31	84
18:9–14	76
18:18–25	80
18:20	81
19:11–27	102
19:28	99, 102
19:36	103
19:42	103
23:1–12	99
23:6–12	99
23:8	107
23:9	107
23:12	96, 107 164
23:50–51	109
23:50–56	173
24:5	174
24:11	174
24:12	174
24:21	173, 211

John

	21, 106, 107, 174
2:19	178
6	165
11	170
11:45–53	106, 165
18:31	106
18:33–36	107
18:37	107, 108
18:39	108
19:6	108
19:12	108, 164
19:15	108, 166
19:16	108

Acts

	129, 176, 183
1:1–3	183
1:3–11	174
1:8	183
7–9	183
7:58	183
8:1	183

Romans

	126, 186, 194, 204, 205
1–3	201, 203, 204, 206
1:16–17	187, 188, 189, 198, 202
1:17	187
1:16—3:31	187
1:17	189, 198
1:18	190–92, 197, 198, 201
1:18–32	191, 192, 194
1:18—3:20	189
1:19–20	190
1:20	194
1:21	189, 193
1:22	190
1:22–31	189
1:23	191
1:24	190, 191
1:25	191
1:26	190, 191
1:27	191
1:28	191
1:29–31	191
1:32	191, 193
2	199
2:1	188, 192
2:1–2	193
2:2	192
2:4	193
2:5	193
2:9	193
2:11	193
2:12	193
2:14	194
2:15	194
2:17–23	192
2:23–24	194
2:26	194
3:1	196
3:2	196
3:9	194, 197

Scripture Index

Romans (*cont.*)

3:10–18	196
3:20	127, 188, 196, 198
3:21	187, 188, 204
3:21–24	202
3:21–31	188, 198
3:22	199
3:23	200
3:24	200
3:25	200–202
3:26	202
3:27	202
3:27ff.	192
3:28	203
3:29	203
3:30	204
3:31	187, 204
4	204
5:1–10	202
5:1–11	189
7	197
7:5	195
7:10	195
7:11	195
7:24	196, 198
7:25	196
8:9–11	199
8:38–39	199
9–11	196
11:32	189
13:8–10	194, 195, 204, 205
13:9	192

1 Corinthians

2:8	97

Galatians

	126
1:14	195
2:16	192

Ephesians

6:17	218

Philippians

2	212
3:5–6	195

Hebrews

4:12	218

Revelation

	149, 158, 207–10, 213, 215, 217, 221–23
1	208
1:1	209, 223
1:4	210
1:5	208, 209, 211, 218, 219, 224
1:6	210, 224
1:7	224
1:9	216
1:10—3:22	210
2–3	213, 223
4	210, 212
5	210, 212, 213, 225
5:3	211
5:4	211
5:5	217
5:6–7	211
5:10	224
5:12	212
5:13	212
7:9	216, 224
12:9	213
12:17	213
13	213, 224
13:1–2	213
13:1—14:5	224
13–14	213
13:3	214
13:4	214
13:7	213, 215
13:9	214
13:10	214
13:11	215
13:14–15	215
14:1–5	215

Scripture Index

Revelation (cont.)

14:4	215, 225	19:20	218
15:4	221, 224	19:21	218, 225
16:14	217, 218	21	219
16:16	219	21–22	219
17	218	21:2	220
17:1–3	219	21:4	219
17–18	217	21:5–8	220
17:1—22:5	224	21:9–10	219
17:6	225	21:9–11	221
18:23	217	21:9–14	220
18:24	217	21:12	220
19	217, 225	21:14	220
19:1–2	217	21:22	148
19:1–10	217	21:23	220
19:7–8	218	21:23–24	224
19:11	217, 218	21:24	220, 221
19:11–21	217, 218	21:24–26	208
19:13	218	21:26	221
19:14	218	21:27	221
19:19	218	22:1–5	220
		22:2	221

Subject Index

Abraham, 1, 24, 30–33, 37–38, 43, 49, 52, 66, 69–72, 75, 77, 104, 110, 116, 121, 181, 196, 199–200, 203–4, 206, 220, 223, 228, 230

Anger, 7, 35, 47, 54, 58, 66–68, 108, 180, 189, 197, 201, 202, 227, 229, 230, 239

Assyria, 31, 54, 62, 117, 149, 154–57, 214

atonement ix, 3–5, 7, 9, 10, 19, 21–22, 46, 95, 138–40, 188, 200–201, 226, 233

Babylon, 30–31, 36, 115, 117, 136–37, 149, 154–58, 163, 210, 214, 217, 219–21, 224–25, 228

blood, 11, 29, 32, 45–46, 55–57, 86, 96, 101, 109, 140, 151, 160, 171, 188, 201–2, 209–10, 217, 218, 223–25, 234

bondage, 73, 85–86, 112, 129, 186, 192, 196–98, 200, 202, 204–6, 221, 232

boundary markers, 94, 115–21, 126–27, 167, 169, 175, 177, 192, 194, 197, 200, 203–4

Caesar, 107, 162, 164, 166, 172, 179, 206, 214, 216, 221

capital punishment, death penalty, 3, 5, 8, 11, 13–14, 108, 160

circumcision, 71, 115–16, 119, 121, 126–27, 194, 198–99, 204

commands, commandments, 20, 41–42, 44, 51–52, 54, 73, 81–82, 112–14, 143, 153–54, 181, 188, 192, 195, 197, 199

community of faith, 2, 24, 30–31, 33, 38, 41, 43–48, 50–56, 58–61, 63, 66–68, 74, 77, 79, 82, 97, 98, 100, 113–20, 122, 126–31, 133–35, 137, 139, 141, 145, 150, 151–54, 157–59, 163, 169–72, 178, 180–82, 191, 197–98, 203–4, 206, 228–29, 231

compassion, 6, 30, 33, 35, 37–39, 43, 83, 85, 89, 117, 122, 209, 211

corporal punishment, 2–3, 5, 227

covenant, 32, 35–37, 41, 43–46, 48, 50, 52–55, 58–60, 63, 65–68, 71–72, 74, 113, 121, 123, 125–33, 135–36, 152–59, 161, 169–70, 174, 177, 189, 191, 194, 196, 198, 222, 229

creation, 28–29, 31, 55, 89, 182, 190–92, 194, 198, 205–6, 209–12, 215, 220–22, 225

criminal justice, 2–3, 5, 7–12, 16, 227, 236–37, 240–41

cross, 4–5, 11, 99, 109, 147, 164, 168, 170, 173, 176, 180, 183, 202, 207–8, 211–12, 218, 226, 233

crucifixion, 7, 86, 89–90, 95, 97, 107–9, 112–13, 144, 149, 163–65, 171, 173, 176, 179, 215–17, 223

Subject Index

cultural exclusivism, 21, 87, 92, 110–11, 125, 127, 129, 170–72, 175, 177, 183, 231–32

David, 30, 70–71, 123, 130–32, 146, 152–53, 155, 211, 235
death, 3, 5, 7–8, 14, 21–22, 33, 45–46, 71, 77–78, 90, 85–87, 89–91, 95, 97, 129, 147–48, 151, 154, 156–57, 160, 163, 165–69, 172, 173, 174–77, 179–80, 182–84, 186–87, 189–90, 193, 195–96, 198, 205, 208–9, 212–14, 218–21, 223–24, 226, 231, 232
debts, 17, 74, 142–43, 167

Egypt, 24, 30, 32–36, 38, 40–43, 49, 52–54, 56, 60–61, 65–66, 74, 81, 85–86, 113–14, 119, 131, 133, 139, 149–52, 155–56, 161, 163, 181, 200, 228
Elijah, 30, 50–52, 69–70, 97, 162, 230
exile, 30–32, 36, 37–38, 49, 85, 114–15, 117, 119, 121, 136–37, 139, 149, 154, 156–59, 200, 206, 216
exodus, 30–31, 34–35, 38–39, 41, 48–49, 54, 67, 70, 86, 110, 130–31, 151–53, 155–56, 181, 206, 222, 230

faithfulness, 36–37, 43, 47–48, 57, 65–66, 87, 112, 117, 121, 125, 135–36, 175, 183, 187–89, 194, 196, 199–200, 202–4, 209, 212–13
freedom, 15, 22, 29, 32, 39, 94, 97, 111, 129, 132–33, 135, 148, 151, 192, 202, 205–6, 209–10
fulfillment, 2, 71–72, 94, 115, 210, 214, 220

gift, 21, 23, 33–34, 36, 39, 40, 42–45, 49, 52–53, 59, 64, 66, 70, 76, 80–81, 113, 122, 142, 181, 186, 188, 198–200, 205–6, 224, 228–31, 236
good news, 1–2, 19, 69, 72–73, 75, 77–78, 87, 97, 162, 181, 191, 198, 230
gospel, 1, 21, 77, 84, 87, 162, 182, 184, 187, 189, 196, 198–99, 204, 218
grace, 38, 40, 113, 126, 135, 167, 188, 200, 202
guilt, 6, 9, 12, 18, 56, 62, 68, 95, 106, 120, 123–24, 147, 192, 240

harmony, 21–22, 28–29, 48, 53, 62, 72, 81, 94, 113, 124, 142–43, 206, 221–22, 229, 235
healing, 1, 9, 11, 19, 24, 27–28, 30–31, 33–45, 47, 49, 54, 61–62, 64, 66–68, 77–81, 87, 90–91, 97–98, 100, 101–3, 110, 113, 122, 124–26, 128–29, 144, 161–62, 169, 175–77, 180–81, 183–86, 188, 200, 202–3, 205–6, 211–12, 214–15, 219–21, 223, 225, 227–30, 232–33, 236, 239–40
health, 10, 27–28, 41–43, 46–48, 51, 54, 64, 68, 229, 235
Herod, 96, 104, 139, 141, 143, 146, 160–61, 164
Herod Antipas, 78, 96, 99, 102, 107, 160–61, 164, 171
holiness, 4–7, 9, 11, 19, 21–22, 38–39, 41–43, 47, 66, 68, 72, 77, 83–84, 87, 95, 110, 119, 122–23, 125–26, 135, 169–70, 180–81, 184–86, 197, 201–2, 228–29

Subject Index

honor, 4–5, 7, 20–22, 31, 41, 47, 72, 77, 81, 87, 100, 119, 186, 197, 201–2, 208, 212

identity, 17, 34–37, 60, 72, 75, 79, 85, 92, 95, 103, 107, 114–16, 118–21, 123, 127, 137–38, 152, 159, 169, 173, 176, 178, 195–96, 198, 200, 203–4, 209, 211, 230, 239
idols, idolatry, 2, 21–22, 35, 44, 46, 52, 55–56, 58–59, 60, 64–65, 67, 73, 82, 93–95, 110–11, 114, 154, 156, 158, 168, 189–201, 203–6, 208, 209–10, 215, 222, 223–24, 229
inheritance, 41, 49, 51, 55, 65, 80–81, 83, 150
injustice, 20, 30, 47, 51–61, 64–65, 67, 95, 102, 114, 135, 145, 154, 156, 187–95, 197, 199, 200, 203–4, 206, 221–22, 228–29

Jerusalem, New Jerusalem, 32, 36–37, 54–55, 72, 92, 96–97, 99, 102–4, 112, 130, 132–45, 147–48, 156–57, 161, 170–71, 173, 180, 183, 199, 208, 210, 215, 217, 219–25, 229, 236
John the Baptist, 1, 69, 70, 75–76, 78, 82, 99, 115, 142
Joshua, 30, 52, 70, 75, 161, 230
judgment, 6, 27, 30, 35, 51, 54–56, 58, 84–85, 104, 119–20, 136, 145, 157, 171, 175, 191–93, 217–18, 221, 223, 225, 235–36
justice, 4–6, 8–11, 19, 20–22, 29–31, 38, 41–43, 45–47, 50, 53–55, 58, 60, 62–69, 72, 77, 87, 95, 100–102, 122, 128, 138, 141, 145, 151, 153, 163, 167, 171, 174–75, 179–80, 186–91, 193–95, 197–207, 221, 226–29, 233, 236–41
justification by faith, 3–4, 21, 187–88, 198, 203–4, 226

kingdom of God, reign of God, 1–2, 22, 24, 40, 70, 75–78, 81–85, 97, 100, 107, 109, 113, 124, 161–65, 167, 172, 177, 209–10, 222, 224, 230
kingdom, Hebrew, 30, 35–36, 53–54, 56–57, 114, 136, 153–54, 156, 229
kingship, 30, 41, 46, 50, 54, 99, 103, 107, 136, 152–55, 162, 165, 167, 172

Lamb, 148–49, 207–13, 215–25
law, biblical, 5–9, 20–21, 28, 30, 34, 36, 39–43, 48–50, 52–53, 61, 64–66, 68, 71, 73, 80, 87, 92–95, 97, 100–104, 108, 111–29, 131, 142–43, 150–51, 153, 155, 161–62, 166–67, 170, 177–78, 180, 188, 191–98, 202–6, 223, 228, 232
law, secular, 8–12, 17, 19–20, 107, 109, 235, 238–39
liberation, 28–30, 32–35, 37, 39–40, 42–43, 47, 49–50, 52–54, 56, 58, 64–66, 73–74, 80–81, 85–86, 102, 110, 112–14, 119, 122, 134, 150, 178, 196–98, 200, 204, 228, 230–32, 240
logic of mercy, 19, 20, 83, 85, 87, 124, 188, 197, 227, 230, 236
logic of retribution, 5–7, 10, 13, 16, 19, 21–23, 27–28, 35, 37–38, 42–44, 48, 61, 68, 72, 74, 78, 80, 82–83, 85–87, 89, 91, 94–96, 110, 125, 163, 170–72, 180, 184–5, 226–32, 234, 236

Subject Index

love, 3, 22, 29–31, 33–38, 41–42, 44–45, 47, 49, 53–55, 58–60, 62–66, 68, 73, 75–78, 80, 81–87, 89–95, 98, 100, 102, 112, 114, 129, 173, 175, 180–84, 188, 190–92, 194–95, 197–205, 207–15, 219, 223, 225, 227, 229–30, 232

mercy, 5–6, 19–21, 27–28, 33–35, 37–40, 42, 44, 46–49, 62–68, 70–72, 74, 77, 81–87, 89, 91, 94, 96, 101, 110, 113–14, 116–17, 120, 123–25, 127–29, 141–42, 148, 157, 167, 172–73, 175, 180–82, 184–85, 193, 197–202, 203, 205–6, 227–30, 232–34, 236, 240

Messiah, 71–72, 75, 78, 81, 85, 99, 105–7, 164, 171, 173–74, 177, 179, 184, 195–96, 211, 213

Moses, 1, 20, 24, 30, 32, 34, 39–40, 42, 44, 50, 62, 69, 73, 75, 100, 112, 117, 119, 122, 127, 131, 134, 141–43, 161–62, 200, 223, 228, 230, 232

nations, 12, 24, 32, 56, 59, 74, 104, 112, 116–17, 119, 128, 131–33, 143, 145, 147–48, 152, 154, 156, 158, 178–79, 182, 189, 208, 215, 217, 219–22, 224–25, 229, 231–32, 234, 236

neighbor, 52, 56, 73, 80–82, 94, 114, 134, 181, 192, 194–95, 197, 199, 202–5

nonviolence, 20, 184, 192, 212, 232–33

offerings, 4, 44–47, 52, 59, 61, 63, 64, 66, 76, 116, 118, 135, 139, 140, 160, 201, 228

Paul, 21, 92, 97, 126–27, 183, 187–206, 223

peace, x, 1–2, 18, 30–32, 37, 40, 45, 57–59, 65, 67, 71, 77, 89, 103, 148, 160, 162–63, 165, 171, 180, 191, 206–8, 214, 216, 219, 221–22, 224–25, 227, 231–32, 234, 237, 240

Persia, 115, 136–38, 149, 155, 157–59, 214

Pharisees, 21, 92, 97–104, 106, 112, 115–42, 161, 166–67, 169–71, 183, 192–93, 195, 231

political authoritarianism, 21, 88, 92, 96, 99, 103, 105–7, 110, 134, 141, 149, 154, 158, 161, 163, 165–68, 172, 231–32

Pontius Pilate, 22, 92, 96, 99, 106–9, 113, 147, 160, 162, 164–67, 171, 173, 179, 231

Powers, 22, 28, 77–78, 80, 83, 85–88, 91–96, 99, 102–3, 107, 110–13, 129, 136–37, 151, 159, 166–69, 172, 175–80, 182–86, 191, 198–200, 202, 206–7, 209–10, 215, 217–18, 220, 225, 230–33

priests, 40, 56–57, 59, 61, 69, 92, 103–6, 108, 116, 122–24, 138–40, 142–43, 145, 153, 160, 166, 170, 210, 224

primal story, 28–29, 31, 34, 37, 38–39, 47–48, 228

prison, 9–18, 237

promise, 1–2, 22, 30–34, 37, 39–40, 48, 52, 61, 64–66, 69–70, 72–73, 76, 121, 138–39, 145, 147, 155, 157, 169, 183, 195–96, 200, 214, 220, 228–30

Subject Index

prophetic, prophets, 1, 20–21, 24, 28, 30, 33, 37, 39–40, 46–48, 50–64, 66–71, 73–74, 77, 82, 84, 86–87, 97–98, 100–102, 104, 106–7, 112–16, 121–22, 130–33, 135–38, 141–42, 145, 148–49, 151, 153–57, 161, 177, 179, 184–85, 188, 198, 201, 203–5, 215, 217–18, 223–25, 228–35

punishment, 2–3, 5–11, 14–15, 18–19, 35, 39, 41, 46, 48, 54, 58, 60–61, 77, 83, 94–95, 102, 104, 129, 160, 163, 165, 170–72, 180, 185, 201–2, 208, 222, 227–29, 233–36, 238, 240

purity, 34, 36, 42, 98, 120–22, 125–27, 140, 144–45, 198, 205

reconciliation, 1, 48, 72, 184, 188, 201–3, 206, 226, 237

religious institutionalism, 21, 88, 92, 98, 103, 105, 134, 141, 143, 147–48, 166, 172, 175, 177, 183, 199, 231–32

repentance, 2, 43, 45, 62, 64, 75–77, 104, 118, 193, 230

resurrection, 22, 94, 110, 141, 173–87, 205, 207–9, 212–13, 215, 218, 223, 232–33

restorative justice, 11, 19, 27, 38, 187, 188, 200, 202–3, 206–7, 226, 233, 236–38, 240

retributive justice, retribution, 2–3, 5–12, 16, 18–19, 21–23, 27, 28, 31, 35–39, 43–44, 48, 58, 61, 68, 72, 74, 77–78, 80, 82–83, 85–87, 89, 91, 94–95, 110–11, 125, 128, 149–50, 154, 161, 163, 167, 170–72, 174, 180, 184–86, 197, 200–202, 206, 226–28, 230–40

righteousness, 6, 55, 60, 63–65, 187–89, 203

Roman Empire, Rome, 92, 106–9, 112–13, 115, 119, 129, 149, 155, 158–69, 171, 179, 184, 189, 191–93, 196–97, 199–200, 204, 206–7, 210, 214–16, 222, 224

Sabbath, 49, 74, 103, 115–16, 118–20, 123–27, 129, 140, 169, 170, 173, 178, 231–32

sacred violence, 22, 61, 80, 83, 147–48, 197, 199, 203

sacrifice, sacrifices, 2, 4–5, 19–21, 27–28, 39, 43–50, 52, 59–64, 66–68, 71–72, 74, 76–77, 86–87, 89–90, 94–96, 110, 116, 124, 138–42, 166, 188, 200–204, 213, 223, 226, 228–29, 233

Sarah, 24, 30–31, 33, 37–38, 43, 52, 69, 104, 110, 181, 196, 200, 203, 220, 228

Satan, 96, 128, 162, 213–14, 220, 222

satisfaction, 2, 4–8, 10–11, 20–22, 31, 34, 38, 46–47, 72, 77, 86–87, 95, 110, 171, 201–2, 205, 226, 233

savior, 7, 29, 38, 71–72, 75, 86, 89, 191, 214, 221, 230

shalom, 1–4, 34, 39–40, 45, 54, 57, 75, 135, 153, 172, 206, 222

sin, sinners, sinfulness, 4–7, 9–10, 30, 36–37, 39, 43, 45–46, 57–58, 60–61, 66–68, 73, 76, 80, 83, 85, 87, 89, 95, 97–98, 100, 103, 122, 126–27, 135, 138–39, 143–45, 184, 186, 188–89, 193–98, 200, 201–4, 209–10, 224, 227, 228–29, 235–36

Solomon, 30, 130–34, 136–39, 141, 153–55, 159

Subject Index

soteriology, 21–22, 69, 86–87, 90, 226
swords, 32, 41, 54, 56–57, 65, 105, 154, 165, 191, 209, 213–15, 218, 224–25

temple, 21, 30–31, 36–37, 46, 49, 50, 71, 76, 92–95, 97–99, 103–6, 111–12, 115, 119, 122–24, 129–48, 153–54, 157–61, 166–67, 170–71, 173, 177–78, 180, 201–2, 220, 231–32
theology, ix–x, 2–3, 5–11, 19, 21–24, 36, 41, 43–4, 68, 74, 86, 94, 118–19, 121, 132–34, 142–44, 151, 157, 186–88 205–6, 208, 226–27, 230–31, 233, 237, 240
Torah, 20, 30–31, 35, 38–50, 52–55, 59–61, 63–67, 69, 74–75, 77, 81–82, 84, 86–87, 92, 98, 100–102, 104, 112–19, 123, 125–28, 130–35, 138, 142, 150–56, 163, 169–70, 172, 175–76, 178, 180–82, 184–85, 187, 192, 194–97, 199–200, 203–6, 222–23, 228, 230–32, 235
trust, 2, 20–22, 43, 52, 54, 57–58, 62, 64–68, 77, 81–83, 85, 87, 91, 93–94, 102, 110, 112, 151–52, 154, 156, 162, 165, 168, 179, 187–91, 193–94, 196–99, 201–6, 208–9, 215, 223, 229, 230, 232

vengeance, 6, 10, 35, 63, 126, 184, 205, 223, 230, 232, 239–40
violence, ix, 1–5, 7–8, 11–13, 16–23, 27–29, 31, 33, 40, 51, 55–61, 67, 74, 77, 80, 83, 86–88, 90–91, 94, 96, 101–3, 108, 110, 125, 128–29, 136, 141, 147–48, 160–61, 163, 165, 167, 170, 172, 176–80, 183–85, 189, 191–97, 199, 202–9, 214–15, 219, 224–25, 227–30, 232, 234, 240
vocation, 72–73, 86, 128, 178, 181–84, 206

war, warfare, ix, 2, 5, 27, 32, 41, 57–58, 65, 131, 151, 213, 216–18, 225, 227
wholeness, 3, 11, 25, 27–28, 36, 45, 51–52, 62, 124, 185, 190, 202, 204, 206, 219, 229
wilderness, 34, 37, 39, 65, 72, 75, 133, 162, 179, 219
works of the law, 127, 188, 191–98, 203–4, 206
worship, 38, 44, 46–47, 56, 58–60, 67, 71, 93, 103, 113, 130, 133–37, 146, 148, 150, 190–92, 194–95, 197, 200, 202, 210–12, 214–16, 219, 221, 224–25, 231
wrath, 5–6, 27, 35, 39, 42–43, 54, 58, 68, 76, 82, 86–87, 106, 189–91, 193, 197, 199, 201–2, 205